Path Dependency and Macroeconomics

International Papers in Political Economy Series

Series Editors: Philip Arestis and Malcolm Sawyer

This volume is part of the new series of *International Papers in Political Economy (IPPE)*. The new series will consist of an annual volume on a single theme with four to five papers on a single theme. The objective of the *IPPE* will continue to be the publication of papers dealing with important topics within the broad framework of Political Economy.

The original series of *International Papers in Political Economy* started in 1993 and has been published in the form of three issues a year with each issue containing a single extensive paper. Information on the old series and back copies can be obtained from Professor Malcolm Sawyer at the University of Leeds (e-mail: mcs@lubs.leeds.ac.uk)

Titles include:

Philip Arestis and Malcolm Sawyer *(editors)*

PATH DEPENDENCY AND MACROECONOMICS

CRITICAL ESSAYS ON THE PRIVATISATION EXPERIENCE

POLITICAL ECONOMY OF LATIN AMERICA
Recent Economic Performance

ALTERNATIVE PERSPECTIVES ON ECONOMIC POLICIES IN THE EUROPEAN UNION

FINANCIAL LIBERALIZATION
Beyond Orthodox Concerns.

International Papers in Political Economy

Series Standing Order ISBN 978–1–4039–9936–8

You can receive future titles in this series as they are published by placing a standing order. Please contact your bookseller or, in case of difficulty, write to us at the address below with your name and address, the title of the series and the ISBN quoted above.

Customer Services Department, Macmillan Distribution Ltd, Houndmills, Basingstoke, Hampshire RG21 6XS, England

Path Dependency and Macroeconomics

Edited by

Philip Arestis

and

Malcolm Sawyer

First published 2009 by
PALGRAVE MACMILLAN

Palgrave Macmillan in the UK is an imprint of Macmillan Publishers Limited,
registered in England, company number 785998, of Houndmills, Basingstoke,
Hampshire RG21 6XS.

Palgrave Macmillan in the US is a division of St Martin's Press LLC,
175 Fifth Avenue, New York, NY 10010.

Palgrave Macmillan is the global academic imprint of the above companies
and has companies and representatives throughout the world.

Palgrave® and Macmillan® are registered trademarks in the United States,
the United Kingdom, Europe and other countries.

ISBN 978–0–230–23600–4   hardback

This book is printed on paper suitable for recycling and made from fully
managed and sustained forest sources. Logging, pulping and manufacturing
processes are expected to conform to the environmental regulations of the
country of origin.

A catalogue record for this book is available from the British Library.

A catalog record for this book is available from the Library of Congress.

10   9   8   7   6   5   4   3   2   1
18 17 16 15 14 13 12 11 10 09

Printed and bound in Great Britain by
CPI Antony Rowe, Chippenham and Eastbourne

Contents

Preface

This is the fifth volume of the new series of *International Papers in Political Economy* (*IPPE*). The new series will consist of an annual volume on a single theme with five to six papers on a single theme. The objective of the *IPPE* will continue to be the publication of papers dealing with important topics within the broad framework of Political Economy.

The original series of *International Papers in Political Economy* started in 1993 until the new series began in 2005 and was published in the form of three issues a year with each issue containing a single extensive paper. Information on the old series and back copies can be obtained from Professor Malcolm Sawyer at the University of Leeds (e-mail: mcs@lubs.leeds.ac.uk).

The theme of this fifth volume of six papers is path dependency and macroeconomics in terms of both theory and applications. The papers in this volume were presented at the 5th International Conference Developments in Economic Theory and Policy held at Universidad del Pais Vasco, Bilbao, Spain, 10–11 July 2008.

List of Figures

List of Tables

Notes on the Contributors

Philip Arestis is University Director of Research, Cambridge Centre for Economics and Public Policy, Department of Land Economy, University of Cambridge, UK. He is also Distinguished Adjunct Professor of Economics, University of Utah, USA; Senior Scholar, Levy Economics Institute, New York, USA; Visiting Professor, University of Leeds, UK; and Professorial Research Associate School of Oriental and African Studies (SOAS), University of London, UK and Chief Academic Adviser to the Government Economic Service (GES) Board of Professional Development. He has published as sole author or editor, as well as co-author and co-editor, a number of books and papers in academic journals.

Amitava Krishna Dutt is Professor of Economics at the University of Notre Dame, Indiana, USA. His current research is on models of growth and distribution, uneven development and North–South interaction, consumption and happiness, and post-Keynesian macroeconomics. He is author or editor of a dozen books, and has published extensively in edited volumes and in journals such as *American Economic Review, Cambridge Journal of Economics, Journal of Development Economics, Journal of Post Keynesian Economics, Oxford Economic Papers* and *World Development*. He is a co-editor of *Metroeconomica*.

Marika Karanassou is a Reader in the Department of Economics, Queen Mary University of London, UK. She is also a Research Fellow at IZA, Bonn, and the Economics Editor of *Quantitative and Qualitative Analysis in Social Sciences*. Her research output relates to macroeconomics, applied econometrics, time series analysis, and empirical finance. She has published, among others, in the *Cambridge Journal of Economics, Journal of Economic Surveys, Economic Journal, Papers in Regional Science, European Journal of Political Economy*.

Dany Lang is maître de conférences (assistant professor) at the University of Paris 13, France. He is responsible for the working group 'Post-Keynesian analyses and modelling' at the Centre d'Economie de Paris Nord. He has published papers, among others, in the *Journal of Post-Keynesian Economics*, the *Review of Political Economy* and the *International*

Review of Applied Economics. He teaches mainly macroeconomics and political economy, both in Paris 13 and at the University de Haute Alsace in Mulhouse. Previously, he has taught and led research in various places: the University of Aix-Marseille II and III, the Institute of Political Studies of Toulouse, and the National University of Ireland, Galway.

Alfonso Palacio-Vera is Lecturer in Economics at Complutense University in Madrid, Spain. He has published a number of papers in different academic journals including the *Cambridge Journal of Economics, Journal of Post-Keynesian Economics, Journal of Economic Issues, Metroeconomica, Review of Political Economy, Eastern Economic Journal* and *International Review of Applied Economics*. He has also written several chapters in books published by Edward Elgar Publishing and Palgrave Macmillan. He is a member of the Post-Keynesian Economics Study Group.

Hector Sala is Associate Professor at the Departament d'Economia Aplicada, Universitat Autònoma de Barcelona, Spain and Fellow of the IZA/Institute for the Study of Labor in Bonn, Germany. His research output relates to the macroeconomic modelling of the labour market and of the inflation–unemployment trade-off. His work has been published in journals such as *Applied Economics, Australian Economic Papers, Cambridge Journal of Economics, Economic Modelling, Macroeconomic Dynamics, Journal of Policy Modeling* and the *Scottish Journal of Political Economy*.

Malcolm Sawyer is Professor of Economics, Leeds University Business School, University of Leeds, UK. He was until recently Pro-Dean for Learning and Teaching for the Faculty of Business, University of Leeds, UK. He is managing editor of *International Review of Applied Economics* and on the editorial board of a range of journals. He has published widely in the areas of post-Keynesian and Kaleckian economics, industrial economics and the UK economy. He has authored 11 books and edited 18, has published over 70 papers in refereed journals and contributed chapters over 100 books.

Mark Setterfield is Professor of Economics in the Department of Economics at Trinity College, Hartford, Connecticut, USA. He is an Associate Member of the Cambridge Centre for Economic and Public Policy (Cambridge University, UK), a Senior Research Associate at the International Economic Policy Institute (Laurentian University, Canada), and serves on the editorial boards of various journals, including the *Journal of Economic Education* and *Reivew of Political Economy*.

1

Path Dependency and Demand–Supply Interactions in Macroeconomic Analysis

Philip Arestis
University of Cambridge

Malcolm Sawyer
University of Leeds

Abstract

The chapter commences with an elaboration on the meaning of the notion of path dependency, how path dependency is linked with notions of fundamental uncertainty, non-ergodicity, hysteresis and some of the factors that have been highlighted in the generation of path dependency. The implications of the notion of path dependency for macroeconomic analysis are discussed in terms of the interrelationship between aggregate demand and supply potential and the availability of future resources. The contrast is drawn between these notions of path dependency, which have featured in the heterodox macroeconomics literature with the path independency of mainstream macroeconomics to suggest that they differ substantially with significant analytical implications. Path dependency in macroeconomic analysis is then discussed in relation to the relationship between aggregate demand and supply, labour market, inflation barrier, investment and the capital stock, technological change and demand and supply in economic growth. In all this we draw on ideas, which have long circulated in Keynesian economics, to indicate some of the ways in which the path of demand impacts on the development of supply potential.

JEL Classification: B52, E12

Keywords: path dependency; non-ergodicity; uncertainty; macroeconomic analysis

1

1. Introduction

The starting proposition for this chapter is that in the real world of uncertainty, where the future has yet to be discovered, the economy (however that may be defined) has to be viewed as path dependent; or to put it in another way, 'history matters'. This view is in sharp contrast to the mainstream view of path independence as shown below. The economy evolves (for better or worse) as decisions are made and actions taken, and 'the long-run trend is but a slowly changing component of a chain of short-period situations; it has no independent entity' (Kalecki, 1971, p. 165). There is not some pre-existing route for the economy to follow around which the actual path followed will oscillate. These may sound trite and obvious observations not worth devoting research time to, yet within the context of macroeconomic analysis (which is our main focus here) the path dependency view runs counter to the prevailing manner in which economic analysis is conducted. The latter is firmly based on the idea that there is an equilibrium path around which the economy can travel which essentially pre-exists. Also, that equilibrium path is the basis for the actual path followed by the economy, in the sense that the economy will oscillate around the equilibrium path. Furthermore, when individuals are characterized as acting on the basis of 'rational expectations', part of the information set held by those individuals is knowledge of that equilibrium path. And, more significantly, there is an equilibrium path already 'out there' to which their decisions will essentially have to conform. In most economic analysis where the economy starts and which path it follows through time does not affect the final equilibrium position in these models.

We propose in this chapter to lay out some of the basic reasons for path dependency and then to show how they impact on macroeconomic analysis, and how that analysis can be interpreted to reflect the pervasiveness of path dependency. A major, but not the only, route for path dependency arises from the irreversible effects of investment, the interdependence between aggregate demand and supply and hence the ways in which the course of aggregate demand impacts on the evolution of the economy. In the orthodox approach the equilibrium growth path is essentially supply determined with the implicit assumption that any short-term movements in demand will not affect the growth path. In our discussion here we draw on ideas that have long circulated in Keynesian economics to indicate some of the ways in which the path of demand impacts on the development of supply potential.

We proceed along the following lines. In section 2 we attempt to clarify the notion of path dependency along with the different forms it can assume. In section 3 we discuss its opposite in the form of path independence, the view assumed in most mainstream analysis. The rest of the chapter shows a number of examples that we hope clarify the meanings developed in sections 2 and 3. Path dependency and labour market is the focus of section 4, followed in section 5 by the role of demand, investment and the inflation barrier in path dependency. Section 6 is a brief discussion of the role of research, development and technical change in path dependency, and section 7 brings together discussion of the interaction of demand and supply in path dependency in the context of economic growth. All these aspects are taken on board finally, which enables us to summarize the argument and offer concluding remarks in section 8.

2.   Path dependence

The view that there is path dependency and that the approach to the analysis of the economy, to understanding how the economy evolves and to the modelling of the macroeconomy has to be based on the path dependency perspective, comes from two interrelated propositions. The first is that the future course of the economy cannot be taken to be in any meaningful sense predetermined in which there is some course already set around which the economy will travel. This contrasts with the notion of an equilibrium growth path that can be defined before the action starts and would in effect be known before decisions are made and around which the economy will actually operate. The second is that decisions made in the present and the resulting actions and interactions must have an impact on what happens tomorrow and the decisions made tomorrow and the actions that result. The decisions made are, of course, based on perceptions of the future: those perceptions of the future will in the event turn out to have been incorrect to a greater or lesser extent. This is inevitable in that perceptions and expectations of individuals necessarily differ and there are not mechanisms by which in general the expectations of individuals are reconciled with one another. There is, though, a sense in which the outcomes that come from decisions based on those expectations involve some degree of reconciliation between decisions to provide an outcome. Not everyone's expectations and perceptions can be fulfilled. Further, there will be events in the future that cannot be imagined or indeed predicted. In the words of Donald Rumsfeld 'there are known knowns – there are things that we know that we know. There are known unknowns. That is to say, there are things that we now know we don't know. But there are also unknown unknowns – there are things we do not know we don't know' (Statement at a Defense Department Briefing on 12 February, 2002).[1] Although Donald Rumsfeld was often mocked for this (and many other) sayings, it does convey an essential point, namely that there will be events and outcomes in the future that people cannot now even envisage. We can form expectations about what can be imagined but not about those that cannot be imagined.

The rational expectations hypothesis involves the essential similarity of expectations between individuals with some differences arising from differences in the information set that individuals possess. But the underlying model of the economy on which rational expectations of individuals are generally based is in effect assumed to be known to all, and hence there is a similarity of expectations across individuals. A particular significant feature of rational expectations approach is that the future path of the economy is taken to be already mapped out and essentially known to individuals (that is, individuals' expectations on the future deviate from what eventually arises only to the extent of non-systematic errors). There is assumed to be a situation of risk (that is, individuals' decisions and actions are based on the probability distribution of future events). This can be contrasted with a situation of uncertainty in the Keynesian and Knightian sense that arises from the essential unknowability of the future, but there is risk in the sense of a probability distribution surrounding future events.

In this chapter we use the term path dependency in preference to any notion of hysteresis (see Setterfield's chapter in this volume for much more extensive discussion). In doing so we hope to emphasize that not only does 'history matter' but that the economy is moving through time and the path (or paths) followed gradually open up and evolve: there is in effect no turning back even if some decisions can be reversed. The term hysteresis has been sometimes used to convey notions that there are alternative equilibrium positions, which can be attained depending on the route followed. It can also be used to focus on issues of reversibility vs. irreversibility, whereas there is a sense in the path-dependent approach that there is a passage through time and time itself is irreversible. The hysteresis approach in effect asks the following type of question. Suppose that a 'position of interest', which we will label Yn (this could be something like the 'natural rate' of unemployment, or in the initial example drawn from physics the magnetic charge of an iron bar), which changes according to an equation such as $Yn_t = Yn_{t-1} + f(Z_{t-1})$ and hence the position of Yn_t can be solved back to give $Yn_t = Yn_0 + \sum_{i=1}^{t} f(Z_{t-i})$. The question can then be asked as to whether if $\sum Z_{t-i} = 0$, does the expression $Yn_t = Yn_0$ then hold? In the much-quoted hysteresis effects in magnetism, the equivalent of $\sum Z_{t-i} = 0$ is imposed by the experimenter. In the context of much macroeconomic analysis there may be some presumption that $\sum Z_{t-i} = 0$; a notable example that is rather pertinent to what we discuss below would be to take Z as a measure of aggregate demand relative to some 'normal' level. Let us treat Yn as some supply-side equilibrium such as the 'natural rate of unemployment'. Then the simple equation $Yn_t = Yn_{t-1} + f(Z_{t-1})$ would suggest that the supply-side equilibrium varies with the level of aggregate demand. However, if there are reasons to think that aggregate demand fluctuates around some 'normal level', then $\sum Z_{t-i} = 0$ and the question then is whether that would imply $Yn_t = Yn_0$.

The main purpose of this chapter is to discuss the ways in which the idea of path dependence impacts on macroeconomic analysis. In doing so, we focus on the idea that the path of aggregate demand impacts on the level of economic activity, which thereby influences a wide range of experiences and of decisions, which in turn have effects on the future of the economy. In particular, the supply potential of the economy is moulded by these experiences and decisions, and hence impacted by demand. In its broadest sense investment can be defined in terms of expenditure incurred in the present, which is intended to bring future gains. Our focus in this chapter will be on the ways in which investment adds to future resources and hence to how the supply potential of the economy evolves.

One of the more obvious topics where path dependency is highly relevant is that of invention and innovation, and the associated changes in products and production processes. The literature on invention and innovation has necessarily long recognized that the time path of the economy, particularly with regard to the level and structure of economic activity (and associated variables), influences the pace and direction of invention and innovation activities. It also, of course, recognizes that each step builds on previous steps, and that one step, for whatever reason that was taken, sets the ground work for the next step; and as Metcalfe (2001) observes, 'As scholars from Marshall … to Kuznets … have recognized, economic activity changes knowledge directly and indirectly and every change in knowledge opens up the conditions for *changes in activity* and *thus further changes in knowledge, ad infinitum*, and in quite unpredictable ways' (p. 570).

From such a view, two significant points emerge. First, the future is inherently uncertain in the Knightian and Keynesian senses. In Keynes's words, the term uncertainty is to be used in the senses 'in which the prospect of a European war is uncertain, or the price of copper and the rate of interest twenty years hence, or the obsolescence of a new invention, or the position of private wealth-owners in the social system in 1970. About these matters there is no scientific basis on which to form any calculable probability whatever. We simply do not know' (Keynes, 1937, p. 214). By contrast, the rational expectations perspective builds on a combination of massive knowledge and computational power by individuals and an essentially knowable future (with risk but not uncertainty recognized). A great deal of macroeconomic analysis has been built on rational expectations and the ability of individuals to foresee the future. The 'new consensus in macroeconomics view' is the most recent embodiment of this as will be readily evident from the pages of Woodford (2003), which is the most comprehensive development of that view.[2] Second, the quote given reinforces a path dependency approach to the analysis of the economy. This is more than the notion, often associated with the hysteresis literature, that a current event may have long-lasting effects on future events but which eventually die away (notably in the literature on unemployment). It is that the future is built on the present and that decisions taken in the present will impact on the future course of the economy.

Martin and Sunley (2006) provide a broad conceptualization of path dependency when they write that 'The key defining characteristic of path-dependent processes and systems is that of "non-ergodicity", which is an inability to shake free of their history. Put another way, a path-dependent process or system is one whose outcome evolves as a consequence of the process's or system's own history ... In economics, there are three main, interrelated, versions of this idea: path dependence as technological "lock-in" (associated mainly with the work of Paul David), as dynamic increasing returns (particularly championed by Brian Arthur), and as institutional hysteresis (as advanced, for example, by Douglas North and Mark Setterfield)' (p. 399).

Pierson (2000), writing in the context of political science, argues that the concept of political processes as path dependent 'is often employed without careful elaboration. This article conceptualizes path dependence as a social process grounded in a dynamic of "increasing returns"' (p. 251). Pierson (op. cit.) remarks that for some theorists, 'increasing returns are the source of path dependence; for others, they typify only one form of path dependence'. Further, 'increasing returns dynamics capture two key elements central to most analysts of intuitive sense of path dependence. First, they pinpoint how the costs of switching from one alternative to another will, in certain social contexts, increase markedly over time. Second, and related, they draw attention to issues of timing and sequence, distinguishing formative moments or conjunctures from the periods that reinforce divergent paths. In an increasing returns process, it is not only a question of what happens but also of when it happens' (p. 251). Pierson (2000) continues by saying that 'specific patterns of timing and sequence matter; a wide range of social outcomes may be possible; large consequences may result from relatively small or contingent events; particular courses of action, once introduced, can be almost impossible to reverse; and consequently, political development is punctuated by critical moments or junctures that shape the basic contours of social life' (p. 251). In our discussion below we do not pay much regard to 'critical moments or junctures' or to the occurrence of economic and social crises. This is not because we wish to overlook crises, and indeed would see the occurrence of a crisis as a stark illustration of the way in which current events have marked and long-lasting effects notably on the perceptions and actions of individuals and organizations. But we would see the effects of crisis on the path of the economy as a particular example of the general phenomenon of path dependency, albeit that the crisis might have substantial effects (compared with what may have transpired in the absence of a crisis).

This conception of path dependency, in which preceding steps in a particular direction induce further movement in the same direction, is well captured by the idea of increasing returns. In an increasing returns process, the probability of further steps along the same path increases with each move down that path. This is because the relative benefits of the current activity compared with other possible options increase over time. Hence 'the costs of exit – of switching to some previously plausible alternative – rise. Increasing returns processes can also be described as self-reinforcing or positive feedback processes' (Pierson, 2000, p. 252). As Mahoney (2000) argues, path dependence analysis has generally involved 'two dominant types of sequences. First, some path-dependent investigators analyze self-reinforcing sequences characterized by the formation and long-term reproduction of a given institutional pattern. Self-reinforcing sequences often exhibit what economists call "increasing returns". With increasing returns, an institutional pattern – once adopted – delivers increasing benefits with its continued adoption, and thus over time it becomes more and more difficult to transform the pattern or select previously available options, even if these alternative options would have been more "efficient"' (p. 508).

The development of the QWERTY keyboard and its continuing use long after the technical reasons for its design had long disappeared is the perhaps most frequently quoted example of the interaction between increasing returns (in the sense that there are economic gains from the use of adoption of one technology rather than use of competing technologies) and 'lock-in' effects such as committed investments supporting the use of the technology. In the example of the QWERTY typewriter keyboard, the idea clearly was that there were gains from the use of a single design of keyboard, which would have been lost through the use of competing designs and the investments included training of typists in the use of that type of keyboard. Boas (2007) suggests that 'A number of generic features in the history of QWERTY that were incorporated into models of technological development distinguish a path dependent process from the standard neoclassical economic model of markets (Arthur, 1988, 1989). The process is *unpredictable*, characterized by multiple possible equilibria, and it may ultimately achieve an *inefficient* equilibrium due to imperfect information or other sources of market failure. Path dependence is also characterized by *nonergodicity*, meaning that events occurring early in a path are not averaged out and forgotten. Furthermore, path dependent processes result in *lock-in* through increasing returns. The costs of switching to a previously discarded alternative accumulate over time, rendering such wholesale change less and less likely' (p. 37).

Some of the arguments on 'lock-in' effects and increasing returns find strong echoes in the notion of cumulative causation (following Myrdal, 1957 and Kaldor, 1972) whereby there are self-reinforcing and cumulative processes through which 'success breeds success and failure breeds failure'. Particularly applied to regional and national differences, the notion of cumulative causation suggests that a rapidly growing economy stimulates productivity gains (e.g. through operation of Verdoorn's Law or the equivalent), learning by doing, the ability to invest more in capital equipment, education, etc., and of course in the other direction a sluggish economy will suffer from lower productivity gains, etc. There are also forces at work that operate in the direction of tending to reduce inequalities between regions and nations. Myrdal (1957), for example, spoke of 'backwash' effects which 'have a similar effect of increasing inequality' (Myrdal, 1957, p. 28) but also 'spread effects' which work to reduce inequalities between regions and nations.

The 'lock-in' effects and the forces of cumulative causation may help to explain and understand the path, which an economy (or more generally a society) follows – particularly in retrospect, though much less so in prospect. But these 'lock-in' effects and cumulative causation do not set out a definitive path along which the economy must necessarily travel. The path has still to be explored: indeed it may be said that the path still has to be built before it can be travelled along. 'Lock-in' effects imply that there may be a continuation down a particular track: the QWERTY keyboard continues to be used with institutional arrangements having some stable properties. There are, though, a whole host of reasons for not regarding the path 'to be set in stone'. There are what may be treated as 'shocks', which are in effect, as far as the entity being analysed, random events. The analysis of 'lock-in' effects and cumulative causation relate to a specific technology, to a particular regional economy, etc. But that technology, that regional economy, etc., interact with other technologies, other regional economies, and those interactions will clearly have a bearing on the path that is followed.

It is also the case that people have their decisions to make, which may or may not conform to these 'lock-in' effects and the forces of 'cumulative causation'. For example, one aspect of cumulative causation could be seen to be that successful firms earn high profits, which enables them to undertake investment, which further secures their place; but, of course, those firms may decide otherwise. Further, there may be many 'circuits' of cumulative causation, which come into conflict with one another. A firm in one industry may have established first mover advantage in that industry but so will other firms in other industries. Those firms will interact with each other in a variety of ways, and can be viewed as in some conflict with regard, for example, for resources, consumers' spending power, etc. The understanding of any specific example of 'lock-in' would also have to bring into the picture the roles of co-ordination of decisions between firms and government involvement.

Setterfield (2002) argues that 'if growth is inherently self-reinforcing, then this suggests that once "initial conditions" are specified, and in the absence of unexplained shocks, so is the subsequent growth trajectory of the economy' (p. 215). However, in his own work, Setterfield (op. cit.) attaches importance 'to the presence of self-reinforcing, cumulative processes in macrodynamics, but the problem, inherent in models of cumulative causation, of there being "too much cumulation", is avoided. This is achieved by *retaining* rather than dispensing with the notion of equilibrium, and therefore allowing for the existence of point attractors or "centres of gravity" in the economy. Furthermore, Kaldor's cumulative growth schema, central to which is a positive feedback from output growth to productivity growth, is treated as only one source of path dependency in the growth process; others, including sources of *negative* feedback from output growth to productivity growth are also postulated' (pp. 215–16).

Irreversibility is a much more general phenomenon than the focus on technological 'lock-in' may suggest. Indeed, irreversibility is a pervasive feature of (almost) all economic activity. This arises from (at least) two considerations. First, the pre-conditions do not exist that permit the reversal of decisions. If a person buys a tin of baked beans in the local supermarket, it is not usually possible for that person to sell the tin of baked beans back to the supermarket. When (as further discussed below) after investment in machinery (and even more so in human capital) selling the machinery cannot readily reverse investment back to the producer or to other firms (and smashing up the machinery does not return to the initial state). Second, time passes as decisions made at time t cannot be reversed in time t, even if they can be partially reversed in time t + 1. The supply of work is perhaps a good illustration of these two points: a person having sold their labour on day t cannot buy back their labour in any meaningful sense and once day t has passed the labour undertaken on that day cannot be brought back.

These irreversibilities become significant when a decision taken today influences a decision tomorrow. When (as in the example given of the work decision) a different decision on a specified action in similar circumstance can be made at time t + 1, then in a number of respects the decision made at time t is reversed, and the decision at time t may have no lasting effects. But when the decision at time t influences the decision at time t + 1 (usually seen in terms of the decision at time t leading to a similar decision at time t + 1) then elements of path dependency arise. For example, when the decision (and actual experience) to work at time t leads to a similar decision in time t + 1, and when a decision or inability to work at time t would have lead to a different decision at time t + 1, then path dependency comes in.

The path dependency approach is clearly located in historical time rather than in logical time. 'Logical time' is the type of 'time' as treated in models based on the principles of neoclassical economics. This is essentially the comparative statics approach in which an equilibrium is disturbed and the model automatically moves to a new, predetermined, equilibrium. How the system gets to the new equilibrium is of no central concern, in the sense that no attention is given to the process of getting from one equilibrium to the next following the disturbance. By contrast, 'historical time' is the type of 'time' as treated in models, which treat the present as nothing exceptional. It is a moment in the passage from the past to the future, where the latter is of course unknowable.

This is a dynamic process, in which equilibrium is of no concern since it is recognized that such a state does not exist in the real world. The actual process, therefore, of going from situation A to situation B is *path dependent*, and in the process determines the character of situation B rather than the latter being predetermined. And in Mahoney's (2000) view, the 'second basic type of path-dependent analysis involves the study of reactive sequences. Reactive sequences are chains of temporally ordered and causally connected events. These sequences are "reactive" in the sense that each event within the sequence is in part a reaction to temporally antecedent events. Thus, each step in the chain is "dependent" on prior steps. With reactive sequences, the final event in the sequence is typically the outcome under investigation, and the overall chain of events can be seen as a path leading up to this outcome. For a reactive sequence to follow a specifically path-dependent trajectory, as opposed to representing simply a sequence of causally connected events, the historical event that sets the chain into motion must have properties of contingency. Furthermore, the overall event chain itself must be marked by processes of "inherent sequentiality"' (pp. 508–9). Furthermore, Martin and Sunley (2006) suggest, 'path dependence is a probabilistic and contingent process: at each moment in historical time the suite of possible future evolutionary trajectories (paths) of a technology, institution, firm or industry is conditioned by (contingent on) both the past and the current states of the system in question, and some of these possible paths are more likely or probable than others. The past thus sets the possibilities, while the present controls what possibility is to be explored, which only becomes explained ex post' (pp. 402–3).

A central idea in path dependency can be seen in terms of one step being taken which opens up a path into the future where there are initially many steps that could be taken, but one of those is actually chosen. The next step depends on the first step taken. As the path develops, switching from that which has been gradually revealed to another is fraught with difficulties – there may be substantial costs in doing so ('the locking-in effects') and in any case the alternative path is hazy.

Figure 1.1 helps to illustrate this. Starting at point A, a number of alternative steps were perceived as available, and the step was taken which led to B2 (this may have differed from what was perceived to be available). A step could have been taken, which led to B1 (or B3) – though this is hypothetical since the participants would only have had perceptions where their actions would have led, and this route was not actually followed. From B2, assume C1 is followed – the figure illustrates some of

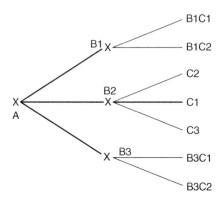

Figure 1.1   Path dependency

the alternatives available. If B1 had been followed, then there may have been alternatives such as B1C1, B1C2, etc.

There is perhaps a tendency to interpret a path such as A B2 C1 in Figure 1.1 as representing 'progress' in some sense: moving forward through time becomes moving forward in other ways. This tendency is enhanced when there is discussion (as in the 'lock-in' literature) on the efficiency of a specific path compared with some hypothetical alternative. Although much of our discussion below is constructed in terms of the growth of output this should not be taken to preclude negative growth (particularly with regard to per capita income). Cumulative causation, for example, may involve some in a virtuous circle but others in a vicious circle. For some path dependency will involve progress (however that is defined) but for others can involve decline (again, however that is defined). We would also not wish to preclude the equivalent of 'going around in circles'.

This chapter is particularly focused on macroeconomics and path dependency, and from that perspective there are four relevant features of Figure 1.1. First, while individuals at point A will have envisaged aspects of the future, and they will have affected the decisions that were made, the point arrived at B2 will not be exactly as envisaged. Different individuals will have had partial and differing 'visions' of the future; there will be 'law of unintended consequences' in operation. Second (though not evident from the figure), the experience of the move from A to B2 impacts on future decisions and attitudes. This may range from new experiences changing tastes and preferences, experience of success or failure on future expectations and perceptions. Third, there are 'lock-in' effects. These cannot be readily illustrated in Figure 1.1 but we would interpret lock-in effects to mean that if, for example, the path taken had been A to B2 it would be more difficult (costly) to shift to, say, B1C2 than if the path taken had been A to B1, and that having travelled the path to B2 continuation to, say, C1 is more likely than to, say, C2. Fourth, many of the decisions taken between A and B2 are akin to investment decisions in that they have created resources, which yield future benefits (and also form the basis for the next steps). Of course, if the path A to B1 had been followed, then other investments would have taken place.

A particular aspect of path dependence, which arises in the context of macroeconomic analysis, is the irreversibilities on the supply side of the economy that arise from movements in the level and composition of aggregate demand. This stands in contrast with the general mainstream approach in which the underlying growth of the economy is not only determined on the supply side of the economy (and demand has to adjust to that) but also that the equilibrium growth path is in some sense predetermined. Elsewhere one of us (Sawyer, 2009) has argued that 'the independence of demand and supply has been a central proposition in mainstream economics, whether at the microeconomic level where the demand and supply curves only interact through the price mechanism with a separation of the factors influencing demand and those influencing supply or at the macroeconomic level. The AD–AS analysis rather replicates the microeconomic demand and supply analysis. ... The interdependence of demand and supply is closely related with path dependency'. It is the ways in which demand and supply interact in the context of path dependency are the centre of our attention below.

To illustrate, let us suppose there is a main path through a forest, and there are side paths, which deviate from the main path but are such that following a side path would always lead one back to the main path. This is akin to the simplest neoclassical approach in the sense that the path is already there waiting from someone to travel along it, that when someone leaves the main path there are 'forces' leading them back to the path and that there is a unique destination. A form of path dependency could be introduced through the introduction of a second main path leading to a different destination, with side paths linking the two main paths. The final arrival point could then be said to be path dependent – the equivalent of multiple equilibria. The path dependency approach is more akin to undertaking a journey through a forest in which there is no clearly marked path, and it is a matter of hacking through the undergrowth (and perhaps there is no final arrival point – the forest goes on forever!). Each step taken has to build on previous steps and the position reached. There are irreversibilities: if one has hacked down some of the trees, even if one then retraces one's steps the trees do not immediately reappear and the experience of having hacked down some trees may have changed perceptions, etc. There can be the equivalent of locking-in effects: having started in a broadly northerly direction, it is more likely that one continues in that broad direction than suddenly changing to the south, but also that there would be costs of returning to the starting point and then going south compared with continuing to go north.

3. Path independence

The mainstream approach in macroeconomic analysis, whether in a static or a dynamic context, can be portrayed as involving path independence, which is simply the idea that there is an equilibrium position (for a market, an economy, etc.) somehow already defined, is not affected by the actions that individuals take and towards which the economy will generally tend to move. Disequilibrium behaviour is viewed as relevant in establishing whether the market or economy (as the case may be) would or would not move towards the equilibrium position, but with the clear postulate that disequilibrium behaviour has no impact on the equilibrium position itself. This is often reflected in the idea of 'market fundamentals' – there are some fundamental forces, which determine the equilibrium value of say the exchange rate or share prices. The actual route, which the economy follows, differs from that pre-set route but only in terms of stochastic differences which themselves do not impact on the route of the economy. This is readily evident in the rational expectations approach of new classical macroeconomics. An implicit feature of this view of stochastic shocks is that a shock is seen as random and the effects of the shock are reversible. The size and nature of these random shocks average out at zero.

The path-independent approach to growth can be most readily seen by reference to the neoclassical model (derived from Solow, 1956, and Swann, 1956) in which the growth equilibrium condition is $s/v = n + m$ where n is the growth of the labour force (usually taken as equal to growth of population, assuming unchanged population structure) and m rate of (labour-augmenting) technical change, where v is assumed flexible and adjustment of v is the mechanism by which equilibrium is reached. This is generally expressed in terms of the change of the capital–labour ratio k based on an assumed equality between savings and investment, and the identity that the change in the capital-effective labour ratio is equal to change in capital minus change in effective labour, and hence $1/k\,(dk/dt) = s/v - (n + m)$. Equilibrium requires a constant capital-effective labour ratio, hence $s/v = n + m$.

The endogenous growth theory is its simplest form views the adjustment process to involve the rate of technical change. In the AK model, $Y = AK$, hence change in capital stock dK/dt = savings = sAK. The growth of labour productivity is then equal to $(1/Y)(dY/dt) = sA - n$, and in this case A ($=1/v$) does not adjust but rather growth of labour productivity comes out as a residual.

The neoclassical theory of investment (following Jorgenson, 1963) can be seen as emphasizing the role of the cost of capital in the determination of investment. But it also has the feature that investment is treated as readily reversible. Decisions on investment are modelled as being forward looking with well-founded expectations about the future. But any mistakes about the future can quickly be undone as investment is readily reversible. In the 'new consensus in macroeconomics' approach, these features are retained. Woodford (2003) writes that 'the equations of the extended model consist of an IS block (which allow us to solve for the paths of real output and of the capital stock, given the expected path of real interest rates and the initial capital stock), an AS block (which allows us to solve for the path of inflation given the paths of real output and of the capital stock), and a monetary policy rule (which implies a path for nominal interest rates given the paths of inflation and output)' (p. 361). In the new consensus macroeconomics (NCM), which in simplified form reflects the approach of Woodford (2003) and others with its three equation set-up of IS equation, AS-equation in the form of a Phillips' curve) and a monetary policy rule (Taylor's rule), works in terms of an output gap, that is, deviations of output from trend. In doing so, it precludes any effect investment and other decisions may have on the capital stock and productive potential of the economy. Investment in this theoretical framework can be introduced in terms of the expansion of the capital stock, which is required to underpin the growth of income. In effect the future path of the economy is mapped out, and consequently the time path of the capital stock. Investment ensures the adjustment of the capital stock to that predetermined time path. There is then by assumption no impact of the path of the economy on the capital stock. There is not what we may term an independent investment function in the sense of arising from firms' decisions taken in the light of profit and growth opportunities, separated from savings decisions of households. Interestingly enough, Woodford (op. cit.) notes with respect to the same model that 'a more generous view of the basic model would be that it abstracts from the effects of variations in private spending (including those classified as investment expenditure in the national income accounts) upon the economy's productive capacity' (p. 242).

The points we seek to emphasize here are three-fold (though clearly related). First, investment is viewed as readily reversible – the capital stock can be increased or decreased as firms so decide. Even when investment is identified with changes in the physical capital stock, this is a dubious proposition. When investment is more generally considered as expenditure undertaken in the present which yields future benefits and includes investment in education, in research and development, it becomes even more dubious. Second, the effects of investment decisions on the growth of the economy are largely ignored in that the growth rate of the economy is pre-set. Third, the equilibrium growth path of the economy is laid out at the beginning of time and then decisions by individuals and firms are brought into conformity with the requirements of that equilibrium growth path (or what might be thought of as the 'fundamentals').

A major weakness of this mainstream approach is summarized by Phelps (2007) in his introduction to Frydman and Goldberg (2007) when he writes that 'the authors argue that if we aspire to build models that apply to modern economies – economies whose central functioning is the manufacture of change through their innovative activity and their adoption and mastery of the innovations made available – it is contradictory to adopt the rational expectations postulate that whatever change takes place in the future is already knowable and known in the present: that the economic change to be experienced is in a sense predetermined' (Phelps, 2007, p. xiv). It is also argued that

> Yet contemporary model builders embracing rational expectations have been undeterred or unaware of the contradiction: they either specify that there is no change in the world (the world they would describe with their models) or that whatever process of change is going on in the world can be incorporated in their models in a fully predetermined way. This criticism is not a narrow point that would be straightforward to remedy. The authors are not referring to the fact that the archetypal models of an economy enjoying rational expectations equilibrium have built into them an invariant trend-growth path to which the economy is constantly returning (as described by some transition dynamics). It is obvious that such a trend path is predetermined; the possibilities and probabilities are 'prespecified' (in the authors' preferred term). The authors' argument is broader than that. If a rational expectations model supposed instead that the future

was governed by a probabilistic linear birth process, so the model has no trend path to which the economy is tethered, there is still a fundamental predeterminacy: the possible states at a given future date are all known already and there is at present a calculable probability, conditional on the present state, of each such future state's occurrence. In this model too, then, there is implicitly no possibility for the actors in the economy to create something unforeseeable, surprising, genuinely innovative. (Phelps, 2007, p. xvi)

Much has been made of the differences between the (post) Keynesian and Kaleckian views that investment expenditure is the driving force behind aggregate demand and that savings adjust to investment and the neoclassical view that savings are the source of funds for investment, and that investment adjusts to savings decisions (exemplified in the neoclassical growth model). These differences are of considerable significance, but there are other features of the modelling of investment, which are less featured but nevertheless highly relevant for our discussion here. Post Keynesians and Kaleckians would see a key feature of investment is that it is the results from the investment decision that have long-lasting effects and (more significantly here) cannot be readily reversed, and influence the future productive potential. Further, investment decisions today influence tomorrow's capital stock and productive capacity, which forms the background to tomorrow's decisions on investment. In the neoclassical investment function (cf. Jorgenson, 1963) investment decisions depend on relative prices and can be readily reversed (that is, nothing rules out negative investment at the firm level and then by aggregation at the aggregate level). In a post Keynesian/Kaleckian approach, investment decisions are undertaken in an uncertain environment, influenced by past experience and perceptions of the future, and in particular by the macroeconomic environment in terms of capacity utilization, growth and profitability. The path followed by aggregate demand impacts on the macroeconomic environment which has further effects on investment and the future capital stock.

4. Path dependency and the labour market

The representation of the labour market used in most macroeconomic analysis is straightforward. There is a downward-sloping demand-for-labour curve (in terms of the real wage) and an upward-sloping supply-of-labour curve (also in terms of the real wage), and equilibrium in the labour market is given where demand and supply are in equality. In the new classical macroeconomics approach, variations in employment arise from variations in supply decisions arising from movements in wages. The state of being employed or being non-employed (which may be labelled unemployed) comes from the voluntary decisions that individuals make in the face of real wages. The present level of real wages (actual and expected) is then sufficient to predict the levels of employment and unemployment. There is then nothing from the past that is seen to influence today's demand and supply decisions, and hence today's real wage and employment levels. It is an important feature of this approach that employment and unemployment arise from voluntary decisions.

Once it is acknowledged that the level of aggregate demand is significant in the setting of the levels of output and employment, then unemployment has to be viewed as involuntary for many of those who suffer from it and has to be seen as a macroeconomic rather than a microeconomic phenomenon (see Sawyer and Spencer, 2008a). It is then an obvious observation to say that unemployment and employment are demand determined. But this does not in itself create path dependency in so far as it is the current level of demand which determines the current level of unemployment. Path dependency is seen to arise from the effects of the experience of unemployment and employment on people's decisions on seeking work. It also depends on the ability of firms to provide employment, which depends on the productive capacity of the economy, including the capital stock built up from previous investment decisions. Once it is acknowledged that experience matters, then path dependency arises. This could to some degree be introduced into the new classical macroeconomics approach if it could be acknowledged that non-employment arising from misperception of wages but voluntarily chosen nevertheless, changed a person's attitude to work and leisure. But the argument becomes more powerful when unemployment comes through force of circumstance, e.g. from a downturn in aggregate demand. Unemployment may take the form of being registered as unemployed and seeking work but may take a number of other forms such as withdrawal from the work force, early retirement and incapacity. The experience of unemployment particularly when extended for the individual may lead to de-skilling, loss of work ethic, and ill health. Some have highlighted the 'scarring' effects of unemployment, which impact on the future employment and future earnings of workers (see, for example, Arulampalam et al., 2001).

It should be readily acknowledged that it is difficult to reconcile path dependency and 'hysteresis' type of arguments with regard to the labour market within a neoclassical choice theoretic approach. This is so since any measured unemployment would be 'leisure' arising from choices made by workers in the face of present and future expected real wages, and preferences would be taken as fixed. The size of the labour supply will be influenced by legal and social norms and would change over time as those norms themselves change. In terms of demand effects, the level of aggregate demand may not have an immediate effect on the labour supply, though a persistently high (or indeed low) level of aggregate demand could be expected to impact on legal and social norms, and thereby on the labour supply. Hence, pressure might increase for a reduction in normal working hours where very high levels of unemployment exist and persist over time. But the level of aggregate demand would impact on the labour force with high levels of aggregate demand bringing people into the labour force who had previously been in the 'discouraged worker' category, and low levels of demand and subsequently unemployment leading to people dropping out of the labour force or becoming effectively de-skilled. High levels of demand for labour may have a range of effects ranging from 'pulling' people into the work force from the home through to encouraging migration from other countries (for further discussion see Sawyer and Spencer, 2008b).

When there is persistently high unemployment induced by low levels of aggregate demand, individuals perceive unemployment to be widespread and their prospects of securing work to be poor, then they may give up actively seeking work and are then deemed economically inactive. Other workers may be forced to seek work because other family members have lost their job or suffered a drop in wages. With high unemployment, employers will have greater power to increase work time and also work intensity for those still in work. In contrast, unemployment has 'scarring' effects on individuals and there is demoralization felt by workers in the face of heightened job insecurity, which tends to reduce productivity.

In terms of path dependency and hysteresis with regard to labour supply this would require some form of change in tastes and preferences in response to actual experience, which would undermine the assumption of exogenous tastes and preferences made in the conventional neoclassical model of labour supply, and also serves to undermine the separation between the supply of labour and the demand for labour assumed in standard macroeconomic analysis. Layard, Nickell and Jackman (1991) make the neoclassical argument when they argue that

> There is indeed a long-run equilibrium at which both unemployment and inflation will be stable. We shall call this the long-run NAIRU

(non-accelerating-inflation rate of unemployment). But if last year we were above the long-run NAIRU and then fell back to it immediately, we would have rising inflation. There is however some 'short-run NAIRU', which *would* be consistent with stable inflation, and which of course depends on last year's unemployment. In this view of the world there is short-term 'hysteresis', in the sense that past events affect the current short-run NAIRU. But there is no long-term 'hysteresis: there is a unique long-run NAIRU. In the end, the unemployment rate always reverts. And employment adjusts to the size of the labour force. (p. 10)

This contrasts with the more general notion of path dependence, which is pursued here in two major respects. First, there appears here a notion of a pre-existing long-run equilibrium position which acts as an attractor for the short-run equilibrium NAIRU and for the actual level of unemployment. The attractor may be a relatively weak one, but nevertheless acts as a 'pull' for the rate of unemployment. Admittedly, Layard et al. (1991) make the point that the 'long-run NAIRU ... is of course subject to long-term change (e.g. from different benefit systems or wage-bargaining arrangements) and to temporary change (e.g. from changes in oil prices)' (p. 11), but there is clearly here no suggestion that those changes are provoked by the actual course of unemployment. A more institutional view may suggest that the experience of unemployment may have an impact on the nature and design of the unemployment benefit system, for example.

Second, a rise in unemployment can set up many forces, economic, social and political, some of which may tend to push unemployment up further and others tend to reduce unemployment. There may be some reversion towards the long-run average rate of unemployment, but that does not mean that there is no path dependency. Some reversion does not necessarily mean complete reversion, and the long-run average is just that – the average – which need not have equilibrium connotations.

The unemployment rate is, of course, a ratio between (measured) unemployment and the labour force. Even if the unemployment rate were to revert back to some historical average, the meaning and significance of that rate may well be different. Labour force participation can respond to the path of aggregate demand. In that case, the size of the economy (as measured by labour force) changes over time in a path-dependent way (this is illustrated in section 7).

This illustrates a more general point with regard to path dependency and hysteresis. In macroeconomic analysis there are many variables of interest, which are ratios and for which there are clear bounds within which the ratio has to fall. The share of wages is one example, and is clearly bound by zero and unity, and it can be readily argued that the bounds are tighter than that. It is plausible to argue that there are forces within the economy that keep the share of wages within a fairly narrow range. It could then turn out that the share of wages was untrended and the inference made that there are no hysteric effects or any path dependency. In contrast we would argue that even if the share of wages were found to revert to some 'normal' level, there may well still be path dependency with regard to the elements of the ratio, that is, for example, to the real wage productivity of labour, not to mention the overall size of the wage payments and of the economy.

In the context of the labour market, path dependency comes from many sources. The experience of unemployment and employment on the skills, work commitment and attitudes of workers; entry into the labour force and migration to another country in response to employment opportunities are not readily reversed. Some of these effects may be reversed but others are unlikely to be. For there not to be path dependence there would have to be factors which lead reversibility but that scale of the factors exactly offsets the initial changes. For example, if a high level of demand pulled people out of the rural economy into the industrial sector, then for an absence of path dependency there would have to be low levels of demand sufficient to push those people back from the industrial sector into the rural economy.

5. Demand, investment and the inflation barrier

In the context of macroeconomic analysis, there are many features of investment, which are at the same time well known in heterodox macroeconomics; unsurprisingly, though, barely mentioned in many mainstream circles. Still, these features are highly relevant for a path dependency approach to macroeconomic analysis. The first is that the essential property of investment (whether in the form of fixed capital equipment or in the form of say education) is that it is intended to bring future rewards and benefits. Investment, which occurs in the present, is intended to have future effects by the definition of what constitutes investment. This leads to the observation that decisions on investment are strongly influenced by perceptions of the future by the decision maker. But the future is uncertain and inherently unknowable. It is then not a matter of the future setting what is done in the present, but rather postulates about the future influencing what is done in the present, and those actions in the present setting the scene for the future.

The second remark is that, in macroeconomic terms, the level of investment is a significant component of aggregate demand. As such, the level of investment that takes place has a significant impact on the resulting level of economic activity. We may articulate this argument in a simple representation in the equation $s_p P = I$, where s_p is the propensity to save out of profits (P), and I is investment. The conclusion to draw is that profits depend on investment, but the investment that occurs depends on the perceptions of what profits are expected to be.

Third, 'many if not most innovations need to be embodied in new kinds of durable equipment before they can be made effective' (Solow, 1960, p. 91). There is then an intimate link between technical change and investment. Decisions made on investment impact on technical change, if and when innovations are made and if and when new ideas are incorporated into practice.

Fourth, investment takes many forms, and with specific reference to fixed capital formation, it is not just the quantity of investment that is relevant but its quality and structure. The manner in which different sectors of the economy (e.g. manufacturing, agriculture) develop depends on the investment that is taking place in the sector. Further, the nature of the capital equipment (K) and its rate of change (k) are not constant over time. This undermines the use of a single variable for K and k in a model of the economy. Growth is not a matter of more of the same. Even when it is more of the same, the amount of the 'same' (in terms of the capital stock) depends on decisions on investment.

When the growth path is already set, as in the neoclassical growth model, then the growth of the capital stock, which is of course equal to net investment, has to move towards that growth rate. The Keynesian approach to investment involves 'the state of expectations' and in that sense is forward looking. But perceptions of the future are much moulded by present and past experience. There are elements of adaptive expectations with regard to key variables such as profitability and growth prospects.

In this chapter we wish to draw attention to some aspects of investment and capital formation for the supply side of the economy. Investment in many respects links together the demand side and the supply side of the economy in the sense that investment is a major component of aggregate demand and investment is capital accumulation influencing the development of the supply side of the economy. Decisions made on investment depend on a wide range of factors including the state of present and prospective demand, profitability and 'animal spirits' and technological factors. The path followed by the economy as reflected in the variables (and others) just mentioned would then influence the investment that takes place. In turn, the investment that occurs helps to set down the next steps for the economy in terms of the evolution of the supply potential of the economy. We illustrate some of the significance of these arguments by reference to the notion of an inflation barrier. In mainstream analysis notions such as 'natural rate of unemployment' and the NAIRU act rather like inflation barriers in the sense that unemployment lower than the 'natural rate' or the NAIRU is predicted to lead to rising inflation. However, those concepts tend to be associated with the labour market and, more significantly here, are treated as equilibrium levels of unemployment which act as strong attractors for the level of economic activity and which are not influenced by the level of demand (indeed it was that property which lead Friedman (1968) to use the label 'natural rate'). In what follows there is no implication that the inflation barrier acts as a strong attractor (or indeed any kind of attractor). We focus though on the way in which the inflation barrier evolves over time in response to the level and forms of investment.

This discussion of the inflation barrier and path dependency draws heavily on Sawyer (2002) and Arestis and Sawyer (2006). The key point we may borrow from these contributions for the purposes of this chapter is that investment expenditure is influenced by factors such as capacity utilization, profitability, technological opportunities, which themselves depend, in part, on the evolution of the economy. Hence, changes in the capital stock are path dependent. As the capital stock changes, there are clearly changes in productive potential and in cost conditions of firms. This leads to changes in productivity, in prices and thereby real wages.

Figure 1.2 illustrates the argument where the p-curve relates to a relationship between real product wage (at the aggregate level) and output based on pricing considerations, and the w-curve to one also between real product wage and output based on wage setting considerations. The inequalities relate to a view on how wages and prices would change in each of the four segments identified, with the upper inequality based on price determination and the lower inequality on wage determination. The technicalities of the derivation are given in Sawyer (2002).

In this analysis it should be noted that it is the interaction of wage and price behaviour that is portrayed. Point X can be thought of as an inflation barrier and the diagram provides an indication of the ways in which wages and prices behave. Thus in zone A, prices try to rise faster than wages based on price determination, and wages try to rise faster than wages based on wage determination, and hence a wage–price spiral would develop. This diagram does not contain any suggestion that point

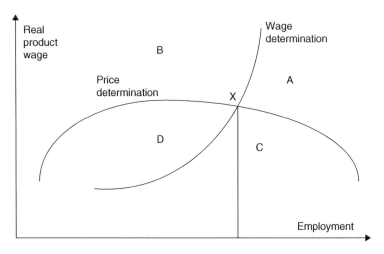

Figure 1.2   Determination of inflation barrier

X will be an attractor for the actual level of economic activity. It rather says that if the economy happens to have a combination of real product wage and output which places it in zone A, then a wage–price spiral develops. Point X may be thought of as some form of equilibrium in the sense that if the economy were at point X then wages and prices would be rising at the same pace, and hence real wages would be constant and inflation not rising (or falling). But there is no presumption that the economy would tend to move towards (or away from) point X. How real wages would change would depend on the relative movement of wages and prices, and how the level of output changes would depend on the impact of changing income distribution on aggregate demand and how government macroeconomic policy evolves (and also other factors such as world demand for exports of the economy concerned).

The most significant point of this approach with respect to path dependency is that the equivalent of point X (the inflation barrier) will be continually changing in response to investment and changes in the capital stock. The productive capacity will be changing, as investment proceeds, and investment will be responding to factors such as profitability, capacity utilization and perceptions of the future. In terms of Figure 1.2, the position of the p-curve depends on the size of the capital stock. Investment that is capacity enhancing (in effect 'more of the same') could be seen to shift the p-curve to the right, whereas investment in new processes which raises labour productivity could be seen as shifting the p-curve upwards.

There are other ways in which the passage of the economy would impact on the inflation barrier. For example, the institutional arrangements with regard to wage formation and employment practices including employment law and industrial relations, would have some impact on the position of the w-curve. The industrial structure and competition between firms could affect the position of the p-curve through their influence on the mark-up of prices over costs. All this stands in contrast to ideas on the 'natural rate of unemployment', which is akin to the equilibrium position based on the demand for and supply of labour.

6. Research, development and technical change

Technical change and the development and implementation of new ideas, introduction of new products and processes are probably the clearest cases for the need for analysis to incorporate path dependency. The discussion above relating to 'lock-in' effects provides examples of the notion that when a new idea is introduced it has subsequent effects on the path of the economy. The whole process of research and discovery involving the development of new ideas, processes, etc. has to build on previous ones. The development of new ideas cannot be other than path dependent.

Technical changes and the development of new ideas and new solutions cannot be foreseen – in effect, if a new idea could have been foreseen it would not have been a new idea! The directions in which new ideas are sought are influenced by many factors: the outbreak of AIDS/HIV stimulates the search for ways to prevent or to cure. But where the preventions or cures will come from cannot be known ahead of their discovery – in the words of Rumsfeld referred to earlier this may constitute 'unknown unknowns'.

There is a close linkage between technical change and fundamental uncertainty. It is because research and technical change involves something new that past experience cannot be used to generate some probability distribution of future events. Rolling the dice many millions of times in the past generates confidence that the probability distribution for future rolls of the dice are such that there is a one-in-six probability for each number on the dice to be rolled. The experience of the discovery and development of electricity does not provide any probability distribution for some future major invention. Technical change involves uncertainty rather than risk.

The quote given above from Phelps (2007) summarizes the essential difficulty, which the novelty of new ideas presents for the path independency and the 'rational expectations' approach. The novelty of new ideas is a major aspect of the essential uncertainty of the future (in the Keynesian–Knightian sense).

In this chapter our focus is on macroeconomic aspects of path dependency, and the ways in which the path of demand and the development of supply potential interact. In the context of technical change, the conditions of demand (whether at the level of the economy or facing a particular industry) are relevant for the pace and nature of technical change in a number of ways. One way, widely drawn upon in the macroeconomics literature, relates to 'learning by doing'. The term 'learning by doing' captures two key features – that there is learning and that there is 'doing'. For the individual, learning involves the acquisition of new (as far as that individual is concerned) knowledge, and there is a sense in which learning is not readily reversible; indeed, there can be a process of unlearning in the sense of lagging behind new developments. The concept of 'learning by doing' though goes further in the sense that what is learnt is often new for society as a whole not merely for the individual. The extent of 'doing' is, of course, related to the level of demand. Verdoorn's Law (using the common terminology though having the status of a 'law' seems rather strong) is generally expressed in terms of rate of productivity change as a function of rate of growth of output, with the assumption that growth of output is demand driven (and that it is positive). In many versions Verdoorn's Law may be limited to certain sectors of the economy (notably manufacturing). In our analysis in the next section we use Verdoorn's Law as an expression of the idea that the pace of change is linked with demand. This is intended to be illustrative rather than definitive, and a fuller analysis would require more exploration of that idea.

There are clearly other ways in which the general conditions in the economy influence decisions made on technical change and research and development, and hence ways in which the path of demand impacts. Research and development does after all have to be financed and, when undertaken by private firms, have to be perceived as profitable (though given the uncertain nature of research and its outcomes the formation of those perceptions also become highly relevant).

7. Demand and supply in economic growth

There are two specific issues that we wish to address in this section that build on our prior discussions. The first is that in a path-dependent world it is possible to construct any type of model of economic growth in that there is no equilibrium growth path 'out there' (as in the neoclassical case); and each step along the growth path depends on the previous steps that have been taken. The second issue is the illustration of ways in which the path of demand influences the evolution of supply, and also how demand factors have a long-term impact on the growth of the economy.

In a path-dependent world where (as illustrated in Figure 1.1) the step taken in time t forms the basis for the steps, which can be taken in time $t + 1$; the path followed by the economy has to be built up step by step. Further, at each stage, decisions have to be made, choices exercised, etc., in some human agency, so that there is no predestination involved. In this section we do not attempt to present a complex model along these lines, but rather to illustrate.

The way we proceed is by a form of construction of possible scenarios, with certain steps being specified and some ways in which the economy tends to change processes postulated to investigate the possible growth path. The emphasis is on the role of demand, and the ways in which supply may change in response to demand.

We start by setting out in this section a basic simple model based on Kaleckian notions in which the demand side plays a key role in the determination of the growth rate. The model assumes a closed economy. These assumptions enable us to raise certain well-known questions and provide a platform for considering the relationship between the demand and the supply sides of the economy in the growth process, and between savings and investment.

The savings function starts from the proposition that s is the propensity to save out of profits, and for simplicity it is assumed that there are no savings out of wages.[3] The savings function is then expressed as:

$$\frac{S}{K} = \frac{smu}{v} \qquad (1)$$

where S is savings, K a measure of the capital stock, s the propensity to save out of profits, m the share of profits in national income, u a measure of capacity utilization and v the capital-(capacity) output ratio. The investment function is assumed to take the form of:

$$\frac{I}{K} = a + b(u - u^*) + cm \qquad (2)$$

where u^* is some measure of 'desired' capacity utilization (as far as enterprises are concerned in terms of costs and profits) and this equation reflects the influence of both capacity and profitability on investment decisions (noting that the rate of profit is equal to $m.u/v$). The coefficient *a* can be thought of as reflecting a range of influences on investment including 'animal spirits' and the technological developments. This is an innocuous looking investment function, which reflects the Kaleckian arguments on the roles of profitability and capacity utilization (Sawyer, 1982, 2002). Besides not including relative prices, it also does not reflect any notion that firms know the future in the sense of holding rational expectations on the future, which are the basis of their decisions. It reflects the effects of current experience on the economy (through capacity utilization and profitability), with that current experience influencing perceptions of the future and that it is demand determined. The inclusion of profitability reflects a number of factors including the availability of internal funds for investment as well as the returns on capital. It is also taken as a proxy for firms' views on future prospects. Since the future is uncertain, future prospects cannot be modelled through some idea of rational expectations but rather has to be based on some projection of current experiences into the future. There is not going to be a one-for-one mapping from current experiences to perceptions of future prospects. There are waves of optimism and pessimism, which can change the balance; in Keynes's terminology 'animal spirits' vary of time in ways not reflected in the macroeconomic variables. The analysis of any specific period based on this type of approach would need to take into account factors such as technological developments and their implications for investment opportunities and the state of 'animal spirits' and the general assessment of future prospects. In the simple framework here we see those factors as being reflected in the coefficient *a*.

The term *d* is used to denote the net injections (into the circular flow of income) from outside the private sector (relative to the capital stock), and as such this includes the budget deficit, and hence *d* can be thought of as the budget deficit relative to the capital stock (in an open economy context *d* would also involve the net export position). We introduce this term to be able to reflect the possible effects of demand on the level of economic activity.

Within a specified period, the Kaleckian equilibrium condition is used to give:

$$\frac{smu}{v} = a + d + b(u - u^*) + cm \tag{3}$$

which can be solved to give the capacity utilization and one-period growth of capital stock, $g_K(t) = I/K$ for time t:

$$u(t) = \frac{(a - bu^* + d + cm)v}{sm - bv} \tag{4}$$

$$g_K(t) = \frac{sm(a + cm) + b(dv - smu^*)}{sm - bv} \tag{5}$$

It is assumed that the 'Keynesian' stability condition holds so that $sm - bv > 0$. The growth rate here is the one period change in the capital stock, and does not imply any trend rate of growth.

The level of capacity utilization would be at its 'normal' level if some combination of a ('animal spirits') and d the fiscal stimulus is sufficient. For $u = u^*$, $(a + d) = (smu^* - cmv)$. The growth rate of the capital stock would then be $a + cm$. Fiscal policy is seen to impact on capacity utilization and on the rate of growth. A given (primary) budget deficit to income ratio will lead to convergence on a debt:income ratio provided that $g > r$, and hence in this model a higher budget deficit is more likely to be sustainable than a smaller one, since the growth rate is higher and hence the condition $g > r$ more likely to be satisfied. Capacity utilization appears as demand determined, and firms are willing to undertake investment even when they have excess capacity, and excess capacity can be a feature of the long-run as well as the short-run and firms are willing to accept excess capacity (where here excess capacity means capacity utilization below the 'desired' capacity utilization, which may be influenced by average costs but also may allow for strategic factors, etc.).

From the position given above, there are clearly many ways in which the variables can evolve over time. We postulate that there are some systematic forces that influence the path along which the economy travels, and that we can in a very simple manner reflect some of those forces in a model. We give two simple examples. First, consider a case where the profit margin changes in response to conditions of demand (as reflected in capacity utilization). This is the simple notion that when demand conditions are favourable firms are able to raise their profit margins, and conversely when demand conditions are less favourable profit margins are under pressure. This could be written as:

$$\dot{m} = \lambda(u - u^*) \quad \lambda > 0 \tag{6}$$

where the dot above a variable denotes the rate of change of the specific variable. This adjustment process could continue until $u = u^*$, and under those circumstances the mark-up could eventually reach a level (provided that the parameters of the model remain unchanged):

$$m = \frac{a + d}{su^* - c} \tag{7}$$

In this model, it should be noted that the profit margin depends positively on the fiscal stimulus d even though capacity utilization has moved to a 'normal level' and could be said to be set on the supply side.

The growth rate of capital stock would then be given by:

$$g_K = \frac{s(a+d)[su^*(a+bd)+cd(1-b)]}{[s(a+d)-b(su^*-c)]} \tag{8}$$

It is again to be noted that the growth rate of the capital stock depends on a range of factors including 'animal spirits' and the fiscal stimulus. This growth rate would reflect the outcome of a process and when reached would have the property of being able to continue. This approach faces a 'knife edge' problem, which may take the following form. If firms find they have excess capacity, and reduce investment, then there is further excess capacity, etc.

Another adjustment process that can be envisaged is when the 'desired' level of capacity utilization changes in the face of experience. Specifically, suppose firms adjust their notions of the 'desired' capacity utilization according to an equation such as: $\dot{u}^* = \vartheta(u - u^*)$, with $\vartheta > 0$. If such a process worked itself out, then desired and actual capacity utilization would be $(a+d+cm)v/sm$ and growth $g_k = a+cm$. In this context, the level of capacity utilization depends on 'animal spirits' (a) and fiscal policy (d); and the growth rate of the economy depends on those 'animal spirits' and on the mark-up (m).

This approach is a representation (in effect an elaboration of the Harrod–Domar model) of the demand-determined approach to growth. This raises the major question of how does the demand determined rate of growth compare with the supply determined rate of growth and what adjustment processes occur to resolve the differences between them.

An equation such as (5) provides a growth rate for the capital stock in time t, and by extension the growth rate of output (based on a given capital-output ratio). Working with a fixed factor proportion approach, the demand for labour (in effectiveness terms) would change in line with output. With employment demand determined, this would imply $L(t+1) = L(t)(1+g_K(t))$. The growth of the effective labour force is labelled g_n hence $N(t+1) = N(t)(1+g_n(t))$. We define (recorded) unemployment rate $ur(t) = L(t)/N(t)$.

The Keynesian approach involves a variety of routes through which the level and the growth on the demand side (and hence growth of output) stimulates the growth of the effective labour force, g_n. High levels of demand help to 'pull' people into the labour force, whereas low levels of demand 'push' people out of the labour force. The arguments associated with 'learning by doing', the application of Verdoorn's law and the stimulus of demand on research and development and investment in education and training, would all suggest that the growth of the effective labour force, whether in terms of a more highly-skilled work force or in terms of increases in productivity, would be related to the growth of demand and capacity utilization. Combining these two elements here we postulate that:

$$g_n(t) = \alpha + \beta g_K(t) + \gamma u(t) \tag{9}$$

The effective labour force would then change over time in accordance with an equation such as this one. The labour force at a point in time would then be given by $N(t) = N(0) \prod_{i=1}^{t} (1 + g_n(i))$. Combining equations (5) and (9) would then give:

$$N(t) = N(0) \prod_{i=1}^{t} (1 + \alpha + \beta \left[\frac{sm(a + cm) + b(dv - smu^*)}{sm - bv} \right] + \gamma u^*) \tag{10}$$

This path for the labour force is clearly built up step by step and can be considered path dependent, as it depends on the value of the parameters in each of the periods an specifically depends on factors such as profit margin, 'animal spirits' and the fiscal policy stance. The level of unemployment then evolves according to the following expression:

$$ur(t + 1) = \frac{L(t + 1)}{N(t + 1)} = \frac{L(t)(1 + \alpha + \beta g_K(t) + \gamma u(t))}{N(t)(1 + g_K(t))} \tag{11}$$

Reference back to equations (4) and (5) would indicate the values taken by g_K and u. At each point in time in this model those variables would be determined by factors such as fiscal stance and 'animal spirits' working through the savings and investment functions. Above we have given two examples of how some of the key variables may vary over time as some form of adjustment process. If those adjustment processes (or others) were at work, then the path followed as described in equations (10) and (11) (and a corresponding one for $Y(t)$) would reflect them. The scale of the economy can be viewed as essentially demand determined and path dependent. By the scale we would mean a combination of the size of the capital stock, the size of the effective labour force and thereby the volume of output. Equation (4) above would indicate how the level of output at a particular time compares with the capacity level of output.

We can also ask the question as to whether there is some 'balanced' growth rate under which output, capital stock and effective labour force would grow at the same pace (and hence capacity utilization and unemployment rate remain constant). This is viewed here as asking the question as to whether that is feasible, and here it does not enable us to say whether such a growth path could be achieved. From equation (9), with the underlying parameters held constant, the balanced growth rate can be readily calculated from $\alpha + \beta g_K + \gamma u = g_K$ as:

$$g_k(1 - b) = a + du \tag{12}$$

Since by reference to equation (4), u depends on fiscal policy, the growth rate of the economy is influenced by fiscal policy, 'animal spirits', and the responsiveness of growth of effective labour force to growth of capital stock and capacity utilization. An alternative interpretation of equation (11) would be that g_k and u refer to the average levels of the variables achieved.

To round off this section we make reference to two other papers which have proceeded in a relatively similar manner. Dutt (2006) develops a Kaleckian style model (that is, one that starts from equations similar to equations (1) and (2) above except that the investment function does not depend on profit margin). His model then allows that the equivalent of the constant a in equation (2) adjusts depending (negatively) on the difference between the growth of employment and the growth of the labour force. Dutt (op. cit.) further allows that changes (growth) in labour productivity depend (positively) on that difference. He draws three implications from his model:

> First, instead of a unique long-run equilibrium, the economy has a continuum of equilibria ... These equilibria are all stable. This implies that the long-run equilibrium position of the economy will depend on where it starts off from. ... Second, starting from a long-run equilibrium ... an exogeneous increase in [constant term in investment function] brought about by expansionary fiscal or monetary policy, or simply an autonomous boost in animal spirits, will imply a move ... In the long run there will be a movement ... implying a higher rate of growth than at the initial equilibrium. Hence expansionary policies and other positive aggregate demand shocks have long-term expansionary effects, although not as strong as short-run expansionary effects. Likewise, contractionary policies have long-run contractionary effects. Third ... the path of economy will depend on the technological responsiveness of the economy ... and by the policy stance of the government and by labour and asset market characteristics. (pp. 326–7)

Palley (1996, 2002) involves an investment function in which investment depends on the growth of demand and capacity utilization (relative to some 'normal' level) in a model in which the growth of output is, as it would be in a endogenous growth theory, equal to the growth of the labour force plus the rate of labour-augmenting technical progress and the elasticity of output with respect to capital (in a Cobb–Douglas production function) times the growth of capital–labour ratio. The rate of technical progress depends on investment and the capital–labour ratio. The level of demand as exhibited in capacity utilization influences investment, which in turn influences the rate of technical change. The growth of output is solved out to depend on growth of labour force and a function of growth of demand, capital–labour ratio and capacity utilization. An equilibrium growth rate (where the growth of demand equals the growth of output) can then be established.

The purpose of this section has been to illustrate the idea that the average growth rate of an economy can be built up from the growth rate in each period of time along with some postulated changes (e.g. in the mark-up of prices over costs). It further has sought to indicate that the average rate of growth depends on what may be termed demand factors and what may be termed supply factors, with the recognition that the evolution of the supply of the factors of production, such as labour and capital stock along with the rate of productivity growth, are dependent on the conditions of demand.

8. Concluding remarks

We have dealt in this chapter with a number of aspects of path dependency. We began with an elaboration on the meaning of the notion of path dependency and contrasted it with path independency. In this respect we have elaborated on how path dependency is linked with notions of fundamental uncertainty, non-ergodicity, hysteresis and some of the factors, which have been highlighted in the generation of path dependency. The implications of the notion of path dependency thereby assembled have been discussed from the macroeconomic analysis point of view in terms of the interrelationship between aggregate demand and supply potential and the availability of future resources. We have also contrasted path dependency as explored in this chapter with mainstream views held about the economy. We have suggested that in the mainstream analysis although the economy is viewed as following a time path, and history may have an important role to play, it does not affect the final equilibrium position in their analysis. Equilibrium theories of the economic system in the mainstream are by far too important. Not so of course in the dependency analysis as demonstrated in this chapter and in the rest of this book.

We have subsequently contrasted these notions of path dependency, which have featured in the heterodox macroeconomics literature, with the path independency of mainstream macroeconomics. For it is the case that the mainstream approach to macroeconomic analysis, in its static or dynamic context, is shown to involve path independence (essentially the idea of equilibrium which in effect exists prior to events). This led us to suggest that these two sets of literature and approach differ substantially with significant analytical implications. Path dependency in macroeconomic analysis is then discussed in relation to the labour market, inflation barrier, investment and the capital stock, and technological change. Building on this analysis we developed argument on the demand and supply in economic growth. Two specific issues have been addressed more closely. The first is that in a path-dependent world it is possible to construct models of economic growth that do not adhere to equilibrium growth path. The second issue concerned itself with the path that demand influences the evolution of supply. Also, how demand factors have a long-term impact on the growth of the economy. In all these cases examined and analysed it is clear that path dependency, and not path independency, is important.

Throughout the analysis in this chapter we have constructed different scenarios in which the economy is faced with different processes that are postulated to investigate the possible growth path. We have focused specifically on two important aspects of path dependency. The first is our attempt to draw on ideas that have long circulated in Keynesian economics. The second is to explore and propose ways in which the path of demand impacts on the development of supply potential. The emphasis is on the role of demand, and the ways in which supply may change in response to demand.

Another interesting conclusion is that fiscal policy has an important role to play and it thus matters a great deal. This is contrary to the currently held view within the new consensus macroeconomics that downgrades the role of fiscal policy to the point of extinction.

Notes

1. The quote is widely available on the web: the precise source is http://www.brainyquote.com/quotes/quotes/d/donaldrums148142.html).

2. We have critically discussed the New Consensus in Macroeconomics on a number of occasions. See, for example, Arestis and Sawyer (2004, 2006, 2008).
3. We would argue that allowing for savings out of wages would complicate the analysis and raise several issues. More specifically these issues are concerned with the use to which workers' savings are put; we wish to avoid these aspects for the simple reason that they do not impact on the arguments concerning the roles of demand and supply. In other words, allowing for savings out of wages would complicate the analysis unnecessarily without changing the basic argument substantially to require a more complex analysis.

References

Arestis, P. and Sawyer, M.C. (2004), 'Can monetary policy affect the real economy?', *European Review of Economics and Finance*, vol. 3, no. 3, pp. 3–26.

Arestis, P. and Sawyer, M. (2006), 'Aggregate demand, conflict and capacity in the inflationary process', *Cambridge Journal of Economics*, vol. 29, no. 6, pp. 959–74.

Arestis, P. and Sawyer, M. (2008), 'A critical reconsideration of the foundations of monetary policy in the new consensus macroeconomics framework', *Cambridge Journal of Economics*, vol. 32, no. 5, pp. 761–79.

Arthur, W.B. (1988), 'Self-reinforcing Mechanisms in Economics', in P.W. Anderson, K.J.A. and D. Pines (eds), *The Economy as an Evolving, Complex System*, pp. 9–32. Reading, MA: Addison-Wesley.

Arthur, W.B. (1989), 'Competing Technologies, Increasing Returns, and Lock-in by Historical Events', *Economic Journal*, vol. 99, no. 1, pp. 116–31.

Arthur, W.B. (1994), *Increasing Returns and Path Dependence in the Economy*, Ann Arbor, MI: University of Michigan Press.

Arulampalan, W., Gregg, P. and Gregory, M. (2001), 'Unemployment scarring', *Economic Journal*, vol. 111, no. 3, pp. F577–84.

Boas, T.C. (2007), 'Conceptualizing Continuity and Change: the Composite-standard Model of Path Dependence', *Journal of Theoretical Politics*, vol. 19, no. 1, pp. 33–54.

Dutt, A.K. (2006), 'Aggregate Demand, Aggregate Supply and Economic Growth', *International Review of Applied Economics*, vol. 20, no. 3, pp. 319–36.

Friedman, M. (1968), 'The Role of Monetary Policy: Presidential Address to AEA', *American Economic Review*, vol. 58, no. 1, pp. 1–17.

Frydman, R. and Goldberg, M.D. (2007), *Imperfect Knowledge Economics: Exchange Rates and Risk*, Princeton University Press.

Jorgenson, D. (1963), 'Capital Theory and Investment Behaviour', *American Economic Review*, vol. 53, no. 2, pp. 247–59.

Kaldor, Nicholas (1955–56). 'Alternative Theories of Distribution', *Review of Economic Studies*, 23(2), No. 61, 83–100.

Kaldor, Nicholas (1972), 'The irrelevance of equilibrium economics', *Economic Journal*, 82, December, 1237–55, reprinted in F. Tagetti and A.P. Thirlwall (eds), *The Essential Kaldor*, London: Duckworth.

Kalecki, M. (1971), *Selected Essays on the Dynamics of the Capitalist Economy, 1933–1970*, Cambridge: Cambridge University Press

Keynes, J.M. (1937), 'The General Theory of Employment', *Quarterly Journal of Economics*, vol. 51, no. 2 (February 1937), pp. 209–23.

Layard, R., Nickell, S. and Jackman, R. (1991), *'Unemployment: Macroeconomic Performance and the Labour Market*, Oxford: Oxford University Press.

Mahoney, J. (2000), 'Path Dependence in Historical Sociology', *Theory and Society*, vol. 29, no. 4, pp. 507–48.

Martin, R. and Sunley, P. (2006), 'Path Dependence and Regional Economic Evolution', *Journal of Economic Geography*, vol. 6, no. 2, pp. 395–437.

Metcalfe, J.S. (2001), 'Institutions and Progress', *Industrial and Corporate Change*, vol. 10, no. 3, pp. 561–85.

Myrdal, G. (1957), *Economic Theory and the Underdeveloped Regions*, London: Duckworth.

Palley, T.I. (1996), 'Growth Theory in a Keynesian Mode: Some Keynesian Foundations for the Theory of Economic Growth', *Journal of Post Keynesian Economics*, vol. 19, no. 2, pp. 113–35.

Palley, T.I. (2002), 'Keynesian Macroeconomics and the Theory of Economic Growth: Putting Aggregate Demand Back in the Picture', in M. Setterfield (ed.), *The Economics of Demand-led Growth: Challenging the Supply-side Version of the Long Run*, Cheltenham: Edward Elgar.

Phelps, E.S. (2007), 'Introduction', to Frydman and Goldberg (2007).

Pierson, P. (2000), 'Increasing Returns, Path Dependence, and the Study of Politics', *American Political Science Review*, vol. 94, no. 2, pp. 251–67.

Sawyer, M. (1982), *Macroeconomics in Question*, Brighton: Harvester-Wheatsheaf.

Sawyer, M. (2002), 'The NAIRU, aggregate demand and investment', *Metroeconomica*, vol. 53, no.1, pp. 66–94.

Sawyer, M. (2009), 'The central core of heterodox macroeconomics' in Jonathan P. Goldstein and Michael G. Hillard (eds), *Heterodox Macroeconomics Keynes, Marx and Globalization*, forthcoming, pp. 24–35.

Sawyer, M. and Spencer D.A. (2008a), 'On the definition of involuntary unemployment' *Journal of Socio-Economics*, 37, pp. 718–35.

Sawyer, M. and Spencer D.A. (2008b), 'Labour supply, employment and unemployment in macroeconomics: a critical appraisal', *mimeo*, University of Leeds.

Setterfield, M. (1997), *Rapid Growth and Relative Decline*, London: Macmillan.

Setterfield, M. (2002), 'A Model of Kaldorian Traverse: Cumulative Causation, Structural Change and Evolutionary Hysteresis', in M. Setterfield (ed.), *The Economics of Demand-led Growth: Challenging the Supply-side Version of the Long Run*, Cheltenham: Edward Elgar.

Setterfield, M. (2009), 'Path Dependency, Hysteresis and Macrodynamics', this volume.

Solow, R.M. (1956), 'A contribution to the theory of economic growth', *Quarterly Journal of Economics*, vol. 70(1), pp. 65–94.

Solow, R.M. (1960), 'Investment and Technical Progress', in K. Arrow et al. (eds), *Mathematical Methods in the Social Sciences*, Stanford: Stanford University Press.

Swann, T. (1956), 'Economic growth and capital accumulation', *Economic Record*, vol. 32 (November), pp. 334–61.

Woodford, M. (2003), *Interest and Prices: Foundations of a Theory of Monetary Policy*, Princeton: Princeton University Press.

2
Path Dependency, Hysteresis and Macrodynamics

*Mark Setterfield**
Trinity College, Hartford, CT

Abstract

This chapter explores the meaning and application of concepts of path dependency in macrodynamics, with a particular focus on hysteresis. It is argued that hysteresis is a particular type of (rather than a synonym for) path dependency, and that the concept emerges from features of the adjustment dynamics of economic systems, rather than the non-uniqueness of equilibrium. Distinctions are made between stating (or asserting) hysteresis, characterizing hysteresis, and providing a model of hysteresis. Concrete examples of appeals to hysteresis in macrodynamic analysis are used to illustrate these distinctions. Finally, a case is made for retaining linear unit/zero root models of 'hysteresis' in macrodynamic analysis, as a useful first approximation and alternative to traditional equilibrium analysis.

JEL Classification: E10

Keywords: Hysteresis; path dependency; macrodynamics

1. Introduction

This chapter explores the meaning and application of concepts of path dependency in macrodynamics. Particular attention is paid to the concept of hysteresis – what it is (and isn't), and how hysteresis can and should be used as an 'organizing concept' in macrodynamic analysis. The chapter is thus intended as a 'practitioner's guide' rather than as a literature survey. Its purpose is to discuss what serious considera-tion of path dependency implies for macrodynamic modelling, and to show how hysteresis can and should be incorporated into macrodynamic models – or, in other words, where hysteresis fits into the 'toolbox' of macrodynamic model builders.

Two of the central premises of the discussion that follows are that, properly conceived: (a) hysteresis is a particular type of, rather than a synonym or euphemism for, path dependency, the latter being a broader concept with more general implications for the methodology of macro-dynamic modelling; and (b) hysteresis emerges from reconsideration of the asymptotic stability properties of purported attractors (such as traditional equilibria) rather than their (non) uniqueness (as in popular unit/zero root models of hysteresis), and involves non-linearities and structural change along the dynamic adjustment path of a system. In what follows, conceptual distinctions are drawn between stating (or asserting) hysteresis, characterizing hysteresis, and providing a model of hysteresis. Concrete examples of appeals to hysteresis in macro-dynamic analysis are used throughout to illustrate these distinctions. The relationship between hysteresis and fundamental uncertainty is also investigated, and the potential for reconciling the two is demonstrated. Finally, and despite their having been subject to criticism, a case is made for retaining unit/zero root models of 'hysteresis' in macrodynamic analysis.

The remainder of the chapter is organized as follows. Section 2 discusses the role of organizing concepts in model building, identifying hysteresis as one example of a path-dependent organizing concept, and distinguishing hysteresis from the broader concept of path dependency. Section 3 then scrutinizes the concept of hysteresis as it has been used in macrodynamics. Attention is drawn to the distinction between stating (or asserting) hysteresis, characterizing hysteresis, and providing a model of hysteresis. Two main models of hysteresis are presented: linear, unit/zero root models; and non-linear models of 'true' hysteresis. The former are shown to provide only a crude approximation of hysteresis, failing to capture some of the most important features of the process – features that are clearly discernable in models of 'true' hysteresis. It is also shown that the latter can be reconciled with fundamental uncertainty. In section 4, a case is nevertheless made for *retaining* unit/zero root analysis in macrodynamics. It is argued that, from a pragmatic perspective, unit/zero root models can provide both a useful first approximation of 'hysteresis' effects in macrodynamics, and a valuable alternative organizing concept to that of traditional equilibrium. Finally, section 5 concludes.

2. Path dependency, hysteresis and model 'organizing concepts'

i) What is path dependency?

All formal models are constructed around 'organizing concepts', the most common example of which in macrodynamics (and economics in general) is the concept of equilibrium. Organizing concepts make an important contribution to the architecture of formal models, in the context of which macrodynamic theories are usually articulated. Concepts of path dependency – such as cumulative causation, lock-in and hysteresis – are, like the familiar concept of equilibrium, best understood as model-organizing concepts.[1]

But before we look more closely at specific path-dependent organizing concepts – and in particular, hysteresis – it is important to first contemplate a more basic question: what exactly *is* path dependency?[2] Broadly speaking, a dynamical system displays path dependency if earlier states of the system affect later ones – including (but by no means limited to) anything that can be construed as a 'long run' or 'final' outcome of the system. In other words, path dependency is synonymous with the principle that 'history matters'. In contrast, path independent systems are ahistorical: their configurations (at least in the long run) are unaffected by events in the past. A good example of a path independent system is any system that embodies a 'traditional equilibrium' as its organizing concept. A traditional equilibrium is both defined in terms of exogenous data that is imposed upon the system from without, and displays asymptotic stability (i.e., it is a position to which the system will return following any arbitrary displacement). In other words, traditional equilibrium configurations – or what Kaldor (1934) termed *determinate equilibria* – are 'both defined and reached without reference to the (historical) adjustment path taken towards them' (Setterfield, 1997a, p. 6).[3] It will immediately be recognized from the foregoing that traditional equilibrium is the canonical organizing concept in economic theory, with which organizing concepts based on path dependency are to be contrasted.

ii) What is path dependent?

Once the possibility of path dependency in dynamical systems is admitted, it is reasonable to ask: what features of a system can be affected by path dependency? Of primary interest in this regard are system outcomes – which in the context of macrodynamics would include growth rates, inflation rates, or, indeed, any 'static' macroeconomic variable (such as the level of aggregate output or the general price level) that is understood to result from a prior sequence of adjustments within a macroeconomic system. On this basis, it is tempting to suggest that path dependency is potentially ubiquitous in macrodynamic outcomes – and indeed, this position is defensible. Hence even in formally static models, in which variables are presented as interacting simultaneously and there is no pretense of a temporal ordering accompanying cause and effect statements, it is common to assert that outcomes are the result of a sequential adjustment process. Consider, for example, textbook comparative static exercises performed using the *IS–LM* apparatus, in which the appearance of instantaneous adjustment from one outcome to another is usually accompanied by an intuitive appeal to a series of disequilibrium adjustments that eventually gives rise (thanks to asymptotic stability) to the new outcomes of the system. Even models involving rational expectations – in which instantaneous adjustment is conceived as possible on the basis of agents' knowledge of the formal structure of the system, and hence their prior calculation of the consequences of any change – allow for purportedly inter-temporal adjustment processes. The latter arise whenever decision makers need time to learn the 'true model' of the system they inhabit, when random shocks create 'price surprises' and hence disequilibrium resource allocations that need to be corrected through subsequent adjustments, and/or when systems contain 'pre-determined' variables (i.e., variables whose values are fixed at any point in time – such as the capital stock) that constrain the ability of the system to 'jump' into its final configuration. Moreover, even in the absence of these mechanisms, it should be noted that, absent shocks and the adjustments (instantaneous or otherwise) they necessitate, the cumulative experience of the *same* outcome creates a 'history' that may (in principle) affect the structure of a system and hence its outcomes in the future. Ultimately, then, it can be argued that *all* models postulate sequential adjustment processes of some sort that may give rise to the path dependency of their outcomes (Setterfield, 1995, pp. 11–12).

It is important to note at this juncture that the outcomes discussed above as being susceptible to path dependency may take the form of equilibria. Although it is quite possible for a path-dependent system to produce outcomes that resemble nothing more than an ongoing series of non-equilibrium and non-equilibrating adjustments, it is also possible that a configuration that would ordinarily be associated with a position of equilibrium – such as the 'balance of forces' characteristic of market clearing, or the constant rate of expansion over time characteristic of a steady state – could be the outcome of a path-dependent process.

Of course, said equilibrium configuration will necessarily be a product of the prior adjustment path taken towards it. Nevertheless, what we are suggesting here is that, while the canonical concept of 'traditional equilibrium' as defined earlier is clearly incompatible with path dependency, the concept of equilibrium per se is not. Suppose, then, that we think of traditional equilibria as configurations that can be identified a priori without knowledge of the actual adjustment path taken towards them, and that therefore characterize systems whose dynamics are of secondary importance (because they serve only to guide the system towards a configuration that is independent of the precise sequence of adjustments the dynamics describe). Then following Lang and Setterfield (2006–07, p. 200), we can identify 'path-dependent equilibria' as having the opposite characteristics. In other words, path-dependent equilibrium configurations are influenced by the specific (historical) sequence of adjustments that a system undertakes in the process of reaching or attaining them, as a consequence of which the system's dynamics are of *primary* importance, since they are intrinsic to the very creation of *any* configuration (including those that can be interpreted as equilibria) that the system experiences.[4]

But is this claim – that path-dependent processes can result in 'path-dependent equilibria' – really sustainable? It was stated earlier that path dependency is synonymous with the principle that 'history matters'. But isn't it the case that the concept of an equilibrium always betrays this principle? Hence consider what achieving a state of equilibrium (of any description) involves. However defined, equilibrium is typically conceived as a state from which there will be no endogenously-generated tendency to deviate. And as noted by Setterfield (1997b):

> What this suggests … is that, once we are in equilibrium, history effectively ends; the future is predetermined by the time path corresponding to the equilibrium that has been achieved. The sequence of outcomes of which this time path is composed does not 'matter,' because the absence of any endogenous tendency to change dictates that it cannot affect the subsequent outcomes of the system in any way that would cause deviation from the equilibrium time path. (Setterfield, 1997b, p. 66)

In short, it would seem that achieving a state of equilibrium should be regarded as incompatible with the principle of path dependency.

Closer inspection, however, reveals that this need not be the case. Hence it is not essential – and given the potential ubiquity of path dependency, may not be at all prudent – to treat positions of equilibrium as states from which there can *never* be an endogenously-generated tendency to deviate. This is because, as intimated earlier, behavioural change may eventually result as a response to the cumulative experience of 'states of rest' themselves. This cumulative experience can eventually promote feelings of boredom or a sense of disappointed aspirations (Witt, 1991, pp. 88–9), or (in an environment of non-cooperative inter-action characterized by deficient foresight) a perceived need to change behaviour in order to avoid conceding first-mover advantages to others – even when (as perfect foresight would reveal) neither first-mover advantages nor any intent on the part of others to change their behaviour actually exists (Setterfield, 1997b, p. 67). Any of these factors may create a psychological imperative to change behaviour in response to repeated experience of equilibrium conditions themselves, resulting in an endogenously generated disturbance to the equilibrium (and hence a change in outcomes).[5] It is for this reason that Setterfield (1997a, pp. 68, 70) recommends that once the possibility of path dependency is recognized, all equilibrium states that are postulated as describing the actual outcomes of economic systems be regarded as temporary or 'conditional' equilibria, where 'a conditional equilibrium represents a state of rest brought about by ... (a) temporary suspension of the forces of change endogenous to a system' (Setterfield, 1997b, p. 70).[6] This explicitly allows for the possibility noted earlier – where 'the cumulative experience of the *same* outcome creates a 'history' that may (in principle) affect the structure of a system and hence its outcomes in the future' – thus reconciling (conditional) equilibrium states with the concept of path dependency.[7]

In short, taking path dependency seriously does not involve dispensing with the notion of equilibrium per se.[8] Instead, the possibility of path-dependent systems achieving equilibrium outcomes can be entertained, as long as it is understood that these will be path dependent rather than traditional equilibria, and that all such configurations are necessarily conditional. As we will see in section 3, this observation has been important in the development and use of the concept of hysteresis in macrodynamics. Hence most applications of hysteresis in macrodynamics involve amending the dynamics of traditional equilibrium models, transforming said models into path-dependent systems with outcomes that are still recognizable as equilibria, but now of the path-dependent variety.[9]

It is not, however, only the realized *outcomes* of dynamical economic systems that may be subject to path dependency. Other features of such systems, which are traditionally regarded as datum exogenous to their dynamics, may also be affected by the actual sequence of adjustments undertaken by the system over time. These include any 'ceiling' or 'floor' values of variables that are not defined as a matter of logic,[10] perhaps the most important of which in macrodynamics is the Harrodian natural rate of growth – the maximum rate of growth that an economy can achieve in the long run. The actual rate of growth need not coincide with the natural rate at any given point in time or even in the long run, but (by definition) it is not possible for the actual rate to exceed the natural rate in perpetuity. In other words, the natural rate constitutes a growth 'ceiling'.

The value of the natural rate of growth can be derived by first defining the maximum or potential *level* of real output that can be produced at any point in time as:

$$Y_p \equiv \left(\frac{N_{\max}}{L} \frac{L}{P} P \right) \frac{Y_p}{N_{\max}}$$

where Y_p denotes potential real output, $N_{\max}$ is the maximum feasible level of employment,[11] L denotes the labour force and P is the total population. If we assume that both the maximum rate of employment ($N_{\max}/L$) and the labour force participation rate (L/P) remain constant, the identity above yields the expression:

$$y_p = l + q$$

where y_p denotes the potential (i.e., natural) rate of growth, l is the rate of growth of the population and q denotes the rate of growth of labour productivity.

There is a long tradition in macrodynamics of regarding the determinants of the natural rate of growth – and hence the natural rate itself – as exogenous.[12] Even in contemporary endogenous growth theories inspired by Romer (1986, 1990) and Lucas (1988), in which technical change (and hence the rate of growth of labour productivity) is explicitly modelled, the ultimate determinants of technical change (such as preferences for the accumulation of human capital) are imposed from without. In other words, the natural rate of growth is typically regarded as invariant to the economy's actual experience of growth: it is treated as being path *in*dependent. But authors in the Kaldorian tradition have long regarded this as a mistake, suggesting that, for example, faster or slower actual rates of growth in the recent past can induce faster or slower population growth (through migration) and/or technical change (through dynamic economies of scale).[13] Suppose, then, that we write:

$$q = \alpha + \beta y_{-1}$$

where y denotes the actual rate of growth. This is the Verdoorn law, according to which rapid growth induces technical change and hence increased productivity growth.[14] Substituting the Verdoorn law into the expression for the natural rate of growth devived earlier yields:

$$y_p = l + \alpha + \beta y_{-1}$$

The natural rate of growth is therefore endogenous to the actual rate of growth experienced in the recent past. In other words, the 'ceiling' defining the maximum rate of growth that the economy can achieve is now path dependent.[15]

Although the overwhelming majority of research focuses on the implications of path dependency for the outcomes of dynamical systems, what the discussion above illustrates is that other important features of such systems may also be path dependent. In general, then, consideration of path dependency necessitates that, instead of thinking of the adjustment paths of dynamical systems as being circumscribed or contained by path-independent ceilings, floors or point attractors (such as traditional equilibria), we confront the possibility that all such constructs may be subject to endogenous revision in the course of a system's adjustment through time. In other words, we cannot overlook the possibility that ultimately, in any economic system, 'the only truly exogenous factor is *whatever exists at a given moment of time*, as a heritage of the past' (Kaldor, 1985, p. 61, emphasis in original).

iii) How or why does path dependency arise?

Having established both what path dependency is and what features of a system may be subject to path dependency, we can now investigate more closely *how* or *why* path dependency arises in dynamical economic systems.[16] These issues can and have been addressed philosophically (see, for example, Elster, 1976). But the same issues are also addressed and answered (at least implicitly) by different specific path-dependent organizing concepts, all of which purport to show exactly how earlier states affect later ones (including anything that can be construed as a 'long run' or 'final' outcome).

As intimated earlier, there are numerous concepts of path dependency of which hysteresis is just one. Hysteresis is thus properly regarded as a *particular type of* (rather than a *synonym for*) path dependency – an important point that is, unfortunately, lost on much macrodynamic analysis that uses the term hysteresis. The problem with such analysis is that its use of a specific term (hysteresis) as a synonym for a more general term (path dependency) serves to blur boundaries and obscure the defining features of hysteresis proper.[17] Hence even the otherwise laudable survey by Göcke (2002) begins by identifying hysteresis with the notion that 'transitory causes can have permanent effects'. This most certainly *is* a feature of hysteresis, but it is by no means a defining feature, since it is also a property of other concepts of path dependency (such as cumulative causation). In anticipation of the discussion in section 3 below, what can be said about hysteresis at this point that helps to set it apart from other concepts of path dependency is the following. First, properly conceived, hysteresis is a form of path dependency that emerges from reconsideration of the asymptotic stability of purported attractors (e.g., traditional equilibria) – and in particular, the assumed invariance of these attractors to the precise adjustment path taken towards them – rather than their non-existence or non-uniqueness. In other words, in terms of the classical triad of equilibrium analysis – existence, uniqueness and stability – our 'point of entry' for the study of hysteresis is (or should be) the latter, leading us to focus on properties of the *adjustment dynamics* of a system. Second, properly conceived, hysteresis involves non-linearities and structural change along the dynamic adjustment path of a system. We will also come to see that hysteresis can be associated with more specific properties such as *remanence* and selective memory that are not, in general, characteristic of the broader class of dynamical systems in which 'earlier states affect later ones' and 'transitory causes can have permanent effects' (Amable et al., 1993, 1995; Cross, 1993, 1995).

3.   The concept of hysteresis in macrodynamic analysis

We are now in a position to more fully and thoroughly explore hysteresis and its use as a organizing concept in macrodynamics. The discussion in this section will bear out the assertions made about hysteresis at the end of the previous section by analysing the various guises in which the concept of hysteresis has appeared in macrodynamics. As will become clear in what follows, it is possible to distinguish between stating (or asserting) hysteresis, characterizing hysteresis, and providing a model of hysteresis. Moreover, with the exception of the analytical 'detour' that is created by popular unit/zero root models of dynamical systems, the specific properties of hysteresis alluded to in section 2 become clearer as we progress through this hierarchy of representations of hysteresis.

i) Stating (or asserting) hysteresis

The simplest way of introducing hysteresis into macrodynamic analysis is to simply state or assert its existence in the process of discussing a particular economic phenomenology. A good example of this is provided by Jenkinson's (1987) discussion of 'hysteresis' in the natural rate of unemployment or NAIRU.[18] The following simple model summarizes the essence of the claims made by Jenkinson:

$$\dot{p} = -\alpha(U - U_n) \tag{1}$$

$$U_n = f(U_{-1}), \ f' > 0 \tag{2}$$

where $\dot{p}$ is the rate of change of inflation, U is the actual rate of unemployment and U_n denotes the natural rate of unemployment or non-accelerating inflation rate of unemployment (NAIRU).[19] Equation (1) is a standard accelerationist Phillips curve, according to which inflation will increase (decrease) over time whenever the actual rate of unemployment is below (above) the NAIRU. Equation (2), meanwhile, posits some functional dependence of the NAIRU on the actual rate of unemployment in the recent past.

The significance of this second equation becomes apparent when we consider the effects of a shock to the rate of unemployment, which raises the latter above the value of the NAIRU. The first impact of this shock is to lower the rate of inflation via equation (1) – in other words, the economy moves along an orthodox, negatively-sloped short-run Phillips curve (SRPC), shown in Figure 2.1 by the movement from (U_n, p_1) to (U_1, p_2). Conventional NAIRU theory suggests that in response to this situation, the actual rate of unemployment will move back towards the NAIRU. If we assume for simplicity that this adjustment is completed within a single period, the economy will thus arrive at the point (U_n, p_2) in Figure 2.1, and the dashed vertical line passing through U_n would be interpreted as the (vertical) long-run Phillips curve (LRPC). But according to equation (2), it is the value of the NAIRU that will respond to the increase in the actual rate of unemployment with which we began. Assuming for simplicity that $f' = 1$ – in other words, that the NAIRU adjusts so as to become equal to the actual rate of unemployment established at the start of the exercise – then the actual unemployment rate U_1 can now be identified as the new value of the NAIRU (U_n' in Figure 2.1).[20] This means that, *ceteris paribus*, the economy will remain at the point (U_1, p_2) since, with $U_1 = U_n'$, the system in equations (1) and (2) has now reached a steady state where $\dot{p} = 0$. Clearly, the long run or final

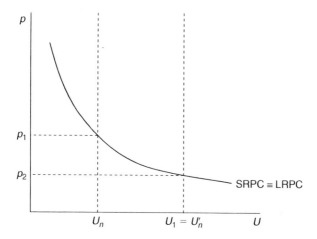

Figure 2.1   Asserting hysteresis in the NAIRU

outcomes of the system depend on events in the past. Had the shock to unemployment with which we began never happened, the economy would still be in equilibrium at (U_n, p_1). But it did happen and, as a result, not only was the economy temporarily displaced from equilibrium, but equilibrium conditions were subsequently recovered at a *different* final equilibrium *position* (the configuration $(U_1 = U'_n, p_2)$). This, it is claimed, demonstrates the workings of hysteresis.

Finally, note that as shown in Figure 2.1, we can join the points (U_n, p_1) and $(U_1 = U'_n, p_2)$ to establish that the shape of the LRPC is negatively sloped.[21] The vertical dashed lines passing through U_n and U'_n have no behavioural meaning – suggesting that NAIRU theory and its associated policy implications (including the purported long-run inefficacy of aggregate demand management) do not survive the introduction of hysteresis effects.[22]

But does the model in equations (1) and (2) actually capture the dynamics of hysteresis? The obvious problem that we confront in trying to address this question is that it is not clear what *causes* U_n to depend on U in equation (2): the function $f(\cdot)$ is a 'black box'. At this point, authors such as Jenkinson (1987) generally appeal to what may be termed 'back-stories' to justify the analytical structure of the model in (1) and (2). For example, suppose that we write:

$$U_n = g(Z), \quad g' < 0 \tag{3}$$

$$Z = h(U_{-1}), \quad h' < 0 \tag{4}$$

where Z denotes some variable affecting the ability or willingness of workers to find work (and hence the value of the NAIRU). For example, Z may be the reciprocal of the insider real wage prevailing in the labour market (assuming that the latter is characterized by insider–outsider relations). It is obvious that substitution of (4) into (3) produces (2) (with $f' = g'h'$), but the advantage that equations (3) and (7) confer on the model is that they furnish a 'backstory' that appears to unpack $f(\cdot)$ and thus justify the results associated with the interaction of (1) and (2). Hence suppose that any increase (decrease) in the actual rate of unemployment from its initial long-run equilibrium value entices insiders to restore long-run equilibrium in the labour market by increasing (decreasing) the insider wage, so that the latter matches the marginal product of labour at the level of employment associated with the new rate of unemployment. For example, insiders may seek to increase the rents they earn in connection with their employment in the event of an increase in unemployment, or maintain the employed status of newly-hired workers in the event of a decrease in employment.[23] These behaviours would remove any incentive for firms to change their pricing and production plans in order to recover conditions of long-run equilibrium by adjusting employment (to reconcile the marginal product of labour with a given insider wage) – because conditions of long-run equilibrium have already been recovered (by adjustment of the insider wage) at the new rates of employment/unemployment. The new actual rate of unemployment with which we began the exercise is thus enshrined as the new long-run equilibrium rate of unemployment, and the NAIRU is described as displaying hysteresis because its value depends on past values of the actual unemployment rate.

But 'backstories' of this nature are of little help if our objective is to identify (and successfully apply) the abstract properties of hysteresis in macrodynamics. Hence even at the end of the preceding exercise, we are left only with the observation that an outcome (in this case, a long-run equilibrium) depends on events in the past. Said outcome is, therefore, clearly path dependent – but is it hysteretic? In point of fact we simply cannot know, without being provided with more details about the system's dynamics that would allow us to point to some feature of these dynamics that can be identified with hysteresis but not with other concepts of path dependency.[24] What this illustrates is that if we are interested in distinguishing hysteresis as a specific concept of path dependency, 'backstories' of the sort identified above are no substitute for a full and proper examination of a system's dynamics. It is for these reasons that the claim that we observe hysteresis in the operation of systems such as equations (1) and (2) can be identified as no more than a *statement* or *assertion* on the part of the model builder.

ii) Characterizing hysteresis

The project of characterizing hysteresis is associated with the work of Setterfield (1997a, ch. 2) and Katzner (1998, ch. 13; 1999). In essence, it comprises an attempt to return to the first principles of economic dynamics in an effort to free the latter from the mechanistic, ahistorical grip of traditional equilibrium analysis and, in particular, the asymptotic stability properties of such equilibria. The concept of hysteresis emerges from this exercise as an alternative (to traditional equilibrium analysis) way of thinking about macrodynamics. In what follows, we focus on the analysis in Setterfield (1997a, ch. 2; 1998b), making periodic references to what Katzner (1999) identifies as the fullest and most pertinent characterization of hysteresis in economics.[25] As will be made clear, these characterizations are essentially equivalent.

The essential insights of Setterfield (1997a, ch. 2; 1998b) can be illustrated in the context of the same NAIRU theory to which we appealed in the previous section.[26] Hence suppose that we begin by rewriting equation (4) as:[27]

$$Z_t = h_t(U_{t-1}) \tag{4a}$$

Defining $dU_i = U_i - U_{i-1}$ for all i, consider now a series of 'cumulatively neutral' changes in U (starting from the initial steady state equilibrium position $U_{t-1} = U_n$), such that:

$$DU = \sum_{t=1}^{n} dU_t = 0$$

In other words, we are forcing U along an adjustment path that leads the variable back to its initial value (U_n). The question, however, is whether or not this is still the steady-state value of U. In other words, at the end of the series of cumulatively neutral changes in U described above, is U 'back in equilibrium'? Or is U_n now merely a disequilibrium value that we are forcing U to attain *en route* to a new long-run equilibrium value, U'_n?

In order to address these questions, suppose initially that:

(a) $h'_t \neq 0$ for some $t = 2, \ldots, n+1$

and:

(b) $DZ = \sum_{t=1}^{n} h'_{t+1} \cdot dU_t = 0$

Condition (a) insists that short-run changes in Z occur as U traverses the cumulatively neutral adjustment path described above. But condition (b) insists that these short-run changes are, themselves, cumulatively neutral – they 'cancel out' over the course of the adjustment path followed by U. Hence the long-run value of Z is unaffected by the sequence of adjustments undertaken by U, so that the long-run value of U is similarly unaffected. In short, when U has completed the cumulatively neutral adjustment path described above and thus regained the value U_n, it is back in equilibrium and the system in equations (1) and (2) will achieve a steady state (with $\dot{p}=0$).

By establishing the path *in*dependence of the NAIRU, this exercise draws to attention an important result: simply making a parameter of a system dependent on the lagged actual value(s) of the systems outcome(s) – as in equations (2) or (4) in the previous sub-section – does not suffice to generate path dependency in the long run or final outcome of the system. This is clearly evident upon closer inspection of the dynamics of equations (1) and (2) discussed earlier. Hence if we assume that $f' < 1$, and then add a third equation describing the lagged adjustment of the actual rate of unemployment towards the NAIRU (as in conventional NAIRU theory), then following the initial increase in unemployment to U_1 depicted in Figure 2.1, subsequent adjustments will 'undo' the revision of the NAIRU that results (in equation (2)) from this initial increase in unemployment, and U will eventually return to its original steady-state equilibrium value, U_n. No amount of 'backstories' designed to provide a behavioural foundation for equation (2) can resolve this problem, which is intrinsic to the dynamics of the system at hand. These observations reinforce our earlier claim that the existence of hysteresis (indeed, *any* form of path dependency) in the modelling exercise in the previous sub-section is merely an assertion.

But suppose that we now retain condition (a) while replacing condition (b) with:

(c) $DZ = \sum_{t=1}^{n} h'_{t+1} \cdot dU_t \neq 0$

As before, condition (a) allows for short-run changes in Z as U traverses its cumulatively neutral adjustment path. But condition (c) now states that these short-run changes are *not*, themselves, cumulatively neutral – they no longer 'cancel out' over the course of the adjustment path followed by U. Hence even though, by construction, we observe $U = U_n$ at the end of the cumulatively neutral adjustment path followed by U, U_n is no longer the value of the NAIRU (so $U = U_n$ will not produce a steady-state outcome in equations (1) and (2)). Instead, defining $Z' = Z + DZ$ where the value of DZ is given by condition (c), the value of the NAIRU is now given (via equation (3)) by $U'_n = g(Z')$. If we assume that the system adjusts towards U'_n during the periods $t = n+1, \ldots, n+s$, and that in so doing the associated changes in U have no cumulative impact on Z (in other words, $DZ = \sum_{t=n+1}^{n+s} h'_{t+1} \cdot dU_t = 0$), then the system will eventually achieve a steady state when $U = U'_n$. Clearly, the long-run outcome of the system has been altered by events in the past (experience of the traverse along the cumulatively neutral adjustment path with which we began): we are observing path dependency. Indeed, according to Setterfield (1997a ch. 2; 1998b), we are observing *hysteresis* which, in light of the preceding analysis, exists 'when the cumulative impact on the structure and hence the long-run outcome of a system of movement along a prior disequilibrium adjustment path is non-zero' (Setterfield, 1998b, p. 292).[28] This structural change is associated with the 'adjustment asymmetries' captured by condition (c), which are in turn associated with *threshold effects*. Hence if events propel a system sufficiently far from its current state that it moves beyond an 'event threshold', condition (c) is triggered and the long-run outcome of the system will be affected. A corollary of this claim is that as long as the system does *not* stray 'sufficiently far' from its current state – i.e., as long as an event threshold is *not* crossed – condition (b) will hold and we will observe *no* change in the system's long-run outcomes. The upshot of all this is the *possibility* (since not all shocks will trigger condition (c)) of a particular type of path dependency (hysteresis), associated with non-linear adjustment dynamics that give rise to structural change in a system that alters its position of equilibrium, all in response to specific prior adjustment paths. Setterfield (1998b) thus argues that the conceptualization of adjustment dynamics in the exercise above is more general than that found in traditional equilibrium economics. Hence traditional equilibrium analysis implicitly treats condition (b) as universal: event thresholds that could trigger condition (c) are not held to exist in the locale of any equilibrium. A more general treatment of adjustment dynamics would take seriously the possibility that such event thresholds do exist (and that research should therefore be devoted to their identification in concrete macrodynamical systems), and that condition (c) may therefore attain – as a result of which what were previously regarded as traditional equilibria would need to be re-interpreted as path-dependent equilibria.

The value of this analysis is that it begins to provide some sense of what is actually involved in generating hysteresis – i.e., how the process of

hysteresis actually works. We learn, for example, that hysteresis is associated with structural change ($DZ \neq 0$ in the example above), induced
by the concrete (historical) experience of a system, that is discontinuous and therefore non-linear. Hence note that hysteresis as characterized
above can be distinguished from other path-dependent organizing concepts, such as (for example) cumulative causation. Cumulative causation
arises when the displacement of a system from some initial position gives
rise not to negative feedbacks (as a result of which the initial position
may subsequently be regained, as in traditional equilibrium analysis)
but to positive feedbacks, so that the initial displacement becomes self-
reinforcing. Note, however, that in the characterization of hysteresis
above, not every displacement from equilibrium will trigger condition
(c). As such, history won't *always* matter: some initial displacements
from equilibrium will be 'self-correcting' – that is, they will restore initial equilibrium conditions in the manner of traditional equilibrium
dynamics – so that no trace of the prior adjustment path will be evident in the long-run outcome of the system. With cumulative causation,
however, any initial displacement becomes self-reinforcing, so *all* history
matters. Moreover, feedbacks need not be positive (as in cumulative causation) to generate hysteresis as characterized above. This is illustrated by
the following example, which utilizes the sort of adjustment dynamics
described in this sub-section. Consider a transitory shock to the supply of
a commodity that increases the price of the commodity far above its initial equilibrium value.[29] Suppose now that this sequence of events creates
a popular aversion to the commodity, as a result of which many buyers
develop a hitherto non-existent preferential attachment to a substitute
commodity. This historically-induced change in preferences will cause a
decline in demand for the original commodity, so that even when (by
hypothesis) initial supply conditions are restored, we will observe a new
(path-dependent) equilibrium price for the commodity that lies *below*
the original equilibrium price. The market for the commodity will now
gravitate towards this new equilibrium price if traditional commodity
market dynamics are present (the price level rises (declines) in response
to excess demand (supply)) and the traverse towards equilibrium is cumulatively neutral with respect to the determinants of equilibrium. In this
case, an initial increase in price results in a subsequent price *decrease* –
i.e., negative feedbacks are operative.

But having established the value of the characterization of hysteresis outlined above, it is also important to note that it suffers certain
drawbacks. For example, it is not clear what explains the event thresholds that trigger condition (c), or where (within the orbit of an initial

equilibrium position) we might expect to find them. Nor is it clear what processes are involved in the time-dependent influence of U on Z summarized in equation (4a) and condition (a). As a matter of logic, allowing that *either* condition (b) *or* condition (c) might hold is more inclusive (and therefore more general) than insisting on the universality of condition (b) (as in traditional equilibrium analysis). But this does not explain why we would expect to observe the event thresholds that distinguish between the applicability of these conditions in economic systems, nor what makes h'_t non-zero.[30] In short, equation (4a), condition (a) and the event thresholds that distinguish between the applicability of conditions (b) and (c) remain 'black boxes'. It is for this reason that the analysis above is described as *characterizing* hysteresis: it takes seriously the project of illuminating the specific properties of hysteresis, but without providing a complete *model* of the process that shows exactly how hysteresis comes about. As a result, it necessarily remains incomplete.

iii) Modelling hysteresis

We now turn to the project of explicitly modelling hysteresis. It is possible to distinguish between two separate branches of this project – one which focuses on the presence of unit or zero roots in linear dynamical systems, and a second which, starting from contributions to the physical sciences, purports to describe 'true' hysteresis. As we shall see, the project of modelling hysteresis has not always succeeded in advancing our understanding of the properties specific to hysteresis as a particular form of path dependency.

a. The unit/zero root approach

The unit/zero root approach to modelling hysteresis involves postulating the existence of unit or zero roots in systems of linear difference or differential equations. In terms of NAIRU theory, the unit root approach to modelling hysteresis can be illustrated if we replace the Phillips curve in equation (1) with:[31]

$$\Delta p = -\alpha(U - \gamma U_{-1}) + Z \tag{1a}$$

where $\gamma > 0$ and Z captures influences other than the rate of unemployment on Δp. Note that (1a) can be rewritten as:

$$\Delta p = -\alpha(1 - \gamma)U - \alpha\gamma\Delta U + Z$$

In other words, equation (1a) essentially postulates that both the level *and* the rate of change of unemployment impact negatively on the rate of change of inflation.

Consider now a constant rate of inflation – i.e., $\Delta p = 0$. Substituting into (1a) yields:

$$U = \gamma U_{-1} + \frac{Z}{\alpha} \tag{5}$$

Suppose further that we set $U = U_{-1} = U^*$ and $Z = \overline{Z}$. Substituting into equation (5) and solving for U^* yields:

$$U^* = \frac{\overline{Z}}{\alpha(1 - \gamma)} = U_n \tag{6}$$

Notice that the value of U^* so-derived is associated in equation (6) with the value of the NAIRU, U_n. It is straightforward to verify that this association is appropriate by substituting the expression in equation (6) into equation (1a) and noting that the corresponding solution to (1a) is $\Delta p = 0$. The upshot of our analysis thus far, then, is that we can identify a unique equilibrium rate of unemployment associated with steady-state inflation. If this unique equilibrium is asymptotically stable, then we are dealing with a path-independent, traditional equilibrium system in which the long run or final outcome (the equilibrium rate of unemployment) is both defined and reached without reference to the path taken towards it.

Suppose, however, that we set $\gamma = 1$. In other words, the first-order difference equation in (5) is characterized by a unit root. This assumption means that equation (6) cannot be solved for U^*. Instead, based on equation (5), we must be content to write:

$$U = U_0 + \frac{1}{\alpha} \sum_{i=1}^{t} Z_i \tag{7}$$

where U_0 denotes the unemployment rate in some initial period, 0. In equation (7), U depends on the initial unemployment rate, U_0, together with the entire past history of the variable Z (captured by $\sum_{i=1}^{t} Z_i$).[32] This is true even in the 'long run', which can now only be interpreted as a period of calendar time observed whenever $t > n$ for some n that is deemed sufficiently large. In the unit root approach, the result in (7) – which makes the unemployment rate at any point in time dependent on earlier states of the system described in (1a), and thus involves path dependency – is called hysteresis.

Note that in the more general case where $\gamma < 1$, equation (7) becomes:

$$U = \gamma^t U_0 + \frac{1}{\alpha} \sum_{i=1}^{t} \gamma^{t-i} Z_i \qquad (7a)$$

Equation (7a) may appear, at first, to have the same properties as equation (7). But closer inspection reveals that this is not the case: in (7a), the dependence of U on its own past history (summarized by U_0 and the history of Z) is strictly transitory. Hence in the limit, the value of U in equation (7a) tends towards the value U^* in equation (6).[33] The result in equation (7a) is referred to as *persistence*. Hence according to the unit root approach, hysteresis in dynamical systems is a special case, arising whenever we observe a unit root (such as $\gamma = 1$ in the example above). We may, nevertheless, observe persistence in the more general case, according to which the value of an outcome will depend on past events over some discrete interval of time. But in the long run persistence disappears, and the outcome will converge onto a value (such as U^* above) that is defined and reached independently of the path taken towards it. Ultimately, then, there is no path dependency of any description in systems with persistence – they simply describe the gradual adjustment of traditional equilibrium systems towards their long run or final outcomes.

As intimated earlier, the essential difference between unit and zero root analyses is the choice of discrete or continuous time (i.e., the use of difference or differential equations to explain the motion of a dynamical system). A good example of a zero root (continuous time) system is provided by the following model, based on Lavoie (2006). Hence consider the following system of equations built around the now familiar accelerationist Phillips curve in equation (1):

$$\dot{p} = -\alpha(U - U_n) \qquad (1)$$

$$U = \beta + \varphi r \qquad (8)$$

$$r = r_n + \delta(p - p^T) \qquad (9)$$

$$\dot{U}_n = \eta(U - U_n) \qquad (10)$$

where r denotes the real interest rate, p^T is a target rate of inflation set by the central bank, and:

$$r_n = \frac{(U_n - \beta)}{\varphi}$$

is the Wicksellian natural rate of interest. Equations (1), (8), (9) and (10) describe a New Consensus model of the economy (see, for example, Clarida et al., 1999; Woodford, 2003). The model consists of an accelerationist Phillips curve accompanied by an IS curve (equation (8)), and a Taylor rule describing the conduct of monetary policy (equation (9)). It is also hypothesized that the NAIRU is endogenous, being sensitive to any deviations of the actual rate of unemployment from the current value of the NAIRU itself (equation (10)).

It follows from combination of equations (1), (8) and (9) that:

$$\dot{U} = -\alpha\varphi\delta(U - U_n) \tag{11}$$

Equations (10) and (11) together constitute a system of two simultaneous differential equations in two variables (U and U_n). Note that steady-state equilibrium in equations (10) and (11) requires that:

$$\dot{U} = \dot{U}_n = 0$$

This equilibrium condition yields the same isocline from equations (10) and (11), specifically:

$$U = U_n \tag{12}$$

Note that the result in equation (12) provides us with an equilibrium value for U, while in tandem with equations (8) and (9) it yields $r = r_n$ and hence $p = p^T$. This is the standard equilibrium configuration of a New Consensus model. However, the behaviour of the system when it departs from this equilibrium configuration is less standard, thanks to the operation of equation (10). Consider, then, Figure 2.2 below, which depicts the isocline in equation (12). Assume that the economy begins in equilibrium at point A, but that it now experiences a transitory shock to the unemployment rate which, in consequence, rises to $U = U_1 + \varepsilon$. Figure 2.2 depicts the behaviour of the economy subsequent to this shock, resulting from the operation of equations (10) and (11). On one hand, the actual unemployment rate moves back towards the initial value of the NAIRU (as shown by the horizontal movement away from point B in Figure 2.2), as in conventional NAIRU theory. But on the other hand, the value of the NAIRU itself is revised upwards, as a result of $U_1 + \varepsilon > U_n = U_{n1}$ in equation (10). This is captured by the vertical movement away from point B in Figure 2.2. The upshot of these dynamics is that the economy moves back into equilibrium at point C in Figure 2.2.

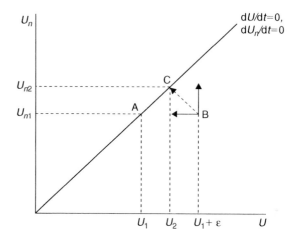

Figure 2.2 Response to a shock in a zero-root system

Clearly, this involves a new equilibrium value of the unemployment rate (i.e., a new value of the NAIRU, $U_n = U_{n2} = U_2$) – an equilibrium position that would not have been attained were it not for the precise prior sequence of events (specifically, the disturbance ε).[34] Equations (1), (8), (9) and (10) therefore describe a path-dependent equilibrium system rather than a traditional equilibrium system. In the zero root literature, this result is called hysteresis.

Analytically, the result depicted in Figure 2.2 can be explained as follows. First, note that equations (10) and (11) can be written in matrix form as:

$$\begin{bmatrix} \dot{U} \\ \dot{U}_n \end{bmatrix} = \begin{bmatrix} -\alpha\varphi\delta & \alpha\varphi\delta \\ \eta & -\eta \end{bmatrix} \begin{bmatrix} U \\ U_n \end{bmatrix} \tag{13}$$

The Jacobian matrix of the system in (13) is:

$$J = \begin{bmatrix} -\alpha\varphi\delta & \alpha\varphi\delta \\ \eta & -\eta \end{bmatrix}$$

from which we can see that $|J| = 0$ and $Tr(J) = -(\alpha\varphi\delta + \eta) < 0$.[35] Finally, we can calculate the Eigen values or characteristic roots of this matrix as:

$$\lambda = \frac{-Tr(J) \pm \sqrt{[Tr(J)]^2 - 4|J|}}{2} \tag{14}$$

$$\Rightarrow \lambda_1 = 0, \quad \lambda_2 = \alpha\varphi\delta + \eta$$

As is clear from the solution to (14) above, one of the characteristic roots of the Jacobian matrix in (13) is zero. This is the zero root from which zero root models take their name, and which gives rise to the result depicted in Figure 2.2 that is associated in these models with hysteresis.

Note, then, that once again, hysteresis is presented as a special case (contingent this time on the existence of a zero root in dynamical systems characterized by linear differential equations). The zero root in (13) will disappear if, for example, equation (10) is replaced with what Lavoie (2006) describes as the conventional 'missing' equation of the New Consensus, $U_n = \overline{U}_n$, according to which the NAIRU is an exogenously given constant. The resulting system would be a path-independent, traditional equilibrium system that will converge towards the equilibrium configuration $U = \overline{U}_n, p = p^T, r_n = (\overline{U}_n - \beta)/\varphi$. We will observe *persistence* in this system if adjustment towards its equilibrium configuration is not instantaneous. But the result associated with hysteresis depicted in Figure 2.2 will disappear.

By formulating explicit models of dynamical systems, unit and zero root analyses claim to locate the exact source of hysteresis in these systems – namely, the existence of unit or zero roots, respectively. While this clarity is, in and of itself, a virtue, it also reveals all of the shortcomings of unit and zero root models of hysteresis – shortcomings that can be readily understood in terms of the characterization of hysteresis reviewed in the previous sub-section. Hence notice that in the analysis above, so-called hysteresis results ultimately arise from the *non-uniqueness* of equilibrium, rather than from any re-consideration of the traditional *asymptotic stability properties* of equilibrium. This is clearly evident in Figure 2.2, where the isocline described in equation (12) draws attention to the continuum of equilibrium positions that exists in the dynamical system from which it is derived. Each equilibrium position on this continuum has conventional asymptotic stability properties (albeit within a *very* limited locale of the equilibrium position itself), and the *structure* of the underlying system (and hence the equilibria towards which it can, in principle, converge) is invariant with respect to its adjustment dynamics.[36]

Second, unit and zero root analyses apply to *linear* dynamical systems. No consideration is given to the possibility of non-linearities, which, according to the characterization of hysteresis reviewed earlier, are essential for generating hysteresis effects. In fact, linearity is the source of the (misleading) result associated with unit and zero root analyses, which suggests that the phenomenon of hysteresis is a special case. This can be illustrated by referring back to conditions (b) and (c) in the previous sub-section, and noting that if $h_i' = h_j' = h'$ for all i, j – which will *always* be the case when $h(.)$ is linear – then:

$$DZ = \sum_{t=1}^{n} h_{t+1}' dU_t = h' \sum_{t=1}^{n} dU_t = 0$$

since $\sum_{t=1}^{n} dU_t = 0$ by hypothesis. In other words, absent some discontinuity in the relationship between U and Z – which cannot exist if $h(.)$ is linear – condition (c) is impossible.[37] Instead, a so-called hysteresis result can only emerge if we postulate the special case of a unit or zero root. As was previously illustrated, persistence is the more general case phenomenon associated with unit and zero root models. But persistence is just non-instantaneous disequilibrium adjustment in an otherwise traditional equilibrium system – it barely merits singling out and naming as a distinct analytical phenomenon.[38]

Finally, unit and zero root systems display irreversibility. In other words, 'one may disturb ... [the] system with an exogenous shock of Δx in a control variable x, wait for whatever adjustment takes place and, then, disturb it again with a new shock – Δx, and find that the second end-state does not correspond to the initial one' (Dosi and Metcalfe, 1991, p. 133). This is clearly illustrated in Figure 2.2, in which the second end-state U_{n2} clearly does not correspond to the first (U_{n1}) despite the fact that the disturbance to the unemployment rate, ε_1, is strictly transitory. The same property is captured in equation (7). Hence suppose that we observe $Z_i = 0$ for all $i \neq n$ in equation (7). In other words, we are assuming that $\Delta Z_n = Z_n - Z_{n-1} = Z_n$, and $\Delta Z_{n+1} = Z_{n+1} - Z_n = -Z_n$. Evaluating equation (7) under these assumptions reveals that for all $i \geq n$ we will observe:

$$U = U_0 + \frac{1}{\alpha} Z_n$$

As remarked by Amable et al. (1993, p. 129), this justifies the claim that in unit and zero root systems, 'transitory causes can have permanent effects'. But note that a shock/counter-shock sequence in a unit or zero root system, in which both the initial shock and subsequent counter-shock are transitory, of the same magnitude, but of opposite sign, will always completely 'wipe' the memory of the system. The initial outcome will be restored leaving no trace of the historical adjustment path of the system. Unit and zero root systems can thus be said to display 'super reversibility'.

Once again, this result can be demonstrated with reference to equation (7). Hence suppose that we now observe $Z_i = 0$ for all

$i \neq n, n+s$ in equation (7), where $Z_n = -Z_{n+s}$. In other words, we assume that $\Delta Z_n = Z_n - Z_{n-1} = Z_n$ and $\Delta Z_{n+1} = Z_{n+1} - Z_n = -Z_n$ as before, but we now also assume that $\Delta Z_{n+s} = Z_{n+s} - Z_{n+s-1} = -Z_n$ and $\Delta Z_{n+s+1} = Z_{n+s+1} - Z_{n+s} = Z_n$. Evaluating equation (7) under these assumptions reveals that for all $i \geq n+s$ we will observe:

$$U = U_0$$

But there is no need to expect super reversibility in systems displaying hysteresis. This is evident from the characterization of hysteresis discussed in the previous sub-section. Hence in the parlance of the previous section, there is no necessary implication that two consecutive cumulatively neutral sequences of changes in U, that begin with a change in U of the same magnitude but of opposite sign, will restore the initial long-run equilibrium value of U. Rather, their exact impact will depend on two things. The first is the initial position of the system relative to the event thresholds that are ultimately responsible for triggering discontinuous changes in the values of long-run outcomes in response to prior disequilibrium adjustment paths. Hence despite their symmetry, there is no reason to believe that *both* sequences of cumulatively neutral changes in U will necessarily propel the system across event thresholds. The second is the precise quantitative impact of crossing event thresholds on the determinants of the value of the long-run outcome. Hence even if event thresholds *are* crossed during *both* the shock and countershock sequences of cumulatively neutral disturbances postulated above, there is no reason to believe their impacts on the long run value of U will necessarily 'cancel out'. In short, it is (once again) the *linearity* of unit and zero root systems that gives rise to the 'memory wiping' super reversibility result derived above. With non-linearities in the adjustment dynamics of the system, this result disappears.[39]

Of course, none of this remedies the fact that, as noted earlier, the characterization of hysteresis discussed in the previous sub-section suffer failings of its own. But fortunately, both the super reversibility result discussed above, together with the various other shortcomings of unit and zero root models of hysteresis, are successfully addressed by models of 'true' hysteresis. It is to these models that we now turn our attention.

b. 'True' hysteresis

Models of 'true' hysteresis were introduced into economics by Cross (1993, 1994, 1995) and Amable et al. (1993, 1994, 1995), and are based on research in the physical sciences. There are two components to models of 'true' hysteresis: the non-ideal relay associated with Krasnosel'skii and Pokrovskii (1989); and the aggregation effects modelled by Mayergoyz (1986). Once again, it is possible to demonstrate the workings of 'true' hysteresis in terms of a concrete model of labour market dynamics that has important implications for conventional NAIRU theory.

The model developed below draws on Lang and de Peretti's (forthcoming) hysteretic model of Okun's Law. We begin by specifying a non-ideal relay, describing the employment decision of the ith firm at any point in time, t, which takes the form:

$$
\begin{aligned}
E_{it} &= n_i + 1 \quad \text{if } E_{it-1} = n_i \text{ and } y_{it} > y_{iu} \\
&= n_i + 1 \quad \text{if } E_{it-1} = n_i + 1 \text{ and } y_{it} \geq y_{il} \\
&= n_i \quad \text{if } E_{it-1} = n_i \text{ and } y_{it} \leq y_{iu} \\
&= n_i \quad \text{if } E_{it-1} = n_i + 1 \text{ and } y_{it} < y_{il}
\end{aligned}
\tag{15}
$$

where E denotes total employment, n is the initial level of employment, y denotes real output, and changes in employment over time are standardized to the value 1. The second and third rows of (15) describe the conditions under which the individual firm will maintain employment at a constant level from one period to the next. The first and fourth rows, meanwhile, describe the conditions under which the firm will vary employment from one period to the next. It is clear that in all cases, the employment decision depends on the proximity of the actual level of output to two key threshold values, y_{iu} and y_{il}. According to (15), variations in output above or below these thresholds will trigger changes in employment, while variations in output within the same bounds will leave employment unchanged.[40]

The workings of (15) can be illustrated by means of an example depicted in Figure 2.3 below. Assume, then, that we begin at point A, with output given by y_{i1} and employment by n_i. Now suppose that a shock causes output to rise to y_{i2}. Since $y_{i2} > y_{iu}$, the firm raises employment to $n_i + 1$, and so arrives at point B in Figure 2.3. But suppose that the shock to output was strictly transitory, and that in the next period, we observe $y = y_{i3}$. Even though output has fallen back to its original level, it has not fallen below the lower threshold value y_{il}. As a result, the firm continues to employ $n_i + 1$ workers, at point C in Figure 2.3. A transitory shock to output has, therefore, produced a lasting change in the firm's employment – i.e., the non-ideal relay in (15) displays irreversibility.

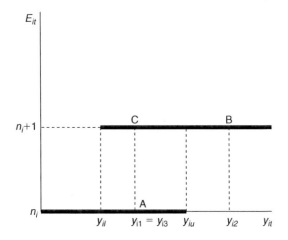

Figure 2.3   The non-ideal relay

Even at this stage of its development, then, our model has succeeded in reproducing the irreversibility property associated with unit and zero root systems. However, the non-ideal real is not the only component of models of 'true' hysteresis. Hence consider now the impact of *aggregating* the employment responses of individual firms captured in (15) across all firms in the economy, as output varies relative to the firm-specific threshold values y_{il} and y_{iu}. This aggregation process is captured by the equation:

$$E_t = \iint f(y_u, y_l) E_i(y_{it}) dy_u dy_l \tag{16}$$

where E_t denotes aggregate employment in period t, the weight function $f(.)$ specifies the relative contribution of firms with specific upper and lower output thresholds (y_u and y_l) to total employment, and $E_i(.)$ denotes the employment functions of individual firms. Total employment is then derived by integrating over the upper and lower output threshold values for individual firms.

The consequences of this aggregation process are best explained in terms of the half-plane diagram (Mayergoyz, 1986) depicted in Figure 2.4. In Figure 2.4, we need only pay attention to the area above the solid diagonal line labelled $y_u = y_l$, since $y_{iu} > y_{il}$ for all i by assumption, so that all individual firms are represented by points above this line. Our analysis starts at point A with $E_i = n_i$ for all i. We assume for simplicity that

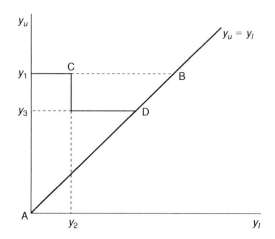

Figure 2.4   Aggregation effects and hysteresis

$y_i = y_j$ for all i, j.[41] Consider now a symmetric shock to output, so that we observe $y = y_1$. All firms for which $y_{iu} < y_1$ – i.e., all firms that lie below the horizontal line y_1B in Figure 2.4 – will now increase their employment to $n_i + 1$. But if a second symmetric shock now reduces output to $y_2 < y_1$, firms below the horizontal line y_1B *and* to the right of the vertical line y_2C (for which $y_{il} > y_2$) will now reduce employment back to n_i. A third shock that raises output again, to $y_3 > y_2$, will cause firms that lie to the right of the vertical line y_2C *and* below the horizontal line y_3D (for which $y_{iu} < y_3$) to expand employment to $n_i + 1$, and so on. As is clear from this analysis, variations in total employment over time – and hence, by extension, the level of aggregate employment at any point in time – are dependent on the precise sequence of shocks to output. A different historical sequence of shocks over the same discrete interval of time would yield a different historical sequence of changes in employment, resulting in a different aggregate level of employment at the end of the interval. The implications of this analysis are clear. Aggregate employment – and by extension, aggregate unemployment – will not automatically converge towards a traditional (path-independent) long-run equilibrium value, as in NAIRU theory. Instead, *ceteris paribus*, the economy will remain at the aggregate level of employment established by the sequence of shocks to output that are traced out in Figure 2.4 – what may thus be interpreted as the new, path-dependent equilibrium rate of employment. In fact, what we have generated in Figure 2.4 is 'true' hysteresis in aggregate employment.

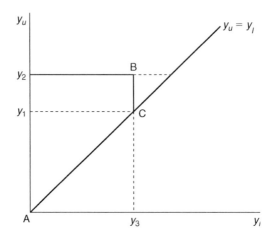

Figure 2.5   Irreversibility

Having constructed a model of 'true' hysteresis, we can now identify some of the properties of hysteresis that it draws to attention. We have already noted that in and of itself, the non-ideal relay in (15) displays irreversibility: a transitory shock to output has a permanent effect on employment. It should therefore come as no surprise that this same property of irreversibility arises from the complete model of 'true' hysteresis depicted in Figure 2.4. This is illustrated in Figure 2.5. Hence suppose that, following an initial increase in output to y_1 (as in the earlier case discussed in Figure 2.4), we now observe an increase in output to y_2 followed by a decrease in output back to $y_3 = y_1$ (i.e., a transitory shock to the level of output). As illustrated in Figure 2.5, this sequence of events will *not* restore the *status quo ante*. Instead, all firms within the rectangle $y_1 y_2 BC$ will have permanently added to employment (since they are characterized by the conditions $y_2 > y_{iu} > y_1$ and $y_3 \geq y_{il}$), as a result of which aggregate employment will be permanently higher (and aggregate unemployment correspondingly lower).

Meanwhile, unlike the unit/zero root models reviewed earlier, our model of 'true' hysteresis does *not* display 'super reversibility'. This is illustrated in Figure 2.6. Suppose that, as in Figure 2.5, following an initial increase in output to y_1 we subsequently observe an increase in output to y_2 followed by a decrease in output back to $y_3 = y_1$ (i.e., a transitory shock to the level of output). But suppose that we now *also* observe a counter-shock of identical magnitude but opposite sign – i.e., a fall in output to y_4 (where $y_4 - y_3 = -(y_2 - y_1)$) followed by a restoration of output

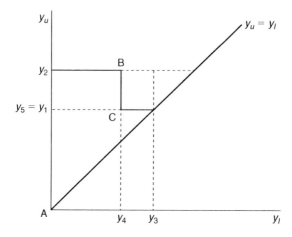

Figure 2.6 Absence of super reversibility

back to $y_5 = y_1$. As illustrated in Figure 2.6, this shock/counter-shock sequence will once again fail to restore the *status quo ante*. This time, all firms within the rectangle $y_1 y_2 BC$ will have permanently added to employment (since they are characterized by the conditions $y_2 > y_{iu} > y_1$ and $y_4 \geq y_{il}$), as a result of which aggregate employment will once again be permanently higher (and aggregate unemployment correspondingly lower). Hence models of 'true' hysteresis display irreversibility but *not* super reversibility. The 'memory' of these systems, and the resulting propensity of past sequences of events to influence future (including long run or 'final') outcomes, is clearly different from that of unit/zero root systems. For this reason, the permanent effects of even transitory sequences of past events on outcomes in 'true' hysteretic systems are given the special name *remanence effects* (see especially Amable et al., 1995, pp. 167–8).

The results in Figures 2.5 and 2.6 highlight that neither the symmetry of a transitory shock *nor* the symmetry of a shock/counter-shock sequence (where both shock and counter-shock are transitory and of identical magnitude but opposite sign) will automatically restore the *status quo ante* in a model of 'true' hysteresis. In so doing, they call attention to the fact that this is because of the adjustment *asymmetries* that characterize this model, arising from non-linearities (specifically, discontinuities caused by event thresholds) in the structure of the non-ideal relay, the assumed heterogeneity of firms in the economy, and the consequent *structural change* that can result from the displacement of a system from any initial state of equilibrium.[42] In other words, in generating the hysteresis results described above, our focus of attention is (properly) on adjustment dynamics and the potential lack of conventional asymptotic stability properties associated with any position that can be construed as an equilibrium, and *not* on the non-uniqueness of equilibrium. Hence note that at any point in time, the equilibrium in a system characterized by 'true' hysteresis may, in fact, be unique. But if the system is displaced from this equilibrium configuration, it may not automatically converge back towards it. Instead, the system may settle at a new – and again, unique – position of equilibrium that has been *newly created* by the structural change wrought by the system's prior adjustment path (see also Amable et al. 1993, pp. 128–31; 1995, pp. 169–72).

Notice that in the discussion above, reference is made to the fact that, following a transitory disturbance, a 'true' hysteretic system *may* not automatically converge back towards its original equilibrium position. Whether or not it will depends on the precise nature of the disturbance itself. To be more specific, the 'memories' of models of 'true' hysteresis are *selective* rather than *complete*, so that what matters for system outcomes are so-called 'non-dominated extrema' rather than the entire past history of the system (Cross, 1994).

In order to substantiate these claims, we begin by turning back to Figure 2.5. Hence suppose once again that starting from y_1, we observe an increase in output to y_2 followed by a decrease in output back to $y_3 = y_1$ (i.e., a transitory shock to the level of output). But suppose now that there are *no* firms within the rectangle y_1y_2BC – i.e., that there are no firms in the economy characterized by the conditions $y_2 > y_{iu} > y_1$ and $y_3 \geq y_{il}$. In this situation, the postulated transitory shock to output will leave total employment unchanged. As intimated earlier, in the event of its being disturbed from an initial position of equilibrium, a 'true' hysteretic system *may* not automatically converge back towards its original equilibrium position – but we cannot completely rule out the possibility that it *will*. Clearly, then, not all history matters. Unlike unit/zero models, in which outcomes are sensitive to *all* past events (as in equation (7)), outcomes in models of 'true' hysteresis depend on only *some* past events. In other words, 'true' hysteretic systems have *selective* rather than *complete* memories.

These properties are further borne out by the events depicted in Figure 2.7. In Figure 2.7, we assume that, beginning at point A, the economy has experienced the same sequence of shocks depicted in Figure 2.4 (y_1, y_2, y_3). But suppose now that this sequence is followed by a further shock, that elevates output to y_4. We will now observe *all* firms for which

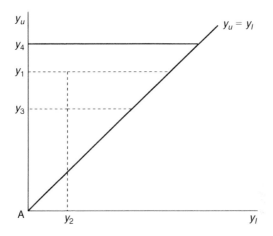

Figure 2.7 'Wiping' the memory: the importance of non-dominated extrema

$y_4 > y_{iu}$ employing at the level $n_i + 1$, regardless of the precise sequence of shocks to output (y_1, y_2, y_3) that occurred in the past. To put it differently, aggregate employment will be exactly the same as it would have been if, starting at point A, output had risen *immediately* to y_4. It is as if the sequence of shocks y_1, y_2, y_3 never happened: the memory of them has been erased or wiped from the system. Once again, then, we are provided with an example of the selective memory of models of 'true' hysteresis, as a result of which not all history matters. More specifically, we have discovered the importance of *non-dominated extrema* for the outcomes of 'true' hysteretic systems. In the parlance of 'true' hysteretic analysis, the shock that raises output to y_4 erases the elaborate effects of what are now the *dominated* extremum values y_1, y_2, y_3 from the system's memory, with the result that aggregate employment depends only on the *non-dominated* extremum value, y_4. Note, then, that just as in unit/zero root systems, it is possible to wipe the memory of a 'true' hysteretic system. But the processes involved in this memory wiping are very different (a shock/counter-shock sequence resulting in super reversibility in unit/zero root models; the dominance of previous extrema in models of 'true' hysteresis), as befits our previous claims that the 'memories' of these systems work in substantively different ways.

While models of 'true' hysteresis are an advance on unit/zero root models, they are not altogether above criticism. For example, some explanation is required for the event thresholds that are crucial to the non-ideal relay. Fortunately, the analytical role played by these event thresholds is made more explicit in expressions like (15) than in the characterization of hysteresis discussed earlier. Hence 'backstories' justifying their existence in specific applications now suffice to fill the remaining gap. For example, it could be argued that in (15), firms are seeking to avoid sunk costs associated with hiring and firing, and that they therefore adjust employment in response to variations in output discretely – whenever the change in y is 'sufficiently large' – rather than continuously.

A more serious problem is that according to authors such as Setterfield (1998b) and Katzner (1999), hysteresis in *social* systems must be understood as a property of *historical time*, in which the future is fundamentally uncertain (Davidson, 1991). These are not issues that models of 'true' hysteresis typically address – likely by virtue of the fact that they are imported from the physical sciences.[43] But the claims of Setterfield and Katzner suggest there is something missing from the model of 'true' hysteresis developed above, that needs to be taken into account when thinking about hysteresis as an organizing concept in macrodynamics.

Fortunately, this omission can again be corrected, once it is recognized that the essence of the problem is methodological. Specifically, models of 'true' hysteresis are typically closed systems. But fundamental uncertainty is properly understood in terms of a quite different ontology – one that presupposes that social systems are structured but *open* (see, for example, Lawson, 2006). It is this aspect of social ontology that must be taken into account when modelling hysteresis in social systems.

An important feature of the characterization of hysteresis reviewed earlier is it shows how this can be achieved. This is because it describes hysteresis in terms of systems that lack intrinsic closure – i.e., systems in which causes need not always have the same effects. Hence suppose that, in terms of the analysis in sub-section 3(ii), we observe both conditions (a) (with $h'_j \neq h'_k$ for some $j, k, j \neq k$) and (c). In other words, the necessary and sufficient conditions for hysteresis both hold. Suppose further that the inter-temporal variations in h'_t cannot be described *a priori* – there is no 'missing equation' that describes changes in h'_t as a time-invariant function of exogenous variables and that could be used to close the system that is being analyzed (Setterfield, 1998b, pp. 293–5; Katzner, 1999, pp. 176–8). In this environment, even if shocks conform to a known stochastic process, it will be impossible to form expectations of (hysteretic) future outcomes without risk of systematic error. Decision makers will find themselves confronting fundamental uncertainty.

Drawing on this analysis, we can now see how models of 'true' hysteresis can be reconciled with fundamental uncertainty, understood as a property of structured but open social systems. For example, we could postulate that the event thresholds in the non-ideal relay are time dependent, and insist on the absence of any 'equations of motion' that would permit foreclosed explanation (and prediction) of their values (and hence those of aggregate hysteretic outcomes) over time. Allied to the assumed *conditionality* of any path-dependent equilibrium (and hence the possibility that the cumulative experience of equilibrium conditions may eventually disturb a system from an initial conditional equilibrium position) this would result in a model of *evolutionary hysteresis* – that is, hysteresis characterized by endogenously-generated structural change involving novelty (Setterfield, 2002, p. 227).

4. The case for retaining unit/zero root analysis in macrodynamics

In section 3(iii)a, it was argued that many of the properties of unit/zero root models fail to conform to those of hysteresis properly conceived. But despite this, a case can be made for *retaining* unit/zero root models in macrodynamics, as a useful first approximation of hysteresis effects and alternative to traditional equilibrium analysis.[44]

In the first place, unit/zero root systems are easy to construct, and easy to compare and contrast with traditional equilibrium systems (there frequently being little analytical difference between the structure of the two, as was demonstrated in section 3(iii)a). Second, unit/zero root models capture at least *some* of the properties of hysteretic systems – including the key property of irreversibility, according to which transitory causes have permanent effects. They are even consistent with the 'errors matter' variant of the theory of decision making under uncertainty. This suggests that any decision made in an environment of risk (where all possible future outcomes and the probabilities with which they will occur are known) that does *not* allow the same decision to be made repeatedly (which would allow the law of large numbers to establish the mathematical expected value of the gamble as the actual average payoff) will be susceptible to the same 'second order' psychological influences – confidence, optimism, 'animal spirits', etc. – as a decision made under conditions of fundamental uncertainty.[45] The classic example of this is a 'crucial' decision that is made only once (for example, betting one's life savings on one roll of a die). But essentially the same problem will confront decision makers faced with forecasting outcomes based on equation (7). Suppose that Z in equation (7) is constant except for transitory shocks, so that we can write:

$$U = U_0 + \frac{1}{\alpha}\sum_{i=1}^{t}(\overline{Z} + \varepsilon_i)$$

or:

$$U = U_0 + \frac{t\overline{Z}}{\alpha} + \frac{1}{\alpha}\sum_{i=1}^{t}\varepsilon_i \tag{7a}$$

Suppose further that decision makers understand that $E(\varepsilon_i) = 0$ and are therefore able to calculate:

$$E(U) = U_0 + \frac{t\overline{Z}}{\alpha}$$

The problem is that even a *transitory* shock to Z ($\varepsilon_i \neq 0$ for some i) will have a *permanent* effect on U in equation (7a). Suppose, for example, that $\varepsilon_i = 0$ for all $i \neq n$. Then for $t \geq n$ we will observe:

$$U = U_0 + \frac{t\overline{Z}}{\alpha} + \varepsilon_n$$

Comparison of this outcome with the expectation described above reveals that the latter will be systematically wrong for all $t \geq n$. In other words, decision makers are vulnerable to systematic expectational error in the event that there is *any* transitory shock to Z at *any* point in time over their forecast horizon. Knowing this, decision makers would be unwise to act solely on the basis of the 'best forecast' of U derived above. Their behaviour will, instead, be influenced by the same psychological influences described by the theory of decision making under fundamental uncertainty.

What this suggests is that a case can be made for retaining unit/zero root analysis as part of the 'toolkit' of macrodynamic modelling, based on appeal to 'pragmatic instrumentalism'. In other words, even if it is understood that unit/zero root systems do not truly reflect the dynamics of hysteresis, they may be recognized as providing a useful first approximation for certain specific purposes – as, for instance, when the analyst is attempting to contrast a traditional equilibrium outcome with one in which 'history matters' in an otherwise familiar system (for examples, see Dutt, 1997; Lavoie, 2006). This is very much like the strategy Keynes adopted when holding constant the state of long-run expectations in order to facilitate exposition of the principle of effective demand in terms of a traditional equilibrium analysis (Kregel, 1976).

Note that the 'pragmatic instrumentalism' described above does not mean that unit/zero root models are *always* justifiable. Instead, it calls for a 'horses for courses' approach to macrodynamic modelling. Hence Lavoie's (2006) zero root model discussed earlier is useful for demonstrating certain limitations of and hidden assumptions in New Consensus macroeconomics. But a zero root model would be fundamentally misleading if our purpose is to describe hysteresis effects in real-world labour markets. On this qualified basis, it can be argued that unit/zero root analysis belongs in a 'big tent' approach to macrodynamic modelling, designed to maximize the useful contents of the practitioners' toolbox.

5. Conclusions

The purpose of this chapter has been to discuss path dependency in dynamical economic systems, and to delineate the features of a specific concept of path dependency – namely, hysteresis. It has been shown that models of 'true' hysteresis are the most acceptable way of using hysteresis as an organizing concept in macrodynamics, by virtue of their superior fidelity to the abstract properties of hysteresis. At the same time, a pragmatic case has been made for retaining unit/zero root analysis, despite its failure to capture some of the most important features of hysteresis properly conceived. Ultimately, then, judicious use of *both* unit/zero root analysis *and* 'true' hysteresis best serves to maximize the extent and value of the macrodynamic modeller's toolkit.

Notes

*An earlier version of this paper was presented at the 5th International Conference Developments in Economic Theory and Policy, Universidad del Pais Vasco, Bilbao, 10–11 July, 2008. I would like to thank conference participants – and in particular, Dany Lang – for their helpful comments. Any remaining errors are, of course, my own.

1. See Setterfield (1995) for a survey of these concepts of path dependency.
2. Obviously, this is a counterpart to the more frequently rehearsed question 'what is equilibrium?' on which see, for example, Setterfield (1997a, p. 5; 1997b, pp. 48–51).
3. See also Lang and Setterfield (2006–07, pp. 198–9) on the concept of traditional equilibrium analysis and Setterfield (1998a) on the contributions of Kaldor (1934).

4. Note that by emphasizing the role of the adjustment path in *creating* (rather than just *selecting*) equilibrium outcomes, the discussion above distinguishes systems with path-dependent equilibria from those with locally stable multiple equilibria. See also Kaldor (1934) and Setterfield (1998a).

5. Note that this is not the same as contemplating the eventual occurrence of an exogenous shock that disturbs an equilibrium. Hence there is always the possibility of explaining an endogenously-generated behavioural change arising from the cumulative experience of equilibrium conditions in terms of the dynamics of the system itself – even if this is only possible *ex post* (as will be the case when behavioural change involves genuine innovation) rather than as an a priori extension of the model of the system (which would allow such change to be predicted). This can never be so in the case of an exogenous shock which, by definition, is imposed upon a system from without.

6. Strictly speaking, one might argue that the *forces* of change have not been suspended at all – rather, it is simply the case that the *manifestation* of these forces in actual change will be absent for discrete periods (during which a specific conditional equilibrium position is maintained), by virtue of the fact that change results from the cumulative experience, over a discrete interval of time, of a particular 'state of rest'.

   Note that the term 'conditional' equilibrium as used here is inspired by Crotty's (1994) concept of conditional stability in Keynesian macroeconomic models. See also Chick and Caserta (1997) on the related concept of 'provisional' equilibrium.

7. It should be noted at this point that the 'suspension of the forces of change' necessary to generate a conditional equilibrium can also be brought about in an entirely artificial fashion by the analyst him/herself. In other words, it is possible to acknowledge the existence of path dependency in the object of analysis, but choose to set it aside. The purpose of this 'locking up without ignoring' path dependency in order to generate a conditional equilibrium is to focus attention on properties of a system other than path dependency (on which see, for example, Kregel, 1976; Setterfield, 1997b; Lang and Setterfield, 2006–07). Of course, it is when path dependency is *not* 'closed down' in this fashion – so that conditional equilibria arise only from a 'temporary suspension of the forces of change' endemic to the system being studied – that path-dependent organizing concepts come into their own as a means for structuring the analysis of a dynamical system.

8. In and of itself this claim is not at all new – it was effectively made by Kaldor (1934) with the introduction of his concept of a definite-indeterminate outcome. Hence, for Kaldor, an outcome may be indeterminate (it cannot be defined and reached independently of the path taken towards it) but nevertheless definite, in the sense that it eventually reaches a (historically contingent) position that has the characteristics of an equilibrium.

9. These include, *inter alia* (and perhaps most famously), hysteretic models of the 'natural' rate of unemployment.

10. Examples of variables for which ceiling and/or floor values *are* defined as a matter of logic include the unemployment rate and the capacity utilization rate, both of which are bounded above and below by one and zero, respectively.

11. This maximum level of employment may be determined by labour market conditions (for example, it may coincide with conditions of labour market clearing or full employment) or by a constraint such as the availability of capital in the context of a fixed-coefficient production technology.

12. See, for example, Solow (1956) and subsequent analyses of growth in this tradition.

13. See, for example, Cornwall (1977) and McCombie and Thirwall (1994).

14. The substance of this claim can be traced back to Adam Smith's famous dictum that the division of labour depends on the extent of the market. See McCombie, Pugno and Soro (2002) for a modern treatment and appraisal of the Verdoorn law.

15. See, for example, Leon-Ledesma and Thirwall (2000, 2002) for empirical evidence relating to this idea.

16. Note that this issue has already been anticipated by our discussion of the natural rate of growth in the previous section.

17. See also Amable et al. (1993, pp. 123–4).

18. Such discussions were by no means uncommon during the 1980s and Jenkinson's paper is but one example of what is identified here as stating or asserting hysteresis. Indeed, the purpose of singling it out is because, judged as an exercise in applied macroeconomics devoted to describing and critiquing NAIRU theory and its implications for macroeconomic policy (rather than as an exercise in identifying the abstract features of hysteresis), it is a model of clarity.

19. The terms 'natural rate of unemployment' and 'NAIRU' are used interchangeably in this chapter, despite the fact that there are arguably important conceptual differences between the two. Fortunately these differences are not central to the analysis that follows, which is why they are overlooked.

20. Note that if we were to rewrite equation (2.) to make the change in the NAIRU depend positively on the difference between the values of the actual rate of unemployment and the NAIRU in the previous period, and then add a third equation to our system describing the adjustment of the actual rate of unemployment towards the NAIRU (as posited in conventional NAIRU theory), then the new steady state value of the unemployment rate (the new NAIRU) would lie somewhere between the U_n and U'_n in Figure 2.1. Figure 2.1 can therefore be thought of as contrasting two extreme cases – full reversion of the actual rate of unemployment towards the NAIRU, and full adjustment of the NAIRU towards the actual rate of unemployment.

21. Once again, were we to rewrite equation (2) to make the change in the NAIRU depend positively on the difference between the values of the actual rate of unemployment and the NAIRU in the previous period, and then add a third equation to our system describing the adjustment of the actual rate of unemployment towards the NAIRU, the LRPC would not be identical to the SRPC (as in Figure 2.1). Instead, its slope would be steeper than that of the SRPC, the precise slope depending on the relative speeds of adjustment of inflation (in equation (1)), of the NAIRU towards the actual rate of unemployment, and of the actual rate of unemployment towards the NAIRU. However, as long as the NAIRU is at least somewhat sensitive to the actual rate of unemployment, the resulting LRPC will always be negatively sloped.

22. See also Cross (1995).

23. Obviously such actions depend on a number of conditions, including the ability of insiders to revise the insider real wage without forcing it above the value of the outsider real wage plus turnover costs – an event that would undermine their own status as employees by making them vulnerable to replacement by outsiders.

24. Note, for example, that in the model developed above, increasing unemployment today means that unemployment will be higher in the future. Such self-reinforcing tendencies are by no means inconsistent with hysteresis, but they are also characteristic of cumulative causation.

25. Katzner (1999) actually identifies *three* 'characterizations' of hysteresis – the one alluded to above that is the focus of attention in what follows, a second that corresponds to the concept of path dependency as defined earlier, and a third that corresponds to the property of irreversibility discussed in section 3(iii).

26. Both of the above-mentioned references are, in turn, based on Setterfield (1992).

    It is useful to continue discussing hysteresis in the context of labour market dynamics in general and NAIRU theory in particular for two main reasons. First, NAIRU theory involves a concrete application of adjustment dynamics in macroeconomics that is universally familiar. Second, it is one of the two main literatures in which appeal to the concept of hysteresis was popularized in economics two decades ago (see, for example, Göcke, 2002, p. 167). However, it is important to bear in mind two things. First, hysteresis is a dynamical process that could, in principle, affect *any* dynamical system: 'the concept of hysteresis refers back to a set of *formal properties*, independently of the various phenomenologies within which it is liable to be encountered (magnetism, ferro-electricity, physical mechanics, various fields of economics, etc.)' (Amable et al, 1993, p. 124). Second, our main interest here is in uncovering the abstract properties of hysteresis, rather than exploring its concrete application to any particular phenomenology.

27. Note that by combining equation (4b) with equation (3) we get:

$$U_n = g(h_t(U_{-1}))$$

which can be written as:

$$U_n = f_t(U_{-1})$$

This is substantively similar to the key equation of motion postulated by Katzner (1999, p. 177), which appears as:

$$x_t = f^t(x_{t-1}, \varepsilon_t) \tag{5K}$$

Indeed, apart from the inclusion of the random disturbance term ε_t, the preceding expression is *exactly* the reduced form that would result from combination of equations (1), (2) and (10) in Setterfield (1998b).

28. This analysis identifies $h'_j \neq h'_k$ for some j, k, $j \neq k$ in condition (a) as the necessary condition for hysteresis to arise, and condition (c) as the sufficient condition for hysteresis. See Setterfield (1998b). This parallels Katzner's

(1999, p. 178) analysis, in which (in the absence of the term ε_t) the outcome in equation (5K) referred to in note 27 above would relapse to a traditional equilibrium outcome if we were to observe $f^t = f^{t-1}$ for all t. Since Katzner (1999, p. 178) describes the latter condition as a 'very special situation', it seems reasonable to infer that he would regard condition (b) in much the same way – which coincides exactly with the interpretation of Setterfield (1998b, p. 292), as discussed below.

29. This example is inspired by Georgescu-Roegen (1950).

30. The importance of this last point arises from the fact that, absent condition (a), there is no possibility whatsoever of condition (c) – i.e., the event thresholds discussed above simply would not exist.

31. Unit root models of hysteresis in the NAIRU can be found in, *inter alia*, Wyplosz (1987), Franz (1990) and Layard et al. (1991).

32. Note that even if Z remains constant over time (as was assumed in the derivation of (6)) equation (7) will become:

$$U = U_0 + t\frac{\overline{Z}}{\alpha}$$

So past events – specifically, initial conditions U_0 and the time, t, that has elapsed since these initial conditions were observed – will still influence the value of U at any point in time.

33. To see this, consider the general solution to the first-order difference equation in (5), which may be written as:

$$U_t = \gamma Ab^{t-1} + \frac{\overline{Z}}{\alpha(1 - \gamma)}$$

where $U_t = Ab^t$. Since the homogeneous function of equation (5) is $U = \gamma U_{-1}$, we can write:

$$Ab^t = \gamma Ab^{t-1}$$

from which it follows that:

$$b = \gamma$$

Substituting this result into the general solution of (5) stated above, yields:

$$U_t = A\gamma^t + \frac{\overline{Z}}{\alpha(1 - \gamma)}$$

Inspection of this last expression reveals that, since $\gamma < 1$ by hypothesis so that $\lim_{t \to \infty} A\gamma^t = 0$:

$$\lim_{t \to \infty} U_t = \frac{\overline{Z}}{\alpha(1 - \gamma)} = U^*$$

as claimed in the text.

34. Using equations (8) and (9), we can see that the new equilibrium configuration will also involve $r = r_{n2} = (\beta - U_{n2})/\varphi$ and $p = p^T$.

35. These results suffice to ensure the stability of the system summarized in equation (13) (as illustrated in Figure 2.2) by appeal to the modified Routh–Hurwitz conditions. See Gandolfo (1997).
36. See also Amable et al. (1993, pp. 128–30; 1995, p. 169) on this property of unit and zero root systems.
37. If $h'_i = h'_j = h'$ for all i, j, then what was identified earlier as the necessary condition for hysteresis is violated.
38. Persistence may, of course, be important in practice if adjustment in a particular traditional equilibrium system is very slow – perhaps even so slow that movement towards equilibrium is slower than the rate at which the data determining the precise position of equilibrium are, themselves, (exogenously) changing. But all of this is already well understood and has been for some time. Hence as Cornwall (1991, p. 107) states, 'if . . . real world change[s] in tastes, technologies and other institutional features are very rapid relative to the rate at which the economy can adjust, the convergence properties of the model take on much less interest and importance than the institutional changes themselves.'
39. More precisely, it will be observed only as a special case.
40. This implies that there must be some local variation in labour productivity, so that different levels of output can be produced by the same number of employees.
41. Note that this does not imply that $n_i = n_j$ because there can be differences in labour productivity between firms.
42. 'Structural change' refers here to change in the *composition* of the economy, as measured by the proportion of all firms operating on the upper (rather than lower) branch of the non-ideal relay depicted in Figure 2.3 – this being a function (as illustrated in Figures 2.4–2.6) of the precise historical sequence of adjustments undertaken by the system in the past.
43. See Cross (1993a) for an exception.
44. See also Dutt (1997) for a sustained argument to this effect.
45. See, for example, Gerrard (1995) on these 'second order' influences on decision making.

References

Amable, B., J. Henry, F. Lordon and R. Topol (1993) 'Unit-root in the wage-price spiral is not hysteresis in unemployment', *Journal of Economic Studies*, 20, 123–35.

Amable, B., J. Henry, F. Lordon and R. Topol (1994) 'Strong hysteresis versus zero-root dynamics', *Economics Letters*, 44, 43–47.

Amable, B., J. Henry, F. Lordon and R. Topol (1995) 'Hysteresis revisited: a methodological approach', in R. Cross (ed.) *The Natural Rate of Unemployment: Reflections on 25 Years of the Hypothesis*, Cambridge, Cambridge University Press.

Chick, V. and M. Caserta (1997) 'Provisional equilibrium and macroeconomic theory', in P. Arestis, G. Palma and M. Sawyer (eds) *Essays in Honour of Geoff Harcourt. Volume 2. Markets, Unemployment and Economic Policy*, London, Routledge, 223–37.

Clarida, R., J. Gali and M. Gertler (1999) 'The science of monetary policy: a New Keynesian perspective', *Journal of Economic Literature*, 37, 1661–707.

Cornwall, J. (1977) *Modern Capitalism: It Growth and Transformation*, Oxford, Martin Robertson.

Cornwall, J. (1991) 'Prospects for unemployment in the 1990s with hysteresis', in J. Cornwall (ed.) *The Capitalist Economies: Prospects for the 1990s*, Cheltenham, Edward Elgar.

Cross, R. (1993) 'On the foundations of hysteresis in economic systems', *Economics and Philosophy*, 9, 53–74.

Cross, R. (1993a) 'Hysteresis and Post Keynesian economics', *Journal of Post Keynesian Economics*, 15, 305–8.

Cross, R. (1994) 'The macroeconomic consequences of discontinuous adjustment: selective memory of non-dominated extrema', *Scottish Journal of Political Economy*, 41, 212–21.

Cross, R. (1995) 'Is the natural rate hypothesis consistent with hysteresis?' in R. Cross (ed.) *The Natural Rate of Unemployment: Reflections on 25 Years of the Hypothesis*, Cambridge, Cambridge University Press.

Crotty, J. (1994) 'Are Keynesian uncertainty and macrotheory compatible? Conventional decision making, institutional structures, and conditional stability in Keynesian macromodels', in G. Dymski and R. Pollin (eds) *New Perspectives in Monetary Macroeconomics: Explorations in the Tradition of Hyman P. Minsky*, Ann Arbor, University of Michigan Press, 105–39.

Davidson, P. (1991) 'Is probability theory relevant for uncertainty?', *Journal of Economic Perspectives*, 129–43.

Dosi, G. and J.S. Metcalfe (1991) 'On some notions of irreversibility in economics', in P.P. Saviotti and J.S. Metcalfe (eds) *Evolutionary Theories of Economic and Technological Change*, Reading, Harwood.

Dutt, A.K. (1997) 'Equilibrium, path dependence and hysteresis in Post-Keynesian models', in P. Arestis, G. Palma and M. Sawyer (eds) *Essays in Honour of Geoff Harcourt. Volume 2. Markets, Unemployment and Economic Policy*, London, Routledge, 238–53.

Elster, J. (1976) 'A note on hysteresis in the social sciences', *Synthese*, 33, 371–91.

Franz, W. (1990) 'Hysteresis in economic relationships: an overview', *Empirical Economics*, 15, 109–25.

Gandolfo, G. (1997) *Economic Dynamics*, Berlin, Springer-Verlag.

Georegescu-Roegen, N. (1950) 'The theory of choice and the constancy of economic laws', *Quarterly Journal of Economics*, 64, 125–38.

Gerrard, B. (1995) 'Probability, uncertainty and behaviour: a Keynesian perspective', in S. Dow and J. Hillard (eds) *Keynes, Knowledge and Uncertainty*, Aldershot, Edward Elgar.

Göcke, M. (2002) 'Various concepts of hysteresis applied in economics', *Journal of Economic Surveys*, 16, 167–88.

Jenkinson, T. (1987) 'The natural rate of unemployment: does it exist?' *Oxford Review of Economic Policy*, 3, 20–6.

Kaldor, N. (1934) 'A classificatory note on the determinateness of equilibrium', *Review of Economic Studies*, 2, 122–36.

Kaldor, N. (1985) *Economics Without Equilibrium*, Cardiff, University College Cardiff Press.

Katzner, D. (1998) *Time, Ignorance and Uncertainty in Economic Models*, Ann Arbor, University of Michigan Press.

Katzner, D. (1999) 'Hysteresis and the modeling of economic phenomena', *Review of Political Economy*, 11, 171–81.

Krasnosel'skii, M.A. and A.V. Pokrovskii (1989) *Systems with Hysteresis*, Berlin, Springer-Verlag.

Kregel, J. (1976) 'Economic methodology in the face of uncertainty: the modelling methods of Keynes and the Post-Keynesians', *Economic Journal*, 86, 209–25.

Lang, D. and C. de Peretti (forthcoming) 'A strong hysteretic model of Okun's Law: theory and a preliminary investigation', *International Review of Applied Economics*, forthcoming.

Lang, D. and M. Setterfield (2006–7) 'History *versus* equilibrium? On the possibility and realist basis of a general critique of traditional equilibrium analysis', *Journal of Post Keynesian Economics*, 29, 191–209.

Lavoie, M. (2006) 'A Post-Keynesian amendment to the New Consensus on monetary policy', *Metroeconomica*, 57, 165–92.

Lawson, T. (2006) 'The nature of heterodox economics', *Cambridge Journal of Economics*, 30, 483–505.

Layard, R., S. Nickell and R. Jackman (1991) *Unemployment: Macroeconomic Performance and the Labour Market*, Oxford, Oxford University Press.

Leon-Ledesma, M. and A.P. Thirlwall (2000) 'Is the natural rate of growth exogenous?' *Banco Nazionale del Lavoro Quarterly Review*, 53, 433–45.

Leon-Ledesma, M. and A.P. Thirlwall (2002) 'The endogeneity of the natural rate of growth', *Cambridge Journal of Economics*, 26, 441–59.

Lucas, R.E. (1988) 'On the mechanics of economic development', *Journal of Monetary Economics*, 22, 3–42.

Mayergoyz, I.D. (1986) 'Mathematical models of hysteresis', *IEEE Transactions on Magnetics*, 22, 603–8.

McCombie, J.S.L. and A.P. Thirlwall (1994) *Economic Growth and the Balance-of-Payments Constraint*, London, Macmillan.

McCombie, J.S.L., M. Pugno and B. Soro (eds) (2002) *Productivity Growth and Economic performance: Essays on Verdoorn's Law*, New York, Palgrave Macmillan.

Romer, P.M. (1986) 'Increasing returns and long-run growth', *Journal of Political Economy*, 94, 1002–37.

Romer, P.M. (1990) 'Endogenous technological change', *Journal of Political Economy*, 98, S71–102.

Setterfield, M. (1992) *A Long Run Theory of Effective Demand: Modelling Macroeconomic Performance with Hysteresis*, PhD dissertation, Dalhousie University, Canada.

Setterfield, M. (1995) 'Historical time and economic theory', *Review of Political Economy*, 7, 1–27.

Setterfield, M. (1997a) *Rapid Growth and Relative Decline: Modelling Macroeconomic Dynamics with Hysteresis*, London, Palgrave.

Setterfield, M. (1997b) 'Should economists dispense with the notion of equilibrium?' *Journal of Post Keynesian Economics*, 20, 47–76.

Setterfield, M. (1998a) 'History versus equilibrium: Nicholas Kaldor on historical time and economic theory', *Cambridge Journal of Economics*, 22, 521–37.

Setterfield, M. (1998b) 'Adjustment asymmetries and hysteresis in simple dynamic models', *The Manchester School*, 66, 283–301.

Setterfield, M. (2002) 'A model of Kaldorian traverse', in M. Setterfield (ed.) *The Economics of Demand-Led Growth*, Cheltenham, Edward Elgar.

Solow, R. (1956) 'A contribution to the theory of economic growth', *Quarterly Journal of Economics*, 70, 65–94.

Witt, U. (1991) 'Reflections on the present state of evolutionary economic theory', in G.M. Hodgson and E. Screpanti (eds) *Rethinking Economics*, Cheltenham, Edward Elgar.

Woodford, M. (2003) *Interest and Prices*, Princeton, Princeton University Press.

Wyplosz, C. (1987) 'Comments', in R. Layard and L. Calmfors (eds) *The Fight Against Unemployment*, Cambridge, MA, MIT Press.

3

Involuntary Unemployment in a Path-Dependent System: The Case of Strong Hysteresis

Dany Lang*
Maître de Conférences, CEPN, Université de Paris 13

Abstract

Hysteresis has been introduced in economics as an alternative to the dominant mainstream models based on the various declensions of the Natural Rate of Unemployment and of the NAIRU. By contrast with the improper interpretations of the concept of hysteresis, many Post-Keynesians have tried to exploit the genuine hysteresis concept used in physics and in other sciences, in order to try understanding the persistence of high unemployment rates in Europe. Hysteresis is one of the most important forms of path dependency in economics. In the presence of hysteresis, the economic system will be characterised by changing equilibria in the aftermath of non-dominated aggregate shocks. In these conditions, the equilibrium unemployment rates change on the basis of the history of past non-dominated aggregate shocks. Rather surprisingly, the authors that have worked in this field up to now have forgotten to examine one of its most important implications: in the presence of hysteresis, unemployment is mainly an involuntary phenomenon. After summing up the main results of the debates on the meaning and the relevance of main definitions of hysteresis in the literature, and underlining the relevance of the concept of genuine hysteresis, we propose a theoretical model for understanding hysteresis in unemployment on the basis of Keynes's concept of effective demand.

JEL Classification: D01, E12, E24

Keywords: Involuntary unemployment; effective demand; hysteresis; path dependence

1. Introduction: hysteresis and unemployment

The term hysteresis comes from the Greek υστερεω that literally means to lag behind. In a contemporary sense hysteresis means, in general, the persistence of an effect while its cause has disappeared. Today, the term hysteresis is well known and used in many fields of knowledge: the hard sciences like physics and biology, but also the social sciences. It is even used in literature, to describe the persistence of a person's love even when the person who is the subject of love has disappeared.

The first scientific application of hysteresis is due to the physician James Alfred Ewing (1881) in his research concerning the thermoelectric properties of metals submitted to shocks, that is, to loadings and unloadings of ferric metals. Ewing showed empirically, and explained theoretically, that the application of an initial shock to ferric metals would modify the characteristics of the electromagnetic field of these metals. This meant that the application of two shocks of the same magnitude but of opposite signs would not bring the system back to its initial position. It also meant that the metals would remember the most important shocks to which they had been subjected in the past. These results put into question Maxwell's equations, which were by then the most important equations of the dominant paradigm in this field of physics. Indeed, following Maxwell's equations, the elements of the ferric metal were supposed to return progressively to their original state after the shock had occurred.

It has been argued by Lang (2008) that there are important analogies between the Maxwellian formalism (the equations used by Maxwell) and the neoclassical theory in economics. Although both references to the Newtonian paradigm *and* to the theory of fields of force are numerous and even omnipresent in the early neoclassical literature, a closer look at this literature reveals that these two branches of science do not have the same *epistemological status*. Indeed, when analysing the writings of the founders of neoclassical economics, one must distinguish between the use of *metaphors* and the *use of formalism*. And if the early neoclassicals used Newtonian and Maxwellian *metaphors* with equal frequency and in similar ways, the Maxwellian system is, nevertheless, privileged because of the appropriation of its *mathematical formalism*. The implicit privilege granted to Maxwellian formalism did not arise by chance. As Mirowski (1989) argues, in the 1860s physics became unified around variational principles and the principle of conservation of energy. Maxwell's construct spread to the francophone world in the 1860s and 1870s, and in England from 1867 on, the starting point being the publication of the textbook by Thomson and Tait (1867). Energy physics had already been presented in some textbooks in the 1860s, and was becoming the most commonly used metaphor for the discussion of the physical world. As a student, Jevons had attended some of Faraday's public lectures at the Royal Institution, and all of the founding fathers of neoclassical theory had received some training in the natural sciences. The reason for the appropriation of the methods, metaphors and equations of physics by early neoclassical economists clearly lies in their desire that economics be conferred the status of a science. To achieve their purpose, the early neo-classicals needed to engage primarily in nomothetical research, that is, in research intended to discover 'universal' economic laws, and, reasonably enough, they looked to the natural sciences for suitable metaphors, methods and equations. As Rod Cross (1995a, p. 128) has put it, 'aping mainstream physics was seen as a means of establishing the scientific credibility of economics, the 1870s seeing the start of a Newtonian revolution in the subject.' Thus, Walras writes that 'the pure theory of economics is a science which resembles the physico-mathematical sciences in every respect' (1954, p. 71), and that 'If the pure theory of economics or the social theory of exchange and value in exchange, that is, the theory of social wealth considered by itself, is a physico-mathematical science like mechanics or hydrodynamics, then economists should not be afraid to use the methods and language of mathematics' (1902, p. 71). Jevons is even more explicit about the importance of the physics of energy for his system, since he considers that 'The notion of value is to our science what that of energy is to mechanics' (1905, p. 50).

From that, Lang (2008) concludes that the bequest of the forefathers of neoclassical economics is path-independence in a Maxwellian fashion, and that more than a century after the writings of the forefathers, the property of path-independence remains embedded in modern economics. It can be found, for example, in the approach that most mainstream economics takes to unemployment. Over the last three decades, almost all models that aim to explain the behaviour of the unemployment rate have included implicit or explicit 'attractionist' dynamics: the observed unemployment rate is supposed to be drawn towards some path-independent equilibrium rate of unemployment. These 'attractionist dynamics' are present in models that have influenced economic policy (see, for example, Friedman, 1968; Kydland and Prescott, 1977; Barro and Gordon, 1983). The implementation of dis-inflationist strategies, as well as the high priority given to central bank independence, is based on the belief that the actual economy will behave as described by these models, that is, in a path-independent, homeostatic and time-reversible manner. And yet, almost 30 years after the implementation of these policies began, the least that one can recognize is that the behaviour of actual economies seldom corresponds to what these models predict.[1]

That is why hysteresis has been introduced in economics. Whereas hysteresis was well known in scientific fields from the nineteenth century on, and economists like Schumpeter, Georgescu-Roegen, Samuelson and Phelps had already used the term occasionally to discuss and explain the functioning of some aspects of economic systems, its first broad usage in economics dates back to the mid-1980s.[2] This broad usage first appeared in the field of the theories of employment at the aggregate level. The concern then was to try to explain something that could barely be justified on the basis of the models proposed by the mainstream paradigm (by the so-called New Classical Macroeconomics which was dominant at the time), whose short and long-run dynamics were based on the natural rate of employment and the Non Accelerating Inflation Rate of Unemployment (NAIRU) frameworks.

Some economists consider that the natural rate of unemployment and the NAIRU is in fact the same thing, or that the differences between the two concepts can be neglected. This is even the case of most of the economists, whether proponents of, opponent to, or neutral towards, the natural rate and the NAIRU. This is the case because of the conceptual proximity of these concepts, due to the fact that the natural rate of unemployment and the NAIRU clearly belong to what we have called above the attractionist theories, and are ensuring the path-independence property. For example, Cross (1995), in a very critical paper concerning the natural rate and the NAIRU concepts, considers that they are fully identical. For Ball and Mankiw (2002), the NAIRU is seen as a synonym for the natural rate of unemployment. A clue for understanding this assimilation may be a remark made by Estrella and Mishkin (1998): the greatest number of the empirical studies, including the famous and reference papers by Staiger et al. (1997), and Gordon (1997) tend to assimilate them, mainly, but not only, for commodity reasons. As a matter of fact, Friedman (1968) himself, in his founding paper concerning the natural rate of unemployment, explicitly talks about acceleration of inflation and acceleration of deflation, to describe the macroeconomic dynamics at work when the current unemployment rate moves away from its natural level.

Anyway, for some other authors, like Jackman and Leroy (1995), Estrella and Mishkin (1998) and Sawyer (1997), the NAIRU and the natural rate are different concepts, and it is therefore important to distinguish them. Different reasons are put forward to justify the necessity to distinguish these concepts. A first one, that we will call the weak version of the distinction, consists in seeing the NAIRU as a generalization of the natural rate concept, just as Tobin (1995) does. Jackman and Leroy (1995) go further: according to them, the NAIRU would be an equilibrium rate of unemployment having similar characteristics as the natural rate, but for which there would not necessarily be any market cleaning. Thus, the NAIRU would be determined solely by real / supply-side variables, exactly as the natural rate, but the NAIRU would be based on a wage bargaining model when a Walrasian general equilibrium model would be underlying the natural rate. Therefore, even if, in both frameworks, demand-side oriented policies would have no other impact than inflationary, involuntary unemployment would be allowed to exist in the NAIRU framework. By contrast, the existence of involuntary unemployment would be theoretically impossible in the models based on the natural rate of unemployment. Anyway, that interesting distinction has an important limit: there are multiple ways of modelling the NAIRU, and the property of involuntary unemployment cannot be found in many of them.

For other authors, the NAIRU would be a generalization of the natural rate of unemployment, in an imperfect competition framework. To put it in another way, whereas the natural rate would only make sense under the hypothesis of perfect competition, the NAIRU would be able to exist in both perfect and imperfect competition frameworks. Anyway, how seducing and clear this distinction can be, reading Friedman (1968), it is easy to show that things are not as straightforward as this distinction tries to make them. Indeed, according to Friedman, the natural rate of unemployment must include the 'actual structural characteristics of the labour and commodity markets, including market imperfections, stochastic variability in demands and supplies, the cost of gathering information about job vacancies and labour availabilities, the costs of mobility, and so on' (Friedman, 1968, p. 8). It is crystal clear that all the elements that Friedman refers to in his seminar paper belong to imperfect competition frameworks. In fact, as argued by Lang (2004), Friedman may have induced that debatable interpretation, since he explicitly refers to the 'Walrasian general equilibrium model' (Friedman, 1968, p. 8) in one of the four definitions of the natural rate of unemployment included in the paper. Indeed, it is worth nothing that the situation usually associated with the Walrasian general equilibrium model is pure and perfect competition.

For Sawyer (1997), the natural rate of unemployment cannot be seen as a particular case of the NAIRU in pure and perfect competition, and for two reasons. First, in a natural-rate framework, the unemployment would, essentially, be the result of matching problems between the labour supply and demand, whereas, in a NAIRU-based model, unemployment would be a proxy for the factors bearing down on wage bargaining, the most important thing, in these models, being the compatibility with a constant inflation rate. Secondly, the natural rate of unemployment could 'be seen as an essentially micro economic phenomenon in the sense that it is based on individual decision making on search behaviour' (Sawyer, 1997, p. 6), whereas the NAIRU would only make sense on a macroeconomic or systemic level, and would not have a counterpart on the individual level. For Sawyer (1997, p. 7), 'it is not possible to observe mini-NAIRUs for each individual and to obtain the NAIRU though summation', whereas the natural rate is nothing else that the summation of search behaviours that can be observed on an individual ground. Summing up, Sawyer argues that the main distinction between the natural rate and the NAIRU is a distinction between the micro and the macro levels.[3]

Whatever the definitions of the natural rate of unemployment and of the NAIRU might be, since the first broad usage of the term hysteresis in economics in the field of unemployment, the dominant paradigm has become the so-called New Keynesian one, in which wage and price rigidities can cause discrepancies in the short run (and possibly in the medium run, in some models) between the current rate of unemployment and the equilibrium rate. But in the long run, the current rate is still supposed to converge to the equilibrium rate (whether it is a natural rate of unemployment or a NAIRU), and the path followed by the economy is supposed to have no influence on this long-run rate (owing to the classical dichotomy between the nominal and the real variables). In both cases, the economic dynamics in the presence of a natural rate of unemployment or a NAIRU can be characterized as attractionist (Lang, 2004), as the current rate of unemployment is always attracted by the equilibrium rate. Following Cross and Strachan (2001) we can write that in this framework the equilibrium rate of unemployment (whether it is a NAIRU or a natural rate) attracts the current unemployment rate

$$u_n A u \qquad (1)$$

According to this equation, it is the natural rate of unemployment ($u_n A u$) that attracts (A) the current rate of unemployment (u).

At the beginning of the 1980s, on the basis of these theoretical frameworks, or at least using these models as theoretical backgrounds and justification, most of the European countries started to implement competitive disinflation strategies. Following the attractionist frameworks, after the implementation of the disinflationist policies (the disinflation shocks), mainly New classical and New Keynesian ones, the current unemployment rate was supposed to go back by its own to the natural rate or the NAIRU of the economy. The dynamics were therefore supposed to be similar to the one that can be found in Maxwell's equations in physics. This was not only the case in the Monetarist models, but also in the more recent models elaborated by the New Classicals and the New Keynesians. For the New Classicals, the adjustment of the inflation rate to a lower level was supposed to be rapid, with only one period cost in terms of unemployment: on the basis of rational expectations models, they predicted that unemployment would only deviate from its natural level while inflation expectational errors that could not be expected remained. For the New Keynesians, the adjustment process was supposed to take some time, and to be more or less sticky, but the current unemployment rate would finally reach the NAIRU at the end of the day, the only price of the adjustment being a temporary rise of the current unemployment rate.

In the mid-1980s, after many years of implementation of the disinflationist strategies, it became increasingly clear empirically that, contrary to theoretical predictions of monetarists and new classical macroeconomists, unemployment showed little sign of getting back to any natural or equilibrium level in most European countries. On the contrary, unemployment remained high and even continued to rise in most European countries. Moreover, among the multiple evaluations of the natural rate and the NAIRU that started to abound at this time, none of them could reach the same conclusion, the evaluations of the natural rate being able to vary considerably among the studies (sometimes up to 5% for a same country, and using similar data). These events have started to cast some doubts on the natural rate and the NAIRU frameworks. Up to now, referring to Lang (2004), we will call these frameworks the attractionist dynamics because in both of those some stable theoretical long-run rate is supposed to attract the current rate of unemployment in the economy.

As a consequence, some economists, who did not believe that the adjustment process would finally take place in the future, have started to put forward another explanation of the persistence of unemployment. This new explanation breaks up with the widespread economic explanations based on models in which there is a long-run convergence of the economy towards a stationary state or an equilibrium growth path. Instead, this new explanation is based on the idea of an accumulation of the consequences of the most important previous shocks that have hit the economy. To put it in another way, while traditional explanations are based on path-independent processes, the new one introduced the idea of path dependence. To describe the time-dependent process, these economists called it hysteresis, in reference to the concept in physics and to Ewing's work. For the authors, strong hysteresis is defined by its two key properties: remanence; and a selective, erasable memory. Remanence means that two successive shocks of the same magnitude, but of opposite signs, do not bring the economy back to its initial state, while the selective, erasable memory implies that only the non-dominated extremum values of the past shocks that have hit the system remain in its memory bank.

The first hysteresis models in this field, the most well known, were constructed in terms of unit roots in the wage–price spiral. Following the seminal papers by Blanchard and Summers (1986, 1988), in many papers about hysteresis in unemployment, and in particular by the end of the 1980s, the term hysteresis is used to mean that there is a unit root in a linear dynamic system. To put it differently, this word is used to refer to a situation where the unemployment rate depends on a linear combination of its past values, and where the sum of the coefficients is strictly equal to one. For example, Alogoskoufis and Manning (1988), starting from an insider–outsider type model where the representative labour union only stands up for the rights of its members, test empirically the following relationship:

$$u_t = \alpha + \beta_1 u_{t-1} + \beta_2 u_{t-2} + \varepsilon_t \tag{2}$$

where u_t represents the rate of unemployment at time t, u_{t-1} and u_{t-2} the rates of unemployment during the previous periods, and ε_t is a white noise. Using annual data for the period 1952–95, for France, Agoloskoufis and Manning (1988) reach the conclusion that $\beta_1 = 0.79$, $\beta_2 = 0.25 \Rightarrow \beta = 1.04$, and statistically significant and hence that there is hysteresis in unemployment in France for that period. This study is very representative of the way that the first economists working on hysteresis in unemployment would usually proceed.

A first remark to be made here is that the residuals being non-stationary, the results of the tests proposed by Agoloskoufis and Manning (1988) are biased. More importantly, a major limit of this kind of modelling is that the unit root condition is extremely restrictive, since it produces cut-and-dried results: either there is a unit root in unemployment, and, according to this definition, one can say that there is hysteresis; or there is no unit root, and the authors using this definition would say that there is no hysteresis, which means that the unemployment rate is supposed to conform to the attractionist-type dynamics described above. Moreover, among the multiple values that the sum of the coefficients can take, the equality to one is a very particular and demanding case. That is why in their original paper Blanchard and Summers (1986) do not use the term hysteresis as a synonym of unit root, but to describe a situation where the degree of the dependence to the past is high, where the sum of the coefficients is close to one, but not necessarily equal to one. Unfortunately, mathematically, the notion of being close is rather hazy. Blanchard and Summers (op. cit.) do not give a clue in the paper how to interpret and translate this notion in empirical tests. That is why, in most of the unit root-type tests implemented in this literature up to now, hysteresis is meant to describe a situation where the sum of the coefficients exactly matches unity. That may be the origin of some misunderstandings, and unsurprisingly the empirical studies where the term hysteresis is used in such a sense come to the conclusion that the hysteresis hypothesis has to be rejected. Indeed, as we said, hysteresis seen as a theory of unit roots corresponds to a very particular case, since the presence of hysteresis is subordinated by the very particular condition that the sum of the coefficients of lagged unemployment is equal to one. As expected, in the search for unit roots, obtaining a coefficient that is exactly equal to one, or not statistically different from unity, seldom happens. And the more complex tests based on the search for unit roots (augmented Dickey–Fuller tests, Phillips–Perron tests, etc.) are nothing else than extended versions of the tests searching for unit roots (see Lardic, 1998). Moreover, following Stanley (2004), univariate unemployment rate series cannot possess a unit root: otherwise, the unemployment rate would occasionally be negative or exceed 100 per cent. Therefore, it is not surprising to notice that even the most recent strategies aiming to find this kind of hysteresis have finally failed to do so.

There are multiple issues caused by the characterization of hysteresis as the presence of a unit root. As should be clear from the previous definition, hysteresis seen as a theory of unit roots corresponds to a very special case, since the presence of hysteresis is subordinated to the very particular condition that the sum of the coefficients of lagged unemployment is equal to one. This is a rather harsh hypothesis, and unsurprisingly the empirical tests of this hypothesis cannot lead to good results. As expected, in the search for unit roots, obtaining a coefficient that is exactly equal to one is rare. And the more complex tests based on the search for unit roots (augmented Dickey-Fuller, Phillips-Perron, etc.) are nothing else than extended versions of unit root tests (see Lardic, 1998). Moreover, following Stanley (2004), univariate unemployment rate series cannot possess a unit root. Otherwise, the unemployment rate would occasionally be negative or exceed 100 per cent. Therefore, it is not surprising to notice that even the most recent strategies aimed to find this kind of hysteresis have finally failed to do so. For example, Fève et al. (2003) have proposed a testing strategy for unemployment hysteresis as the joint restriction of a unit root in the unemployment rate and no-effect of the level of unemployment in the Phillips wage equation. On the basis of the previous remarks, it is not surprising to read that the empirical application of their model leads to rejection of the null hypothesis of wage hysteresis for most of our sample of OECD countries. The most surprising result of this application is that the authors have finally managed to find such kind of hysteresis for some countries, in particular the Scandinavian ones.

Moreover, in unit root hysteresis models, there seems to be a major inconsistency between the stories told at the microeconomic and at macroeconomic ground. Indeed, on the one hand, reading the multiple available papers about the empirical evaluations of hysteresis, the equations that are commonly used for the empirical tests are consistent with a variable equilibrium rate of unemployment, but they are also consistent with reversible processes. On the other hand, the processes presented in the loss of skills and the depreciation of the physical capital theories are clearly irreversible. This is one of the reasons why the story that is referred to when justifying the structural equation put under test is almost every time the insiders–outsiders story, since the outsiders can become insiders again.

This remark has important implications concerning the economic policy consequences of the presence of hysteresis seen as a theory of unit root. Indeed, the first proponents of the hysteresis concept, in particular Blanchard and Summers, were presenting the concept as an alternative theory to the theories based on the automatic adjustment of the economy to its natural rate. On this basis, hysteresis was supposed to be a tool in favour of Keynesian policies. This is only partially true. But the macroeconomic model based on unit roots is inconsistent with most of the stories told on the microeconomic ground. If the loss of skills, the depreciation of the physical capital, or the insiders–outsiders models are telling stories that correctly fit what happens in reality, it would be true that the current unemployment level could become structural, but the contrary would not be true, because all of these processes are irreversible. In that case, the best way to fight unemployment would be, on the contrary, to implement structural-type policies like the neoclassical ones that have been implemented during the past decades. For example, if the insiders–outsiders story is the good one, the best remedy would probably be to break the labour unions and to lower the wages in order to allow the outsiders to become competitive; if the story of the loss of skills is true, the unemployed that are excluded from the labour market must be trained via active employment policies, or employed in low-paid jobs in order to get back the work habit and to raise productivity. These may justify, for example, some exemptions granted to the employers on some kinds of jobs. All these policies are clearly structural-type ones. In the case of the depreciation of the physical capital, employers have clearly no interest in hiring new employees when the recovery is under way, so the economic solution may be much more complex, and should be based on the motivation to invest. If there are Keynesian solutions to that problem, there are also many classical ones. One of the major lacunae of the literature on the unit root-type of hysteresis is that it has not mentioned this important aspect of the problem at all.

Moreover, to find a unit root in time series is rather harsh. So, when the message of the model is that there is hysteresis if and only if there is a unit root, and otherwise that there is a unique and stable equilibrium towards which the system converges in the long run, the logical conclusion of most tests will necessarily be that there is no hysteresis, and that the natural rate of unemployment/NAIRU-type stories are closer to the true model of the economies.

For all these reasons, it is not certain that hysteresis seen as a theory of unit roots would allow rehabilitating Keynesian policies, despite what proponents of this kind of approach have claimed. Rather, seeing hysteresis as the presence of a unit root process may reinforce the neoclassical view that there is an adjustment process to a stable natural rate of unemployment or NAIRU, even if the adjustment takes time and may be slow. That is why Stanley (2004) prefers to think about hysteresis as being the alternative to the natural rate of unemployment, its falsifying hypothesis. Indeed, aware of these problems, when applying meta-analysis tests on the hysteresis concept, he defines unemployment hysteresis as a convenient low-level empirical generalization that represents what the Natural rate hypothesis is not.

Another major drawback of the unit root models comes from the property, in these models, that the system is supposed to keep in its memory *all* the previous shocks that have hit the economy, whatever the amplitude of these shocks. The memory of such economic system is materialized here by the value of the time-dependent natural rate. In the presence of full hysteresis (unit root), all shocks that have hit the economy are kept in the memory bank of this natural rate. As Cross puts it, this particular natural rate is like an elephant. Following Amable et al. (1990), such unit root processes would be characterized by the infinite persistence of the shocks on the system. That is also why we should characterize the hysteretic process seen as a unit root as a process of inverted attraction, or a super path-dependent process: compared to the kind of attraction present in the NRU and the NAIRU models, the unit root proponents have simply inverted the sense of causality between the current unemployment and the equilibrium unemployment rate (Cross, 1996). Economically, if there were such a kind of hysteresis, this would mean that every little economic slowdown or recovery would cause the current natural rate as well as the big recessions and the strongest recoveries. Of course, little fluctuations do not have the same impact as big shocks, but they are supposed here to influence the path of the equilibrium unemployment rate anyway, in a linear way, that is, proportionally. This is a rather extreme hypothesis. We must add to this that these processes are fully reversible: two opposite successive shocks bring the equilibrium value back exactly to its initial level (Amable et al., 1990). This seems to be contradictory to the stylized facts concerning the economic events that have taken place in Europe since the 1980s, and, as we have said, with the microeconomic foundations of the models.

Another issue with the definition of hysteresis in terms of unit roots is the progressive sliding of the vocabulary. When some economists working on the unit root version of hysteresis became aware that searching for a unit root is searching for a case that is rather extreme, and econometrically difficult to find in time series, they started to use the term in a broader and looser sense. For example, in the famous book by Layard et al. (1991), the term hysteresis is used to describe what the first unit root proponents would have called persistence. Some of these economists then talked about partial hysteresis, gradual hysteresis, or persistent persistence, or other close concepts, to name the same situation, that is, the one where the sum of the coefficients is close to, but less than one. In fact, all these concepts are rigorously equivalent. They point to the idea that the adjustment process to the natural rate of unemployment or the NAIRU is slow and sticky, but finally takes place in the long run. In that case, the dynamics is the same as the one that can be found in the New Keynesian models, and there is no need for a new concept like hysteresis to express the idea that the adjustment process is simply sticky. As Setterfield (1997, p. 25) puts it, '[i]n spite of its sometimes elaborate interpretation in the context of the unit root characterization of hysteresis, the notion of persistence is simply a rediscovery of the idea of sequential disequilibrium adjustment.'

Later on, taking into account the major theoretical and empirical issues raised by the unit root models, more refined models of hysteresis have tried to introduce the idea of endogenous changes, or to reconstruct hysteresis as a general case in economics. Two kinds of approaches have to be distinguished. The first approach, due to Roed (1997), views hysteresis as a process of endogenous change. The second approach may be characterized as the Setterfield–Katzner approach.

Starting from the considerations that the definition of hysteresis must be such that transitory shocks have permanent effects; that the past history must matter; and that the equilibrium should be path dependent, Roed (1997) defines hysteresis in unemployment starting from the following reduced form:

$$u_t = f(U_{t-1}, y_t, x_t, X_{t-1}) \tag{3}$$

where u_t is the contemporaneous unemployment rate, $f(\cdot)$ is a fixed function, x_t is the vector of all contemporary exogenous variables (including error terms in stochastic models), while U_{t-1} and X_{t-1} contain the sequences of past realizations of u and x that is deemed appropriate.[4] Last, y_t is the vector of structural change, which is supposed to be invariant to the history of the unemployment rate. Roed defines the absence of hysteresis as the following. If we suppose that the vector of exogenous variables remains constant in time ($x_t = x \,\forall\, t \geq 0$), and assuming the absence of any disturbances to the system, the unemployment rate is said to be non-hysteretic if it converges to a number that is independent of the past behaviour of the system. In that case, the model converges to a path independent, but not necessarily unique, equilibrium rate of unemployment. Formally, this definition can be transcribed as following:

$$\lim_{t \to \infty} [u_t | U_{t-1}, X_{t-1}] = u(x, y) \tag{4}$$

As one can see, this equation is fully consistent with the three approaches: the natural rate of unemployment; the NAIRU; even the TV-NAIRU (time-varying NAIRU) approaches. Hysteresis is then defined in the negative: for Roed, there is hysteresis if the previous equation is violated, and the system yields, in the best-case scenario, a path-dependent equilibrium rate. In that case, temporary shocks may have permanent effects and the equilibrium is path-dependent. This definition, which is very general, includes the unit root approach of hysteresis, but also embodies many other possible dynamics of the economic system. This allows Roed to include under the hysteresis banner economic models that are not formulated explicitly in terms of hysteresis. It also helps him to exclude from this field of research models that use this term in a non-relevant way, for example the ones that are using the term hysteresis in a loose sense, that is, to mean that the convergence towards the equilibrium is slow, but that the equilibrium, supposed to be unique, is finally reached at the end of the day.

Nevertheless, however important this definition may be, it is also very general and can embrace a wide range of economic models. Roed himself recognizes that giving this very general definition of hysteresis, which includes non-linear models with a limited number of equilibria, is problematic, as many non-linear models tend to predict the existence of a limited number of distinct and stable equilibria; and this does not seem to fit the record of European unemployment rates very well. Roed himself also underlines a major flaw in his own definition: as the unit root definition of hysteresis and its derivatives does, Roed's definition forgets about not only the idea of path dependence, but also some of the most important and interesting properties of the genuine definition of hysteresis put forward below. Roed's definition is not only compatible with the unit root definition, which, as we have already seen, has important limits. This general definition may also be, in some models, compatible with situations where the natural rate of unemployment or the NAIRU are still attracting the current unemployment rate. This is very annoying: in that case, there is no need to appeal to the hysteresis concept, which is supposed to introduce alternative analyses. Last, another major flaw of this definition is its lack of measurability. Since it is very general, it can fit very different hysteretic models, which in turn may correspond to many different empirical applications and to very different econometrical tools.

The second approach, which views itself as alternative to the unit root definition of hysteresis, can be characterized as the Setterfield–Katzner approach, as it is mainly based on the seminal works by Setterfield (1993, 1997) and Katzner (1993, 1999). Although these papers are separate, the definitions used in all these papers are very close. Based on the critique of the unit root definition, the Setterfield–Katzner approach tries to reconstruct hysteresis as a general case. Hysteresis is then seen by these post-Keynesian economists as a process of disequilibrium adjustment. More precisely, hysteresis is viewed as a process characterized by changes in the dynamic path followed by the economic system. The equilibrium(ia) of the system may never be reached because the variables underlying it change during the dynamic process. The starting point of this characterization of hysteresis is the critique of the unit root definition. The modelling starts from a general characterization of the mainstream hysteresis (unit root hysteresis), which can be defined, using a linear functional form:

$$X_t = \Omega W_t \tag{6}$$

$$W_t = f(X_{t-1}, Z_t) = \alpha + \beta X_{t-1} + \gamma Z_t \tag{7}$$

where X is an endogenous variable, W an alleged exogenous variable. The coefficients and the variable Z are treated in this model as genuinely exogenous. Substituting (7) into (6), and defining $v = \Omega \alpha$, $\mu = \Omega \beta$ and $\phi = \Omega \gamma$, yields:

$$X_t = v + \mu X_{t-1} + \phi Z_t \tag{8}$$

The long run is defined here as the point in time when, in the absence of hysteresis the economy, following the usual attractionist dynamics, reaches the steady state. The previous equation may be solved by setting $X_t = X_{t-1} = X^*$ (where a star over a variable means that it is a steady state value). Provided that $\mu \neq 1$, the solution is the usual steady state value:

$$X^* = \frac{v + \phi Z^*}{1 - \mu} \tag{9}$$

In this framework, there is what may be termed mainstream hysteresis, that is unit root hysteresis, if and only if there is a unit root ($\mu = 1$) in which case (8) cannot be solved as previously, but needs the rewriting of the full dynamics of the system, as we have done in the first section of this chapter. Starting from equation (8) and considering this equation period after period, this yields:

$$X_t = X_0 + tv + \phi \sum_{i=1}^{t} Z_i \tag{10}$$

In this equation, the endogenous variable depends on the whole history of the exogenous variable Z: every shock will remain in the memory bank of the system. Considering the issues examined in this chapter, X_t corresponds to the unemployment rate of the economy as a whole.

Setterfield (1997) starts his critique of this mainstream characterization of hysteresis by considering that, in order to be able to reach the steady state (as characterized by equation (9)), an implicit hypothesis has to be fulfilled: the speed of adjustment of X towards the equilibrium must be fast relative to the speed at which the data underlying this equilibrium are themselves changing. Anyway, if the convergence towards X is long enough to allow the data underlying the determination of the long-run equilibrium to change, then the long-run equilibrium will not provide an appropriate description of the configuration of the system at any point in time. In that situation, the important value of X is the contemporaneous one. In the Setterfield–Katzner approach, the changes in the data are not autonomous, but arise from the deep endogeneity of data to the independent variable and the absence of Lucasian deep parameters, on which, upon substitution, a conventional steady state could be established. The dynamics of the system will then be described by the successive equations:

$$X_t = v + \mu X_{t-1} + \phi Z_t$$
$$X_{t-1} = v + \mu X_{t-2} + \phi Z_{t-2}$$
$$X_1 = v + \mu X_0 + \phi Z_1 \tag{11}$$

As, this time, μ may take any value between 0 and 1, the full dynamics of the system at time t, obtained by successive substitutions, is characterized by the following equation:

$$X_t = \mu^t X_0 + v \sum_{i=1}^{t} \mu^{i-1} + \phi \sum_{i=1}^{t} \mu^{i-1} Z_i \tag{12}$$

This equation means that, at any moment, the value of the endogenous variable depends on its prior adjustment path. For Setterfield and Katzner, it characterizes hysteresis as a general case: it is seen as a situation where the value of X, at any time, depends on the previous adjustment path.

To fully understand the extent of this concept of the hysteresis, an appeal to the concept of deep endogeneity is helpful. Following Setterfield (1997, p. 29), 'a central point of the hysteresis critique of traditional equilibrium analysis is to question whether conventional "data" can in fact be regarded as exogenous in this manner. Might it not be preferable to interpret such traditional "data" as tastes, technology and institutions as being endogenous to the economic outcomes they are held to explain?' That is why, following the author, the deep endogeneity of the data may be sufficient to generate hysteresis. Moreover, all variables underlying the equilibrium need not be deeply endogenous in order to generate hysteresis. The distinction between the extent of deep endogeneity and its nature is fundamental. Following Setterfield, the key issue is not the extent, but the nature of the endogeneity, and in particular the way that the adjustment of the deeply endogenous variables is modelled.

The main advantage with the Setterfield–Katzner definition of hysteresis is also one of its most important drawbacks: the gain in generality. By gaining in terms of generality, their definition of hysteresis loses some properties of genuine hysteresis underlined below. For that reason, it is not certain that using the term hysteresis to refer to the Setterfield–Katzner dynamics is relevant, even if the model indubitably belongs to the same family. Moreover, this definition of hysteresis also poses difficulties that are not necessary drawbacks, but which cause issues that still have to be solved. First of all, determining the starting point of the dynamics (the time zero) may not be easy. The choice may always be seen as arbitrary. More importantly, determining which variables can be considered as being deeply endogenous and how to model these variables and to consider their nature is not an easy task. Last, it may be very tricky to implement this definition of hysteresis empirically, even using complicated computational devices. Nevertheless, the fact that, to our knowledge, these tasks have not been done yet does not mean that they are impossible to do, but rather that they remain on the agenda for future macroeconomic analysis.

Finally, some economists, also belonging to the post-Keynesian School, the most prominent being Rod Cross, have introduced in economics the original definition of hysteresis, the only one used in sciences, such as physics or biology. This definition may be characterized indifferently as strong hysteresis (Amable et al., 1993, 1994; Cross, 1993a) or, as we will do from here on, as genuine hysteresis (Göcke, 2003). Considering this very definition, the multiple other definitions given to hysteresis in economics may be considered as bastard (Cross, 1993a), since none of them embed the core properties of genuine hysteresis.[5] By contrast to these bastard definitions, genuine hysteresis is used by authors in the post-Keynesian tradition, and more precisely on the Robinsonian and Kaldorian branches of post-Keynesianism, to model systems in which past shocks can have effects on the real economy even a long time after their resorption. In genuinely hysteretic systems, the equilibria will be shaped by the dynamics of the system, that is, by the most important aggregate shocks. Technically, these most important shocks will be called the non-dominated ones, that is, positive of negative shocks that have not been overtaken by more important shocks. The authors working on genuine hysteresis have shown that, in the presence of this phenomenon, the natural rate of unemployment and the NAIRU frameworks do not make sense. In the presence of genuine hysteresis, the most important steps taken in the short run will help shape the dynamics of the system and therefore its equilibria. In these conditions, nominal shocks can have real effects and the discretionary economic policies will exert an influence on the equilibrium outcomes by changing these outcomes (Cross, 1995), provided that the economic shocks are sustained enough to overcome the past negative shocks that have hit the economy (Lang, 2004). Therefore, the hysteresis models provide good arguments in favour of interventionist monetary and budget policies. These policies have to be all the more sustained that the past negative shocks that had hit the economy are important quantitatively.

Nevertheless, rather surprisingly, the authors working on genuine hysteresis in unemployment have forgotten to examine an important implication of the concept: it can be shown that, in genuinely hysteretic systems, unemployment is mainly an involuntary phenomenon. If unemployment was always voluntary, how could there be hysteresis if what happens (unemployment) has been freely chosen by those who are unemployed? To put it differently, and to use Keynes's vocabulary, in genuinely hysteretic systems, the unemployed are willing to work at the current wage prevailing in the economy, but they cannot find jobs because of the lack of effective demand. Showing this is the main point of this chapter. Reading the papers of the authors who have worked on genuine hysteresis in unemployment, it is clear that the idea that unemployment is mainly involuntary is an implicit assumption of genuinely hysteretic models (see for example Cross et al., 1998; Hallet and Piscitelli, 2002). But, to our knowledge, the idea that unemployment is involuntary in genuinely hysteretic models has never been made explicit up to now in the literature. Moreover, it is often argued against genuinely hysteretic models that on the microeconomic level the presence of decision thresholds, that is a necessary condition for the presence of hysteresis, is an *ad hoc* device, as this is assumed, but not really based, on sound economic foundations and rationale. In fact, it is unfair to authors like Dixit (1989) and Booth et al. (2002), who have established solid foundations for the presence of such thresholds, but it is true that genuinely hysteretic models lack micro-foundations formulated in post-Keynesian terms.

The purpose of this chapter is to try to remedy these deficiencies by showing how involuntary unemployment can emerge, in genuinely a hysteretic system, as a consequence of the lack of effective demand. We intend to make a first step in providing new foundations, in terms of lack of effective demand, of the micro-foundations of hysteretic models, and to draw the most important implications for macroeconomic policies.

The remainder of this chapter is organized as follows. In section 2, we introduce and define genuine hysteresis in greater details, and we propose a hysteretic model in economics, which, following the works by Cross (1993, 1995) and Cross et al. (1998), is based on the hysteretic models framed, in physics, by Krasnosel'skii and Pokrovskii (1989) and Mayergoyz (1991). In section 3, the foundations of the model presented in section 2 are developed by introducing an amended version of Keynes's concept of effective demand as a rationale for the presence of hysteresis at the microeconomic level. Section 4 examines the economic policy consequences of our model. Some concluding remarks follow in section 5.

2.   Genuine hysteresis: definition and framework

According to the rigorous mathematical definition of hysteresis, due to Krasnosel'skii and Pokrovskii (1989) and Mayergoyz (1991), a process that has a memory of past shocks must possess two key properties to be characterized as hysteretic, that is, in the vocabulary used here, as strongly hysteretic. These properties are *remanence* and a *selective, erasable memory*. By definition, remanence occurs when the application of two successive shocks of the same magnitude, but of opposite signs, does not bring the system under consideration back to its initial position. The selective, erasable memory property means that only the non-dominated extremum values of the past shocks that have hit the system remain in its memory bank. To put it differently, in the presence of a selective, erasable memory, only the most important past shocks will matter. By contrast, in attractionist models, in the long run, the system would not keep any memory of shocks. By contrast, in the unit root-like definitions of hysteresis, the system would keep an elephantine memory of the shocks (Cross, 1993b): every shock, whatever its importance, will remain in the memory bank of the system.

Many economic applications of the genuine hysteresis framework have been proposed in economics, such as, for example, in the fields of the analysis of exchange rates (see Amable et al., 1991) or the analysis of the violations of the law of one price in the case of E-commerce (Cross and Lang, 2004). More particularly, and more interestingly for our purposes in this chapter, some works apply the strong hysteresis model to the understanding of the unemployment problem (see in particular Cross et al., 1998; Hallet and Piscitelli, 2002; Lang and De Peretti, 2009).

In this section of the chapter, we propose an amended version of these models, in order to be able to introduce more solid microeconomic foundations based on a microeconomic transposition of the concept of effective demand. In hysteretic models, the microeconomic level has to be distinguished from the macroeconomic one. The macroeconomic behaviour is not a simple sum of all microeconomic ones, and similar properties at both levels bear different meanings at the two levels.

The microeconomic framework

In genuinely hysteretic models, in order to be able to derive the aggregate hysteretic dynamics, we first have to consider the activity functions of individual, heterogeneous elements. In our model, these elements (whose generic usual name in mathematics is hysterons), are what we have chosen to christen here as potential units of labour. The set of all potential units of labour represents all the jobs that can potentially be created in the economy as a whole, that is, at the macroeconomic level.

For each of the potential units of labour, the employers will decide, in the wake of economic shocks, whether they fill the position and therefore employ a person, in which case the status of the potential units of labour is E_i (employed potential unit of labour); or not to fill the position, the state of the potential units of labour in this case being U_i (unemployed potential unit of labour). When the position of a potential unit of labour is E_i, this potential unit of labour will be characterized as active; otherwise, it will be said to be inactive (that is when its state is U_i).

All potential units of labour react to a common macroeconomic shock, denoted ε. We do not give any explicit content to this shock here, as we want to focus on the hysteretic behaviour of the system and its properties rather than on the nature of the macroeconomic shock, that will vary from author to author. This shock can be either one of supply or demand. In this kind of model, as will be clear below, it does not matter whether the shock is anticipated or not. All that is required is that the intensity of the shock, and therefore the level of the relevant variable, is known by all the agents.

Any potential unit of labour will be fully characterized by two different thresholds. The potential units of labour are also heterogeneous in that all of them will have different thresholds from one to another. For a particular potential unit of labour i, a_i will denote the threshold that the aggregate shock hitting the economy (ε) has to cross in order to induce a potential unit of labour i that was previously inactive to switch from the U_i to the E_i position, that is, from unemployment to employment. Similarly, b_i will denote, for the particular potential unit of labour i, the threshold that must be crossed in order to switch from the E_i position to the U_i position.

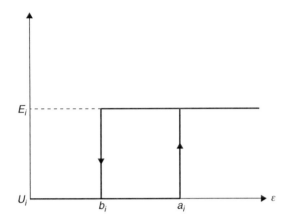

Figure 3.1   The behaviour of a potential unit of labour

Therefore, at any time, for each potential unit of labour, depending on the common macroeconomic shocks, three decisions can be taken: to switch from inactivity to activity (from U_i to E_i); to become inactive while it was previously active (i.e., to switch from E_i to U_i); or to remain in the previous position (whether E_i or U_i). In this model, adjustments are discontinuous in that a threshold value has to be crossed in order to induce a potential unit of labour to switch, on the basis of the two different threshold values a_i and b_i. By construction, for all the potential units of labour, $a_i > b_i$. From now on, in order to lighten the notation, we will denote the thresholds a and b. This microeconomic framework is illustrated in Figure 3.1.

The microeconomic model has two important properties. First, the past history of the system matters: for any value bounded by a and b, in order to determine whether the potential unit of labour is active or not, it is necessary to know the initial state of the potential unit of labour (E_i or U_i), and the number of times the system has switched over a, or under b. To put this another way, between the two thresholds, a and b, there is no way of knowing a priori whether the potential unit of labour will be active or not. This is usually interpreted as the presence of a memory of the system at the microeconomic level. Secondly, there is a remanence effect, illustrated in Figure 3.2. If, initially, the potential unit of labour is inactive, and if a shock brings the system from position 0 to position 1, then is followed by another shock that brings the system back to its initial position, the potential unit of labour will become active, and remain in

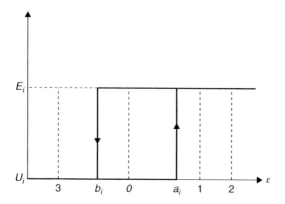

Figure 3.2 The remanence effect at the microeconomic level

the active state even if the relevant economic variable returns to its initial value. Nevertheless, on the microeconomic level, this remanence effect is limited. Indeed, if there is a shock from position 3 to position 0, followed by another shock of the same magnitude in the opposite direction, the potential unit of labour will end up inactive, since the threshold b_i will have been crossed. This is the case because the inactivity threshold b will have been crossed. Therefore, the remanence effect is limited. It does not necessarily depend on the magnitude of the common macroeconomic shock: what matters more at the microeconomic level is whether or not the threshold values (a_i and b_i) have been crossed.

This basic microeconomic framework is the foundation of macro-economic dynamics, where the most important past economic shocks (the non-dominated ones) remain in the memory bank of the current unemployment rate.

The macroeconomic framework

At the aggregate level, the economy as a whole is represented as a set of a large number of potential units of labour. Each potential unit of labour will be characterized and represented by its two switching values a and b. The only hypothesis made here is that, as the potential units of labour are heterogeneous, there are significant variations in these switching values. Under these conditions, the set of all potential units of labour can be represented in Mayergoyz's (1991) diagram, illustrated in Figure 3.3. In this diagram, each potential unit of labour is represented by its two characteristic two threshold values, (b, a); and the triangle T, defined by the first bisector and the extreme values $b = b_0$ and $a = a_{FCU}$ represent the

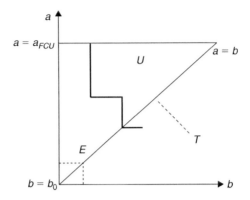

Figure 3.3   The staircase partition between unemployment and employment at the macroeconomic level

set of all potential unit of labour in the economy. As we saw earlier, by construction, for each potential unit of labour, $a > b$, since the activity threshold is necessarily higher than the inactivity threshold. a_{FCU} is the activity threshold for the most demanding potential unit of labour, and corresponds therefore to the full utilization of capacities in this economy. Note that, even if the point of full capacity of utilization (FCU) is reached, this may, or may not, mean that the economy has reached the full employment level, as it may be the case that, even when all physical capacities in the economy are used, some people will remain jobless, if there is a physical capital shortage. The active potential units of labour belong to the domain marked E, representing the total level of employment in this economy, while the inactive potential units of labour operate inside the area U (the unemployment level in the economy). The frontier between U and E will necessarily take the form of a staircase, the coordinates of the stairs corresponding to the past local non-dominated minima and maxima of the economic shocks.[6]

The economy depicted in this diagram will retain in its memory bank the sequence of past shocks in a selective manner. The memory is *selective and erasable*, in that only non-dominated shocks remain in the memory bank of the system. At the macroeconomic level, the *remanence effect* is different from the one already examined at the microeconomic level: in the Mayergoyz diagram (illustrated in Figures 3.2 and 3.3), two different growth shocks of the same size but of opposite signs will never bring the system back to its initial position, whatever the importance of these shocks is. Indeed, after a positive growth shock, some potential units of labour will become active, and will remain active even after a negative shock of the same magnitude, whatever the magnitude of the shock. This is also true for negative shocks followed by positive ones: some potential units of labour that were initially active will now remain inactive. But, in all cases, after two shocks of the same size but of opposite signs, the macroeconomic system, that is, the levels of employment and unemployment, will necessarily change.[7] Economically, this means that the reactions of the economy to positive and negative shocks are asymmetric. Therefore, in our framework, the fluctuations of employment in reaction to shocks will not be the same during booms as during recessions. Moreover, the economic system as a whole, and, more precisely, the employment and unemployment levels, will be path dependent. On the whole, two different shocks of the same size but of opposite signs will not bring the system back to its initial position, whatever the importance of these shocks.[8]

The *erasable and selective* character of the memory can also be understood on the basis of Mayergoyz's diagram. The memory is erasable in that only non-dominated shocks will remain in the memory bank of the system. Indeed, let us suppose that the memory bank of the system is represented by the dotted line in Figure 3.3, and that, later on, there is an important negative shock that deteriorates the state of the relevant macroeconomic variable to a value lower than that experienced during any of the preceding periods. Because of the selective memory property, this minimum value of ε is a local minimum. It will erase from the memory bank of the economy all the coordinates of the staircase partition associated with the (now dominated) previous values of ε. This erasing process is illustrated by the new partition between the active and inactive firms marked by the solid vertical line that can be seen in Figure 3.4.

On a more formal level, at any time t, given the distribution of firms between the two domains (E and U), and given the past values of the common macroeconomic shock, the aggregate hysteretic activity function can be written as following:

$$h[g(t)|I_{t-1}] = \iint\limits_{A(t)} e_{ab}[\varepsilon(t)|I_{t-1}]f(a,b)dadb \qquad (4)$$

where $\varepsilon(t)$ is the common macroeconomic shock variable at time t, and e_{ab} is the activity dummy of the potential unit of labour i: $e_{ab}=0$ if the state of the potential unit of labour is U; $e_{ab}=1$ if this state is E. $f(a,b)$ describes the distribution or density function of the potential units of labour, each potential unit of labour being characterized by its pair of

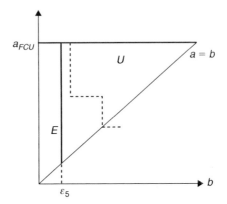

Figure 3.4   An illustration of the selective memory property

switching values (a, b). I_{t-1} is the information set on the state of the system at time $t - 1$. h is the hysteretic transformation function.

3.   Involuntary unemployment in hysteresis models

At this stage, one may ask what is the link between the model summed up above and Keynes's concept of involuntary unemployment. The usual reply to this relevant question is that it must underlie the microeconomic behaviour in some way, but this way has never been made explicit in the literature – at least to our knowledge. Therefore, the relationship would go through the economic foundations of the microeconomic framework illustrated in the previous section.

In this chapter, we want to show that the link between the strongly hysteretic model and the Keynesian foundations proposed here goes through the economic justification of the existence of the discontinuous adjustments in terms of effective demand. Indeed, the combination of two economic phenomena is necessary to justify the existence of the thresholds, and to explain why they are crossed: the presence of *sunk costs* of hiring and firing, and Keynes's original principle of *effective demand*. As the rationales for and economic effects of the presence of sunk costs are already very well documented (see, among others, Dixit, 1989, or Dixit and Pindyck, 1994), we will insist in greater extent here on the most important argument of this chapter, that is, on the introduction of Keynes's principle of effective demand as a sound foundation for the microeconomic model.[9]

Keynes (1936, p. 25), defines the principle of effective demand on the basis of the intersection, at the macroeconomic level, of what he calls the aggregate supply function and the aggregate demand function. Nevertheless, these concepts have nothing to do, in Keynes's writings, with their current economic meaning in macroeconomics, in particular in the aggregate supply–aggregate demand (AS–AD) model that can be found in textbooks. Keynes defines aggregate supply, aggregate demand, and the resulting concept of effective demand, as follows:

> Let Z be the aggregate supply price of the output from employing N men, the relationship between Z and N being written $Z = \varphi(N)$, which can be called the *aggregate supply function*. Similarly, let D be the proceeds which entrepreneurs **expect** to receive from the employment of N men, the relationship between D and N being written $D = f(N)$, which can be called the *aggregate demand function* ...the volume of employment is given by the point of intersection between the aggregate demand function and the aggregate supply function; for it is at this point that the entrepreneurs' expectation of profits will be maximised. The value of D at the point of the aggregate demand function, where it is intersected by the aggregate supply function, will be called *the effective demand*. (Keynes, 1936, p. 25; emphasis in italics in the original text; emphasis in bold added)

It is to that concept of effective demand that we refer here. Now, let us introduce sunk costs and a microeconomic transposition of this principle of effective demand in our model, in order to justify the presence of the thresholds on the microeconomic level. For doing so, let us define SC_i as the sunk cost for the ith potential unit of labour in the economy. As, in general, hiring and firing decisions seldom have the same cost, SC_i, the sunk costs for the ith potential unit of labour, will have two different components: the sunk cost of hiring, denoted SCH_i; and SCF_i, the sunk cost of firing. Now, on the basis of Keynes's principle of effective demand, let us denote Z_i the aggregate supply price of the output obtained when filling one particular of labour (except for SC_i, excluded from this supply price, as it has to be distinguished in our model). Let D_i be the proceeds, which entrepreneurs *expect* to receive from the filling of one particular of labour.

In this framework, the thresholds for activity and inactivity of the potential units of labour described in the previous section will be defined as follows. The activity threshold a_i corresponds to the point where the proceeds which entrepreneurs expect to receive from the filling of one particular of labour correspond to the aggregate supply price of the output net of the sunk cost of hiring, plus the latter costs. This can be written $D_i = Z_i + SCH_i$. Similarly, the inactivity threshold b_i will be defined such as the point where the proceeds which entrepreneurs expect to receive from the filling of one particular of labour correspond to the aggregate supply price of the output net of the sunk cost of firing, plus these sunk costs, which is written as $D_i = Z_i + SCF_i$.

On the basis of this simple model based on the combination of the transposition of the principle of effective demand and on the presence of sunk cost, we now have a simple but solid foundation of the microeconomic model examined above. In this framework, the particular of labour i will become active when D_i will be greater than $Z_i + SCH_i$; the same of labour will become inactive when D_i will be lower than $Z_i + SCF_i$. For the values of D_i such that $Z_i + SCF_i \leq D_i \leq Z_i + SCH_i$, it will be necessary to know what the initial position of the potential unit of labour was, and whether one of the threshold will have been crossed previously.

The macroeconomic consequences of this are quite clear: since the thresholds will be determined on the basis of sunk cost and effective demand considerations, the employment and unemployment levels in the economy as a whole (the partition between U and E in Mayergoyz's diagram) will depend, in a path-dependent fashion, on the past history of the economic shocks that have hit the economy. Effective demand, through its contribution to the thresholds a and b of all the potential units of labour, will be, with the presence of sunk costs, the rationale of this path dependence. In other words, in this amended model,

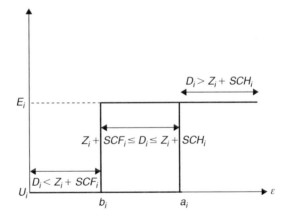

Figure 3.5   Sunk costs, effective demand, and thresholds

effective demand will determine the shape of the staircase partition in this economy.

The introduction of effective demand in the model also adds another important dimension in this model. Indeed, as the switching decisions now depend on D_i, it means that, as in Keynes (1936), the employment level in the economy will now be fully dependent on the subjective expectations of entrepreneurs (the animal spirits), who, accordingly with the general framework of the *General Theory* and with the post-Keynesian universe in general, do not have any rational basis for computing what the future will be. Therefore, radical uncertainty is introduced this way in hysteresis models: we simply don't know what the future is going to be. Entrepreneurs have to make decisions on D_i in the dark.

On the whole, adding these new microeconomic foundations allows us to underline and reinforce the post-Keynesian nature of these models, as effective demand and radical uncertainty are introduced in a framework that is already fully path-dependent.

4. Implications for economic policies

Since the 1990s, it is usually argued in papers about genuine hysteresis in unemployment that strong hysteresis would bring back into favour the Keynesian macroeconomic policies, but this is often said in conclusion and left for future research. The framework introduced here may help in making a first step in this direction. In the usual hysteretic framework (the one without the foundations introduced here), and looking at Mayergoyz's diagram, the stimulation of the economy by the government has to be important enough in order to erase the past history of the economy, that is, the staircase partition (shaped by the positive and the negative shocks). This is a major economic policy implication, as it means that the macroeconomic stimulation must be *important enough* in order to succeed, which could help explain why some Keynesian policies of the 1970s or at the beginning of the 1980s have failed. But this does not give any clue concerning the *channels* through which the economic stimulation should proceed in order to be successful. The foundations of the microeconomic framework introduced here give us some clue, as a stimulation of effective demand will have an effect both on the aggregate variable at the microeconomic level *and*, at the microeconomic level, it will change the threshold by making the expectations of the entrepreneurs more optimistic. This means that the usual channels underlined by the Post-Keynesian literature, in particular the ones that operate through income distribution (see for example the work of Hein and Vogel, 2008), can be reintroduced here. This is a task for future research.

5.   Concluding remarks

This chapter has summed up the main arguments in favour of the usage of the genuine hysteresis definition of hysteresis in economics, by contrast with the other multiple definitions that can be found in the economic literature. We then introduced a novel declension of the genuine hysteresis model in terms of employment and unemployment, in order to introduce path-dependence in the equilibrium path of unemployment. We then tried to introduce new post-Keynesian foundations for these hysteresis models, which are among the most important category of path-dependent models. In our model, the path-dependent level of unemployment at the aggregate level depends on the non-dominated economic shocks that have hit the economy, and this path-dependence is triggered by the combination, on the microeconomic level, of sunk costs of hiring and firing and a transposition of Keynes's principle of effective demand. Obviously, this declension is closer to Keynes's concept, as it includes the subjective expectations of proceeds by entrepreneurs and true uncertainty. Last, we have drawn the main economic policy implications of this model.

In our model, as in Keynes (1936), there is still no reason to believe that, in general, the point where all potential units of labour will set their effective demands will correspond to full employment. This conclusion is even reinforced here, with the presence of a fully path-dependent level of employment (which corresponds, in our macroeconomic model, to the staircase partition between the employment and unemployment areas). In the general case, in this path-dependent economy, there will be involuntary unemployment, and there is no reason to think that the particular equilibrium reached at any time will correspond to full employment. This might even be the case in the very particular case where, in the aftermath of a very strong positive shock (strong enough to erase all the past history of the system), the point corresponding to full capacity utilization is reached, and, therefore, when a large positive economic shock is able to erase all the previous past history of the system. In our model, even when the economy reaches full employment, the neoclassical models and their predictions may be wrong; whereas Keynes (1936) states that they may be right.

The usual economic policy implications of hysteretic models is that economic policies should seek to erase the previous non-dominated growth shocks, which implies that economic policies intended to reduce employment should be sufficiently sustained to erase the negative shocks that remain in the memory of the economic system. Our model allows us to conclude that, in this framework, this can be done by stimulating effective demand, which can be achieved here in two ways: first, by reducing the sunk costs and the other determinants of the aggregate supply price of the output; secondly, and maybe more efficiently, by stimulating the proceeds which entrepreneurs expect to receive from the employment, which is a psychological variable. In this model, it is clear that an expansionist budget policy will have a positive impact on the employment level not only in the short run, but also in the medium and long run since this policy will induce many potential units of labour to switch to the upper branch, and therefore will change the equilibrium on the macroeconomic level in a positive fashion. In the presence of genuine hysteresis, the classical dichotomy vanishes, and expansionary policies, provided that they are sustained enough, will contribute to the reduction of unemployment, in the short, medium and the long run.

Notes

*   The author wishes to thank Mark Setterfield and all the other participants in the 5th International Conference on Developments in Economic Theory and Policy for their helpful and relevant remarks on a preliminary version of this chapter.
1. For Lang (2008), it would therefore seem that the work of 'choosing one's legacy' to do, in economics, the same kind of work that has been done in physics, biology and chemistry, where the inheritance bequeathed by the previous generation is routinely subjected to critical scrutiny so that the science can progress. One result of this process has been the abandonment of path independence in the hard sciences.
2. For a more detailed history of the hysteresis concept, see Cross (1993a) and Lang (2004).
3. If Sawyer's distinction between the natural rate of unemployment and the NAIRU is very clear and interesting, one must nevertheless underline an important limit of it: it is not fully consistent with the original papers about the natural rate of unemployment. Indeed, Friedman does not make any explicit reference to individual behaviours, or to any microeconomic reasoning, even if the reference to 'the resolution of a Walrasian general equilibrium system' lets it be understood that there is an underlying microeconomic model. One can hardly deny that the research programme opened by Friedman opened onto the job search models. These models are trying to find micro-foundations to the NAIRU. Nevertheless, for obvious reasons, no reference to the matching models can be found in Friedman's (1968) paper.
4. Unfortunately, the author does not make explicit what he means by 'appropriate'.
5. Many economists would argue that the application of physical concepts to economics, *per se*, is devoid of any interest, and they would be right. We have chosen to analyse and apply the concept of hysteresis to economics because there are reasons to think that this concept has interesting properties that may help us to understand the behaviour of unemployment. This definition also

provides the macroeconomic analysis with dynamics that are alternative to the ones present in the natural rate – NAIRU frameworks. These attractionist dynamics (Lang, 2004) have failed to explain the behaviour of unemployment in the developed countries. Moreover, on a theoretical ground, the attractionist dynamics are rather discredited considering the number of issues they are generating, as well as on the theoretical, the empirical and the epistemological levels. The strong definition of hysteresis is examined and developed because its application may be relevant when coming to the examination, analysis and understanding of the puzzle of unemployment. At least, applying it to this problem may help us assess it relevance. This is the case because this definition has some important properties that the other hysteresis concepts do not share.

6. The proof of this is provided in Appendix 1.
7. The proof of this is given in Appendix 2.
8. We do not develop this framework to any great extent here because these developments are already well known. For further explanations, and a more detailed illustration of the way genuinely hysteretic systems work and of their properties, see Cross (1993a), Setterfield (1997), Lang (2004), and Lang and De Peretti (2009).
9. Note that other rationales, closer to the more familiar foundations of hysteresis on the microeconomic level, can be found in the literature concerning discontinuous adjustments and in some papers on the effects of hiring and firing costs (see for example Booth et al., 2002). Note that this literature, which is closer to the usual neoclassical microeconomic models of profit and utility maximization, can nevertheless in such cases provide rationales, through microeconomic foundations, for the presence of path dependence and hysteresis at the macroeconomic level, though the relationship between the two is almost never examined in this literature.

References

Alogoskoufis, G. and Manning, A. (1988) 'Wage Setting and Unemployment Persistence in Europe, Japan and the USA', *European Economic Review*, 32 (2–3), pp. 698–706.

Amable, B., Henry, J., Lordon, F. and Topol, R. (1990) 'Une tentative d'Elucidation d'un Concept Flou: l'hystérésis', *Actes du colloque annuel de l'AFSE*, pp. 135–46.

Amable, B., Henry, J., Lordon, F. and Topol, R. (1991) 'Strong Hysteresis: An Application to Foreign Trade, *Document de Travail de l'OFCE*, 91(3).

Amable, B., Henry, J., Lordon, F. and Topol, R. (1993) 'Unit-Root in the Wage-Price Spiral is Not Hysteresis in Unemployment', *Journal of Economic Studies*, 20 (1/2), pp. 123–36.

Amable, B., Henry, J., Lordon, F. and Topol, R. (1994) Strong Hysteresis versus Zero-Root Dynamics, *Economic Letters*, 44, pp. 43–7.

Ball, L. and Mankiw, G. (2002) 'The NAIRU in Theory and Practice', *NBER Working Paper*, 8940, May.

Barro, R. and Gordon, R. (1983) 'A positive theory of monetary policy in a natural rate model', *Journal of Political Economy*, 91, pp. 589–610.

Blanchard, O.J. and Summers, L.H. (1986) 'Hysteresis in Unemployment', *European Economic Review*, Papers and Procedings, 31, pp. 288–95.

Blanchard, O.J. and Summers, L.H. (1988) 'Hysteresis and the European Unemployment Problem', in Summers, L.H. *Understanding Unemployment*, M.I.T. Press.

Booth, A., Chen, Y.F. and Zoega, G. (2002) 'Hiring and firing: a tale of two thresholds', *Journal of Labour Economics*, 9(20), pp. 217–48.

Cross, R. (1993a) 'On the foundations of hysteresis in economic systems', *Economics and Philosophy*, 9(1), pp. 53–74.

Cross, R. (1993b) 'Hysteresis and Post Keynesian Economics', *Journal of Post Keynesian Economics*, 15(3), pp. 305–8.

Cross, R. (1995a) 'Metaphors and time reversibility and irreversibility in economic systems', *Journal of Economic Methodology*, 1, pp. 123–34.

Cross, R. (1995b) 'Is the natural rate hypothesis consistent with hysteresis?', in Cross, R. (1995) *The Natural Rate of Unemployment: Reflections on 25 Years of the Hypothesis*, Cambridge University Press.

Cross, R. (1996) 'The Natural Rate: An Attractor for Actual Unemployment, or an Attractee?', *Scottish Journal of Political Economy*, 43(3).

Cross, R., Darby, J., Ireland, J. and Piscitelli, L. (1998) 'Hysteresis and unemployment: a preliminary investigation', *CEPR/ESRC Unemployment Dynamics Workshop Paper*.

Cross, R. and Lang, D. (2004) 'Habits, hysteresis and the law of one price: the case of E-commerce', *CEDERS Working Paper*.

Cross, R. and Strachan, D. (2001) 'Three Pillars of Conventional Wisdom, *Review of Political Economy*, 13(2), pp. 181–200.

Cross, R., Piscitelli, L., Grinfeld, M. and Lamba, H. (1998) 'A test for strong hysteresis, *Computational Economics*, 15, pp. 59–78.

Dixit, A. (1989) 'Entry and exit decisions under uncertainty', *Journal of Political Economy*, 97(3), pp. 620–38.

Dixit, A. and Pindyck, R. (1994) *Investment Under Uncertainty*, Princeton University Press.

Estrella, A., Mishkin, F.S. (1998) 'Rethinking the Role of NAIRU in Monetary Policy: Implications of Model Formulation and Uncertainty', *NBER Working Paper*, 6518, April.

Ewing, J.A. (1881) 'On the Production of Transient Electric Currents in Iron and Steel Conductors by Twisting them when Magnetised or by Magnetising them when Twisted', *Proceedings of the Royal Society of London*, 33, pp. 21–3.

Fève, P., Henin, P.Y. and Jolivaldt, P. (2003) 'Testing for Hysteresis: Unemployment Persistence and Wage Adjustment', *Empirical Economics*, 28(3), pp. 535–52.

Friedman, M. (1968) 'The Role of Monetary Policy', *American Economic Review*, 13(1).

Göcke, M. (2003) 'Various Concepts of Hysteresis Applied in Economics', *Journal of Economic Surveys*, 2(16), pp. 167–88.

Gordon, R. (1997) 'The time-varying NAIRU and its implications for economic policy', *Journal of Economic Perspectives*, 11(1), pp. 11–32.

Hallet, A.J.H. and Piscitelli, L. (2002) 'Testing for hysteresis against nonlinear alternatives', *Journal of Economic Dynamics and Control*, 27, pp. 303–27.

Hein, E. and Vogel, L. (2008) 'Distribution and Growth Reconsidered: Empirical Results for Six OECD Countries', *Journal of Economics*, 32(3), pp. 479–511.

Jackman, R. and Leroy, M. (1995) 'Estimating the NAIRU: The Case of France', *Actes du Congrès Annuel de l'AFSE*, September, Paris.

Jevons, W.S. (1905) *Principles of Economics*, London: Macmillan.

Katzner, D.W. (1993) 'Some Notes on the Role of History and the Definition of Hysteresis and Related Concepts in Economic Analysis', *Journal of Post Keynesian Economics*, 15 (3), pp. 323–45.

Katzner, D.W. (1999) 'Hysteresis and the Modelling of Economic Phenomena', *Review of Political Economy*, 11(2), pp. 171–81.

Keynes, J.M. (1936) *The General Theory of Employment, Interest and Money*, Macmillan Press, 1973.

Krasnolsel'skii, M.A. and Pokrovskii, A.W. (1989) *Systems with Hysteresis*, Springer Verlag.

Kydland, F. and Prescott, E. (1977) 'Rules rather than discretion: the inconsistency of optimal plans', *Journal of Political Economy*, 85, pp. 473–91.

Lang, D. (2004) *Hysteresis in Unemployment*, (PhD. Thesis), Université de la Méditerranée.

Lang, D. (2008) 'Why economists should choose their inheritance: the example of physics and path-independence in economic systems', *Review of Political Economy*, July.

Lang, D. and De Peretti, C. (2009) 'A Strong Hysteresis Model for Okun's Law: Theory and Preliminary Investigation', *International Review of Applied Economics*, forthcoming.

Lardic, S. (1998) *L'hystérèse en Economie, Théorie et Mesure*, PhD. Thesis, Université de ParisX – Nanterre.

Layard, R., Nickell, S. and Jackman, R. (1991) *Unemployment: Macroeconomic Performance and the Labour Market*, Oxford University Press.

Mayergoyz, I.D. (1991) *Mathematical Models of Hysteresis*, Springer Verlag.

Mirowski, P. (1989) *More Heat than Light: Economics as Social Physics, Physics as Nature's Economics*, Cambridge University Press.

Roed, K. (1997) 'Hysteresis in Unemployment', *Journal of Economic Surveys*, 11 (4), pp. 339–418.

Sawyer, M. (1997) 'The NAIRU: A Critical Appraisal', *International Papers in Political Economy*, 6 (2), pp. 1–40. Reprinted in P. Arestis and M. Sawyer (eds) *Money, Finance and Capitalist Development*, Edward Elgar, pp. 220–54.

Setterfield, M. (1993) 'Towards a Long-run Theory of Effective Demand', *Journal of Post Keynesian Economics*, spring, 22 (2), pp. 331–56.

Setterfield, M. (1997) *Rapid Growth and Relative Decline: Modelling Macroeconomic Dynamics with Hysteresis*, Macmillan.

Staiger, D., Stock, J.H. and Watson, M. (1997) 'The NAIRU, Unemployment and monetary policy', *Journal of Economic Perspectives*, 11, pp. 33–49.

Stanley, T.D. (2004) 'Does Unemployment Hysteresis Falsify the Natural Rate Hypothesis? A Meta-Regression Analysis', *Journal of Economic Surveys*, 18(4), pp. 589–612.

Thomson, W. and Tait, P.G. (1867) *A Treatise on Natural Philosophy*, Cambridge.

Tobin, J. (1995) 'The Natural Rate as New Classical Macroeconomics', in Cross, R. (1995) *The Natural Rate of Unemployment: Reflections on 25 Years of the Hypothesis*, Cambridge University Press.

Walras, L. (1909) 'Economique et mécanique', *Bulletin de la Société Vaudoise de Sciences Naturelles*, 45, pp. 313–25.

Walras, L. (1954) *Elements of Pure Economics*, Allen & Unwin.

Appendix 1 The staircase partition at the macroeconomic level

This appendix is intended to show that the frontier between the areas of active and inactive potential units of labour will necessarily take the shape of a staircase (accordingly with Mayergoyz's 1991 results). The coordinates of the stairs of this staircase partition correspond to the past local non-dominated minima and maxima of the common shock variable, ε.

To show this, let us consider the sequence of aggregate shocks illustrated in Figure 3.6. Let us consider the evolution of a relevant macroeconomic (shocks to the economy) and 'periods' of time. Note that here, the definition of the 'periods' do not correspond to the usual one. The period is defined here as the interval on the horizontal axis between two peaks, that is, between two non-dominated local extrema (one minimum and one maximum, or vice versa).

In Mayergoyz's diagram, the entry thresholds of the potential units of labour are represented on the horizontal axis, and the exit thresholds on the vertical axis. Therefore, the booms (the positive shocks) will be represented on the horizontal axis and the busts (the positive ones) on the vertical one, accordingly with the theoretical framework presented above.

Let us suppose that, at time t_0 (the initial state of the economy), there is full employment in this economy, so the E (active) zone corresponds to the whole Mayergoyz's triangle T. During the interval of time $[t_0, t_1]$, a bust (a negative shock) takes place and the relevant determinant of

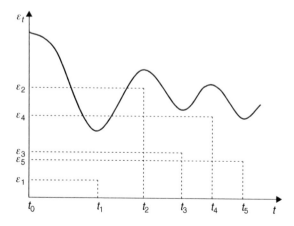

Figure 3.6 A sequence of aggregate shocks

macroeconomic activity is slowing down. Therefore, at t_1, which corresponds to the first minimum, all potential units of labour for which $\varepsilon(1) \leq b_i$ become inactive. To put it differently, during $[t_0, t_1]$, people are fired by the employers. Obviously, during this period, the potential units of labour for which $\varepsilon(1) \geq a_i$ do not become active, since they were already active previously, from the original state on. The fact that some potential units of labour become inactive implies the appearance of the U (unemployment) zone, as illustrated on Figure 3.7.

During the interval of time $[t_1, t_2]$, there is a boom: the economic situation of the economy is getting better, and when the relevant macroeconomic variable reaches its next maximum (its value then being $\varepsilon(1)$), a certain number of potential units of labour that were inactive at t_1 have become active again. This is the case for the potential units of labour having an entry threshold such as $a_i \geq \varepsilon(2)$. With the boom, employers have started hiring again.

The graphical representation of this situation can be seen on Figure 3.8. In this figure, the U domain, corresponding to the level of unemployment in this economy, diminishes progressively. The frontier between the U and E areas is now shaped by the history of the system, that is, by the first peak and the first hollow $\varepsilon(1)$ and $\varepsilon(2)$. More precisely, during the interval of time $[t_1, t_2]$, the size of the U area diminishes (and the E area increases) by a right-angled triangle determined by $\varepsilon(1)$, $\varepsilon(2)$, and the lower boundary of Mayergoyz's triangle. In Figure 3.8, the arrows represent the dynamics of the system between t_1 and t_2.

The time interval $[t_2, t_3]$ sees the relevant macroeconomic variable slow down again. Subsequently, all potential units of labour for which $\varepsilon(3) \leq b_i$

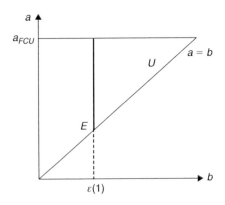

Figure 3.7 The effect of the first negative aggregate shock

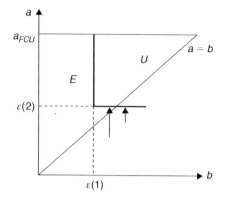

Figure 3.8 The effect of the second aggregate shock

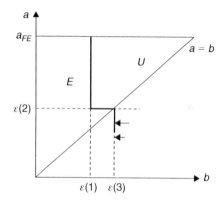

Figure 3.9 The effect of the third aggregate shock (bust)

will become inactive again during this period. This dynamics is illustrated by the arrows oriented to the left. To put it differently, employers fire people again, progressively, every time the exit threshold of their respective potential units of labour is reached. This is the case until the next hollow is reached (at time t_3). The graphical result is the horizontal component of the stair that corresponds to $\varepsilon(3)$ on the horizontal axis (see Figure 3.9). The selective memory property is illustrated in this figure: in this economy, the partition between unemployment and unemployment (the U and E areas) is fully determined by the peaks and the hollows of the common macroeconomic variable.

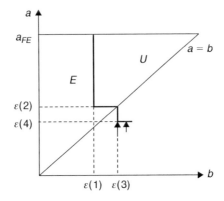

Figure 3.10   The effect of the fourth growth shock

As the relevant macroeconomic variable starts to go up again during $[t_3, t_4]$, all potential units of labour for which the entry threshold is such as $\varepsilon(4) \geq a_i$ hire again. This boom will provoke the appearance on of a new horizontal component of the stair (see Figure 3.10).

The slowing growth during the interval of time $[t_4, t_5]$ is interesting since it allows illustrating further the erasable and selective memory property. Indeed, this period is characterized by a recession, which is more severe than the previous one, but less severe than the first one. Therefore, the hollow reached at t_5 is lower than the previous recessionist peaks, but higher that the first recessionist peak ($\epsilon(3) < \epsilon(5) < \epsilon(1)$). The result will be the erasing of a part of the previous memory of the system, as illustrated in Figure 3.11. In this figure, the full line illustrates the staircase partition at time t_5, and the dotted bold line corresponds to the part of the staircase partition (at t_4) that has been erased from the memory of the economic system.

Figure 3.11 illustrates a fundamental property of genuinely hysteretic systems, the erasable and selective memory of the system, according to which only non-dominated aggregate shocks remain in the memory bank of the system.

Appendix 2   An illustration of the remanence effect at the macroeconomic level

This appendix is intended to illustrate the remanence effect at the macroeconomic level. According to this major property of genuinely hysteretic systems, if a macroeconomic shock occurs, and is followed by

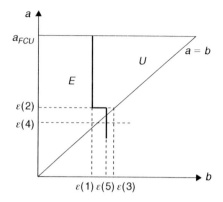

Figure 3.11 The effect of the fifth aggregate shock

another shock of the same magnitude but of opposite sign, the economy will never end up in its initial position. This contrasts with what happens at the microeconomic level, where the potential units of labour can end up in their initial state if one of the thresholds is crossed in the wake of the first shock and the other is crossed as a consequence of the second shock, of the same size but of a different magnitude.

To illustrate remanence at the macroeconomic level, let us suppose that, stating from the state illustrated in Figure 3.3, where the staircase partition between the E and the U domains is already shaped, the economy is hit by a negative shock followed by a positive one of the same magnitude. In order to give a full illustration of the property of remanence, we will suppose that these successive negative and positive shocks are less intense than the two most important negative ones, but that the negative shock is more important that the previous negative shock that had hit the economy, as illustrated in Figure 3.12.

In Figure 3.12, the dotted line indicates the previous staircase partition between U and E, or more precisely the part of the previous staircase partition that is erased by the new shock in ε_{t+1}. Let us suppose now that the next positive shock is of the same magnitude, as illustrated in Figure 3.13.

From Figure 3.13, it is clear that the final partition between E and U will not be the same as before the two successive shocks of the same magnitude. The shaded area corresponds to potential units of labour that would have been employed before the shocks, and that are not employed anymore after them. If we had chosen a positive shock followed by a negative one, the final effect would be the reverse one: a shaded area

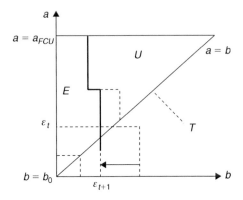

Figure 3.12   An illustration of the remanence effect (1/2)

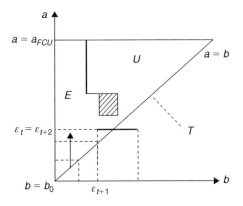

Figure 3.13   An illustration of the remanence effect (2/2)

corresponding to people who used to be unemployed before the shock, and who end up employed afterwards.

Note that what we have shown here is always true, whatever the importance of the shocks may be. In hysteretic systems, there is always a remanence effect, which means, at the macroeconomic level, that two different shocks of the same size but of opposite signs will never bring the system back to its initial position, whatever the importance of these shocks.

4
Path Dependence, Equilibrium and Economic Growth

Amitava Krishna Dutt
University of Notre Dame, USA

Abstract

The *process* of economic growth is often viewed as a dynamic and path-dependent one in which history matters, but the *theories* and *models* of economic growth normally invoke the concept of equilibrium, albeit, a dynamic one. Recently there have been attempts to introduce path dependence into theories and models, including models of economic growth, which allow history to have an important role in determining the path of the economy. This chapter discusses why path dependence may be a desirable property of models and, to do so, it develops a taxonomy of different methods with which path dependence has been or can be incorporated in models. Using this taxonomy, it discusses how the introduction of path dependence in growth models can change our understanding of the nature and determinants of, and policies for, economic growth.

JEL Classification: O41, E12, B40

Keywords: Economic growth, path dependence, equilibrium, hysteresis, aggregate demand, income distribution

1. Introduction

Economic growth is often considered to be a dynamic process, in which 'history matters', and where outcomes are 'path dependent'. However, most growth-theoretic models invoke the concepts of equilibrium and steady state, in which the economy converges to some equilibrium, albeit a dynamic one. Where the economy starts and which path it moves along does not affect the final equilibrium position in these models. All this is particularly problematic for heterodox growth theories, because heterodox economists often try to distance themselves from the orthodox economists' fixation with equilibrium methods, and insist that growth is a dynamic process in 'historical' time where the past is irreversible, while at the same time developing what may be called equilibrium theories of growth.[1] In fact, several economists who may be called mainstream or orthodox economists have developed models in which history has an important role to play.

This chapter examines the reasons for, and implications of, introducing path dependence in heterodox models of economic growth. To do so, it discusses different methods with which some form of path dependency has been introduced into formal models, and for each of these methods, it (1) examines some applications of these methods to heterodox growth theories, (2) discusses their plausibility, and (3) assesses what these methods can contribute to our understanding of growth processes.

The word 'heterodox' can be interpreted broadly to mean analysis which is not 'orthodox' or neoclassical, but this requires some definition of the term 'neoclassical'. That term has been used in a variety of ways. One is to interpret it in a methodological sense to refer to analysis that explains behavior in terms of optimization. Another is to interpret it as analysis that views the economy in a particular way, that is, one in which the economy operates by fully utilizing its resources, such as labor and capital. We will sidestep, but roughly rely on, these definition issues by in most part focusing attention on heterodox theories of growth which have been described as drawing on post-Keynesian and Marxian analysis, in which unemployment and excess capacity are the general features of the economy, where distributional and aggregate demand issues are relevant, and in which behavioral regularities rather than explicit optimization are used to depict behavior. Interpreting heterodox in this way has the added virtue of narrowing the class of models we will examine in this chapter. However, we will sometimes briefly discuss other heterodox growth models to illustrate particular issues.

The rest of this chapter proceeds as follows. Section 2 provides a preliminary discussion of the reasons for introducing path dependency in growth analysis. Then, in section 3, it starts with a simple model of equilibrium growth to explore in what sense such models imply path dependence and in what sense they do not. In sections 4 through 8 it examines five alternative methods with which path dependence can be incorporated into growth models. Section 9 concludes by commenting on the implications of these methods for the plausibility of mechanisms which give rise to, and the major implications of, path dependence for heterodox growth theory.

2. Why path dependence?

We start with a preliminary examination of the reasons which are sometimes given for wanting models to exhibit path dependence.

One reason is that it brings models closer to the intuitive idea that what happens and what we do now determines where we end up. This idea seems to be entertained even by economists, who have had heavy exposure to equilibrium models, but is probably more strongly held by non-economists. Although I know of no formal survey on this question, a few informal surveys I have conducted support this observation.[2]

A second reason relates to what can be called the 'closedness' of models of economic growth. Equilibrium models imply that the economy ends up in a position determined entirely by the structure of the model and is independent both of factors not dealt with in the model, and of the starting point and temporary shocks experienced during the time-path of the economy. This deterministic approach is argued to be problematic because it seems to 'close' the model rather than leave it 'open' for factors that are not considered within the analysis. This 'closedness' can be criticized both because it has no role for human agency and free will, and because it restricts attention to a small set of factors included in the analysis. This problem cannot be removed by introducing white noise into the models, since free will and other factors cannot and should not only have a random role in affecting outcomes. Having some form of path dependency may provide a plausible way of allowing human agency and 'external' factors have a more systematic role to play.

A third relates to problems with the notion of equilibrium, especially in dealing with growth issues. Among heterodox economists Nicholas Kaldor and Joan Robinson have been particularly critical of the notion of equilibrium which they associate with the neoclassical approach, and find to be problematic in the presence of uncertainty and increasing returns. Robinson (1962, p. 23) discusses her problems with the concept of equilibrium by distinguishing between two kinds of economic 'arguments':

> One kind ... proceeds by specifying a sufficient number of equations to determine its unknowns, and so finding values for them that are compatible with each other ... The other type of argument specifies a particular set of values obtaining in a moment of time, which are

not, in general, in equilibrium with each other, and shows how their interactions may be expected to play themselves out.

In the first type of argument the equations may in fact determine a path through time, but 'the time through which such a model moves is, so to speak, logical time, not historical time' (1962, pp. 23–4). Although she admits that one can learn much from '*a priori* comparisons of equilibrium positions, they must be kept in their logical place. They cannot be applied to actual situations; it is a mortal certainty that any particular actual situation which we want to discuss is not in equilibrium' (1962, p. 25). 'As soon as the uncertainty of the expectations that guide economic behaviour is admitted, equilibrium drops out of the argument and history takes its place' (Robinson, 1974, p. 48). Kaldor, examining the determinateness of equilibrium in a static neoclassical demand–supply model early in his career, defines an equilibrium to be indeterminate if 'the successive moves undertaken in order to reach equilibrium will influence the nature of the final position' (Kaldor, 1934, p. 41). Later, writing on neoclassical economic theory, with its assumption of constant returns to scale, and given preferences, technology, and factor supplies, Kaldor writes:

> The very notion of 'general equilibrium' carries the implication that it is legitimate to assume that the operation of economic forces is constrained by a set of exogenous variables which are 'given' from the outside and stable over time. It assumes that economic forces operate in an environment that is 'imposed' on the system in a sense other than being just a heritage of the past – one could almost say an environment which, in its most significant characteristics, is independent of history. (Kaldor, 1972, p. 382)

He writes than even when attempts have been made to analyse growth and development using equilibrium theory, such attempts 'have not succeeded in transforming it into a sequence analysis in which the course of development is dependent on the path of evolution' (Kaldor, 1975, p. 401).

A final issue relates to economic policy. If outcomes are path dependent, economic policy-makers, by affecting what happens along the path of the economy during the growth process, can affect the outcome, presumably for the better. If the outcome is not path dependent, however, there is little that policy-makers can do to affect outcomes.

To what extent are these legitimate reasons for introducing path dependence in economic models and in models of economic growth in particular? It is difficult to evaluate these reasons without a more precise understanding of what we mean by that concept. To make the concept more precise we will examine alternative formal ways in which it has been introduced into models which do not otherwise exhibit this property. The next section discusses equilibrium models to explore in what sense they do not exhibit path dependence by examining a specific heterodox growth model. The subsequent sections will examine alternative ways of addressing the issue of path dependence.

3.   Models of equilibrium growth

Consider a simple standard heterodox model of economic growth in a closed economy which produces one good that can be used for both consumption and investment purposes with two factors of production, homogeneous capital and labor (see Dutt, 1990). Government fiscal activity and asset markets are, for simplicity, not explicitly considered. The production process requires labor and capital as fixed proportions of output, where a_0 and a_1 are the required amounts of labor and capital per unit of output. For simplicity we assume that all firms are identical and consider a representative firm. There is an unlimited supply of workers and capitalist firms hire workers according to the needs of production, there being no long-term labor contracts. Capital, once installed by investment, has to be kept by the firm. This implies that

$$L = a_0 Y \tag{1}$$

and

$$K \geq a_1 Y \tag{2}$$

where L is total employment (or number of workers), K the stock of output and Y the level of output.

Output can either be consumed or invested, so that we have

$$Y = C + I, \tag{3}$$

where C and I denote real consumption and investment, and total income can go to wage or non-wage income, so that

$$Y = (W/P)L + rK, \tag{4}$$

where W is the money wage, P the price level and r is the rate of profit defined as the value of the difference between income and wage payments as a ratio of capital valued at the price of the good. These two equations are simply accounting identities.

Turning to behavioral equations, wages are entirely consumed and a fraction of profits, s, is saved. This implies that consumption is given by

$$C = (W/P)L + (1 - s)rK \tag{5}$$

Planned investment by firms is given by the equation

$$g = \gamma_0 + \gamma_1 r + \gamma_2 u \tag{6}$$

where γ_i are positive investment parameters, g the planned level of investment as a ratio of capital stock, and u the rate of capacity utilization, Y/K. Firms set the price of their product as a mark-up on labor costs while adjusting output in response to demand, maintaining excess capacity. The price level is thus given by

$$P = (1 + z)a_0 W, \tag{7}$$

where z is the fixed mark-up rate which depends on factors like industrial concentration and the relative bargaining power of workers and firms.

We can now determine the equilibrium values of the variables for this economy. Replacing actual investment, I, by planned investment, gK, equation (3) gets converted from an accounting identity to a condition of equilibrium in the goods market. Substituting equations (1) and (4) through (7) into it we can solve for the equilibrium rate of capacity utilization which equilibrates the goods market, given by

$$u = \frac{\gamma_0}{(s - \gamma_1)\dfrac{z}{1 + z} - \gamma_2}, \tag{8}$$

assuming, using inequality (2), that $u \le 1/a_1$, that is, firms cannot produce more than full-capacity output. The rate of profit, using equations (4) and (7), is found to be given by

$$r = \frac{z}{1 + z} u \tag{9}$$

and its equilibrium value can be found by using equation (8). Assuming, for simplicity, that there is no depreciation of capital, the rate of change in capital stock is given by the level of investment (or saving, which is equal to investment in equilibrium). The rate of growth of capital is therefore given by g, which, using equations (3), (5) and (8), is given by

$$g = s\pi \frac{\gamma_0}{(s - \gamma_1)\pi - \gamma_2} \tag{10}$$

where $\pi = z/(1 + z)$ is the share of profit in income. The determination of equilibrium can be shown graphically in Figure 4.1. The g^S line is the savings function given by the equation $S/K = sr$ which is obtained from equations (4) and (5) using the definition of saving, $S = Y - C$. The g^I line is the investment function given by equation (6) using equation (9), which gives

$$g = \gamma_0 + [\gamma_1 + (\gamma_2/\pi)]r.$$

Goods market equilibrium requires that planned investment be equal to saving, so that the equilibrium levels of g and r are determined at the intersection of the saving and investment curves. The lower part of the figure then determines u from equation (9), or $u = r/\pi$.

We may assume that in the short run the level of capital stock, K, is given. In the short run the level of output, and hence the degree of capacity utilization, varies to clear the goods market. The adjustment will be a stable one if, as is standard in macroeconomic models of quantity adjustment, the responsiveness of saving to changes in capacity utilization exceeds that of investment, taking into account the relation between the rate of profit and the rate of capacity utilization, that is, $s\pi > \gamma_1\pi + \gamma_2$. In the long run K changes according to

$$\hat{K} = g \tag{11}$$

where g is determined in equation (10) and which is seen to be a constant. Since u, given by equation (8), remains constant in the long run, the growth rate of Y is equal to the growth rate of K.

This model therefore implies that if the economy is in short-run equilibrium with the goods market clearing, the growth rate of capital and output will be determined and not change in the long run. In this sense the model can be called an equilibrium model; it has no 'dynamics' and no 'path' to equilibrium and is therefore not path dependent.

The generality of this model can seen by modifying it in specific ways to arrive at other heterodox models (see Dutt, 1990). If the parameters

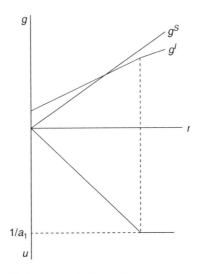

Figure 4.1   Basic equilibrium model of growth

of the model imply full capacity utilization, so that $u = 1/a_1$, further increases in u are not possible because of the shortage of capital. In this case something in the model has to change. A plausible candidate is that excess demand causes the price level to go up which, given the money wage, will reduce the real wage and increase the mark-up, z, to clear the goods market. This which replaces u by z as a variable, has been called a neo-Keynesian model. If, in the resultant model, the money wage cannot fall any further because the real wage has reached its minimum level acceptable to workers, the price rise will be accompanied by a proportionate wage rise, keeping the mark-up constant. In this case the price-adjustment mechanism will also not equilibrate the goods market, and something else in the model has to change. A plausible candidate in this case is that if there is excess demand in the goods market the planned investment of the firms will be unrealized, and actual investment will be given by the level of savings. In this case the mark-up will again be fixed at the level corresponding to the minimum real wage, output will be at full capacity, the investment function will become irrelevant, and capital accumulation will be determined by the level of savings, given by sr. This model has been called the neo-Marxian model. In all of these cases there is assumed to be enough labor to produce the level of output determined by the models. If this is not the case, output growth will be determined by the growth of labor supply, and the real wage will become a variable.

This corresponds to the Cambridge model of full employment growth associated with Kaldor (1955–56) and others. We now return to the basic model.

Although this economy does not have a (long-run) time path for those variables which have equilibrium values, that is, values which satisfy all the equations of the model, it is not difficult to introduce some explicit dynamics into the model to obtain time paths. An example of such dynamics can be obtained by modifying the model as follows. In the short run, in addition to K being given, we assume that g is given instead of being determined by equation (6), as is π (which was always given in the basic model, since z was taken as a parameter). Thus, in this modified model, using equations (1) through (5) and (7), and for the given g, the short-run equilibrium value of u is determined by

$$u = \frac{g}{s\pi} \tag{12}$$

In the long run we assume that g adjusts to differences between g and the desired rate of investment, g^d, according to the equation

$$\hat{g} = \theta(g^d - g), \tag{13}$$

where overhats denote time rates of growth, $\theta > 0$ is a speed of adjustment constant and where

$$g^d = \gamma_0 + \gamma_1 r + \gamma_2 u. \tag{14}$$

The lag in catching up to the desired level can be explained by physical difficulties in quickly getting to the desired level, by a deliberate slow move towards a target of which firms are not very sure, and by slow and adaptive changes in expectations regarding profits and capacity utilization. Changes in the profit share are assumed to depend negatively on the growth rate of employment and the current profit share. Using a linear formulation we have

$$\hat{\pi} = \sigma_0 - \sigma_1 l - \sigma_2 \pi \tag{15}$$

where l is the rate of growth of employment and σ_i are constants, of which σ_1 and σ_2 are positive. Faster growth in employment results in an increase in the real wage and reduces the profit share. A higher profit share dampens the pressures on firms to increase their mark-ups and increases that on workers to increase their wages, thereby reducing the profit share. Since technology is given,

$$l = y, \tag{16}$$

where y is the rate of growth of output. Given the definition of u, we get

$$y = \hat{u} + g. \tag{17}$$

Differentiating equation (12) with respect to time and substituting it and equation (16) and (17) into equation (15) we obtain

$$\hat{\pi} = \sigma_0 - \sigma_1(\hat{g} - \hat{\pi} + g) - \sigma_2 \pi. \tag{18}$$

Substituting equations (9), (12) and (14) into equation (13) we get

$$\hat{g} = \theta[\gamma_0 + \gamma_1(g/s) + \gamma_2(g/s\pi) - g]. \tag{19}$$

Substituting equation (19) into equation (18) we obtain

$$\hat{\pi} = \mu_0 - \mu_1 g - \mu_2 \pi - \mu_3(g/\pi), \tag{20}$$

where

$$\mu_0 = \frac{\sigma_0 - \sigma_1 \theta \gamma_0}{1 - \sigma_1}, \quad \mu_1 = \frac{\sigma_1}{1 - \sigma_1}\left[\frac{\theta \gamma_1}{s} + (1 - \theta)\right], \quad \mu_2 = \frac{\sigma_2}{1 - \sigma_1},$$

$$\mu_3 = \frac{\sigma_1 \theta \gamma_2}{(1 - \sigma_1)s}$$

If we assume that $\sigma_1 < 1$ (that is, the effect of employment growth on wages and hence on the profit share is not too strong), and that $\theta < 1$ (so that the investment lag is not too short), it follows that $\mu_i > 0$ for $i = 1$, 2 and 3. Equations (19) and (20) comprise a dynamic system containing two long-run variables, g and π, that, is the rate of growth of capital stock and the profit share.

To examine the dynamics of this system we use the phase diagrams shown in Figure 4.2 which show the $\hat{g} = 0$ and the $\hat{\pi} = 0$ isoclines. Starting from a point on the $\hat{g} = 0$ isocline, an increase π shifts income from wage earners to profit recipients who have a higher propensity to consume,

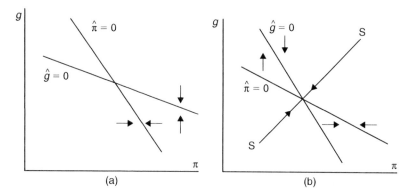

Figure 4.2 Dynamic models of growth and distribution

and reduces the rate of capacity utilization, and hence the desired rate of investment, and therefore reduces $\hat{g}$. When g increases the effect on $\hat{g}$ is ambiguous, since

$$\frac{\partial \hat{g}}{\partial g} = \theta \left(\frac{\gamma_1}{s} + \frac{\gamma_2}{s\pi} - 1 \right).$$

If $s\pi > \gamma_1\pi + \gamma_2$, which is the standard stability condition that the responsiveness of saving to changes in capacity utilization exceeds that of investment, this expression is negative, that is, the increase in actual accumulation does not, through its effect on the profit rate and capacity utilization, increase desired accumulation more than itself, therefore leading to an increase in $\hat{g}$, the expression is negative. In that case the $\hat{g} = 0$ isocline is negatively sloped and the horizontal arrows show the changes in g when the economy is not on that isocline. Turning to the $\hat{\pi} = 0$ isocline, starting from a position on it, an increase in g reduces $\hat{\pi}$ given our assumptions: the increase in g increases output growth and hence employment growth, and exerts an upward pressure on the wage, reducing the profit share. The effect of an increase in π on $\hat{\pi}$ is ambiguous, as shown by the partial derivative

$$\frac{\partial \hat{\pi}}{\partial \pi} = -\mu_2 + \mu_3 \frac{g}{\pi^2}.$$

The increase in π has a direct effect on reducing $\hat{\pi}$, as captured by the first term, but it has an indirect effect of raising it by reducing aggregate demand and investment through the effect of redistributing income to profit recipients, thereby reducing employment growth and wages. Assuming that the direct effect predominates, we need to reduce π to increase $\hat{\pi}$ to satisfy $\hat{\pi}=0$ again. Thus, the $\hat{\pi}=0$ curve is also negatively sloped, and the vertical arrows show what happens to π when the economy is not on it.

Two cases are shown in Figure 4.2. Figure 4.2 (a) (we will consider (b) later) assumes that the slope of the $\hat{\pi}=0$ curve is greater (in absolute value) than that of the $\hat{g}=0$ curve. In this case the 'own' effects of π and g on $\hat{\pi}$ and $\hat{g}$ are stronger than the cross effects from π to $\hat{g}$ and from g to $\hat{\pi}$, that is, the effect of growth in employment on wages and the effect of wages on growth. It can be seen from the figure, and by checking the stability conditions of the model, that the equilibrium at the intersection of the two isoclines, at which g and π attain their long-run equilibrium values, is stable. Thus, there is no path dependence: the initial state of the economy and the particular path along which it travels does not affect the final equilibrium of the economy, that is, where it ends up. If we change the value of a particular parameter, the equilibrium values of the variables will, of course, change. For instance, an increase in γ_0, the parameter representing autonomous investment or 'animal spirits', will shift the $\hat{g}=0$ curve upwards (by increasing desired investment and therefore $\hat{g}$ at each level of g and π) and the $\hat{\pi}=0$ curve downwards (by increasing the rate of change of investment, thereby increasing employment growth and wages and reducing the profit share) in Figure 4.2(a), thereby increasing long-run equilibrium g and reducing π. However, if we restore γ_0 to its original value, the long-run equilibrium values of the variables will return to their former levels: the economy will 'forget' that these changes ever occurred.

Two features of this dynamic model are worth pointing out. One, if we assume in equation (13) that $\sigma_1=0$, the system given by the dynamic equations (19) and (20) with $\mu_1=\mu_3=0$ (and with the $\hat{\pi}=0$ locus in Figure 4.2 vertical) will have an equilibrium, in which g and π are stationary, which is identical to that in the equilibrium model without dynamics, and given the assumptions we have made here, it will be stable. The fact that the two equilibria are the same can be seen by noting that in both models, in long-run equilibrium, the goods market clears, in the dynamic model actual investment is equal to desired investment, so that equations (13) and (14) imply equation (16), and in the dynamic model $\pi=\mu_0/\mu_2$ which is equivalent to the assumption in the equilibrium model without dynamics that distribution is exogenously given. Two, the dynamic model in which $\sigma_1 > 0$ is a modification of the equilibrium model without dynamics which endogenizes income distribution in a non-trivial way, that is, its equilibrium version is not the same as the equilibrium model without dynamics, because income distribution is no longer exogenous but, even in equilibrium, represented by a relation between growth and distribution, as shown in equation (20) with $\hat{\pi} = 0$.

To generalize the property of the absence of path dependence, we use a general continuous-time model involving an n-dimensional vector $x(t)$, which can be written in the form

$$dx/dt = F(x, \alpha), \tag{21}$$

a general first order n-dimensional differential equation system in which the vector α contains m parameters; the time variable, t, has been suppressed.[3] Assume that the solution to the equation $F(x, \alpha) = 0$ exists, is unique and is denoted by x^*, which can be called the equilibrium value of x for the dynamic system given by equation (21). Assume, moreover, that this equilibrium x^* is globally stable. This implies, starting with any initial value of x, say x_0, the dynamic system given by (21) will converge to the equilibrium position, x^*. This in turn implies that the initial position, x_0, which will determine the path of the system over time, does not affect the position of the final equilibrium: x^* depends on the functions F() and on α, and on nothing else. Our dynamic growth model provides a two-variable example.

In the following sections we consider a series of interpretations of how history can be introduced and outcomes made path dependent, using these and other related simple heterodox equilibrium models in which history apparently does not matter.

4. Equilibrium versus path

The first interpretation is to focus on the time path – or the dynamics – of the economy, otherwise keeping the models unaltered. There are at least two senses in which we can examine the path of the economy in the growth model discussed earlier.

The first is in terms of the time path of the economy even in an equilibrium model without explicit dynamics of the variables for which the model finds equilibrium values (see Figure 4.3). Thus, even though the basic model does not have any dynamics for g (because its equilibrium value is determined in short-run equilibrium and does not change in the

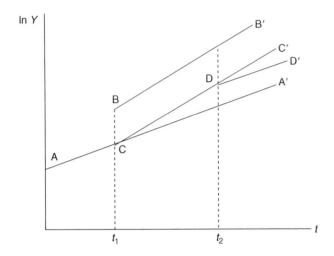

Figure 4.3   The time path in an equilibrium model of growth

long run), it does have time paths in terms of Y and K and other variables such as I. Given the parameters of the model, the time path of Y reflects a constant growth rate, and is shown by the straight line AA'. It is in terms of the growth rates of output and capital that there is no 'path'.

In the model, a parametric change will affect this path. If there is an expansionary aggregate demand shock at time t_1, say an increase in y_0, the level of autonomous expenditure (or an increase in government spending in a model with government fiscal activity), the level of u and Y will increase in the short run (the latter from C to B), and the economy will jump up to the higher output curve, BB'. Thereafter, it will grow at a higher rate as g increases, reflected in the higher slope of BB' compared to AA'.

Moreover, if there is an increase in y_0 at t_1, followed by a decrease in it at t_2 by the same amount, the growth rate of output and capital will rise as shown in the previous comment at t_1, and fall back to its original levels at time t_2. However, the level output is always higher after time t_2 if these changes took place compared to what would happen if y_0 did not change at all. To see this, assume, by choice of units, that initial $u = 1$, or $Y = K$. Thus, before the change in y_0 the time paths of both output and capital are shown by the curve AC. When y_0 increases at time t_1, output jumps to B, but there is no jump in K. After y_0 increases both the output and capital curves have a higher slope reflecting their higher (and equal) rates of growth, but the time path of Y is shown by curve BB' and that of K by curve CC' until t_2. At t_2, when γ_0 returns to its earlier level, the time path of K is shown by the curve DD'. Since capacity utilization returns to its original level, $u = 1$, the output curve is also shown by the curve DD'. Since DD' is everywhere above AA', the output level is higher with the policy changes than without it for all $t \geq t_2$. Thus, a temporary change in aggregate demand has a permanent effect on the economy and, therefore, the model allows for path dependence in levels of output and capital. But these are variables that have *no* equilibrium values. There is no path dependence with respect to variables that arrive at an equilibrium level, such as the rate of growth of the economy.

The second sense in which we can think of a time path for the economy is by analysing explicit dynamic equations and examining the time path of the economy starting from its initial state rather than focusing on the final equilibrium. In general terms, rather than just examine how x^* is determined using what we can call the 'static' system involving equations like

$$F(x, \alpha) = 0 \qquad (22)$$

one needs to analyse the full 'dynamic' systems, given by equation (21). In terms of our growth model, we take the model given by equations (19) and (20) and Figure 4.2, that is, the dynamic model, rather than the one shown by Figure 4.1, that is, the static model.

However, this captures the notion of path dependence in a very limited sense because the solution to the static or equilibrium system, x^*, is the same as that obtained as the equilibrium solution to the dynamic system (in the case in which the change in distribution does not depend on the growth of labor demand, that is, $\sigma_1 = 0$). Given this equivalence, the effect of a change in an element of the parameter vector α will be the same in terms of its effect on x^* in the static or the dynamic model.

Despite this, the analysis of the dynamics does bring us closer to a notion of path dependence in some senses. It allows us to examine what happens along the path (interpreted merely as a sequence of states or, as a sequence of moving equilibria) rather than what happens at the final equilibrium. Consider the evolution of the discrete time analogue of the system given by (21) for two periods, starting from an initial position at x_0. We obtain

$$
\begin{aligned}
x_1 - x_0 &= F(x_0, \alpha), \\
x_2 - x_1 &= F(F(x_0, \alpha) + x_0, \alpha).
\end{aligned}
\qquad (23)
$$

This set of $2n$ equations allows us to solve for $2n$ variables (x_1, x_2). In general the solution will depend on the value of x_0, which implies that the past does matter, even though x^* is unaffected by x_0. We can also examine the effects of changes in elements of α on (x_1, x_2), effects which in general will be different from the effects on x^*. We can use this method for examining the evolution of x for T periods, and obtain the solution (x_1, x_2, ..., x_T), and represent it by its mean, x_M, which in general will depend on x_0. The property that the solution values of x depends only on x_0, and not on the entire prior path, is the result of the deterministic framework used here. If, for instance, the dynamic equation has a white noise error term added to it, one would have to know the entire prior path to solve for the expected value of a value of x.

When is it important to examine the path – which is history dependent – in this manner, rather than focusing only on the final equilibrium, which does not depend on history? Obviously, when the speed of adjustment to the final equilibrium is slow, so that the system stays out of equilibrium for a 'long' time. However, there are at least two problems with using this method. First, the values of x along the path are more difficult to calculate than the values of x^*. Even for the two-period discrete-time case one has to solve for twice the number of variables than one does for the equilibrium. The problem expands – although only linearly – as we consider more periods. It is for this reason that, in general, simulation analysis is more convenient than theoretical analysis when dealing with time paths. Second, it may be misleading to focus attention on a few years, for instance, in a two-period model, since many models have the properties of overshooting or cycles, in which the direction of change from the initial to the next period may be different from the direction from the initial period to the final equilibrium.

There are additional reasons for explicitly examining the dynamics behind the model that are related to issues to be discussed later, and may therefore be briefly mentioned here. First, with explicit dynamics the equilibrium may well turn out to be an unstable one, so that it is inappropriate to conduct analysis as if the economy is always at equilibrium. Second, it reduces the chances of introducing properties of equilibrium states from a priori ideas which may seem plausible, but which are unwarranted given the structure of the economy being modeled. A common example is the set of models which assumes that full employment always exists in equilibrium, such as new classical models and neoclassical (and endogenous) growth models. The assumption of full employment in equilibrium may seem plausible on a priori grounds since it can be argued that if unemployment exists, the money wage will change, which will imply that the situation is not an equilibrium state. One fallacy of this line of thinking is that is does not examine whether a change in the money wage will actually result in appropriate dynamics that will take the economy to an equilibrium with full employment. Keynes (1936) argued that this is not necessarily the case in his discussion of the effects of wage changes, and the issue has been examined by a variety of subsequent writers.

5. Parameters and parametric changes

A second way that history can enter the benchmark model – without changing the model itself – is by interpreting the parameters of the model as being historically determined. More generally, the structure of the models – its equations and parameters – can all be taken to be determined by historical circumstances, and given them, the model determines where the economy will end up. Therefore, history – and the path of the economy in the past – determines equilibrium.

Eatwell (1997) employs this interpretation in arguing that the equilibrium or center of gravitation of the classical/neo-Ricardian model is historically determined. This model determines relative prices for products produced by different sectors and one distributional variable (the real wage or the rate of profit), given input–output ratios in production, sectoral output levels and the other distributional variable. The last elements – the data – of the model are, in this interpretation, historically determined.

A problem with this interpretation is that since all equilibrium models have a set of equations and parameters, all of them by definition give some role to history. Therefore, the interpretation is unable to discriminate between models that give some role to history and those that do not. However, a case can be made that some models pay more careful attention to the historical and institutional details of particular economies, and derive the structure of the model and its relevant parameter values from such an analysis, whereas other models – including many neoclassical ones – use the same structure for all situations, paying insufficient attention to institutional factors which are shaped by historical forces.

A closely related sense in which equilibrium models are taken to incorporate history is when it is explicitly taken into account that their parameters are subject to *changes*, sometimes in ways related to some variables of the model (but sometimes not), and often in ways that are not knowable (even in a probabilistic sense) in advance.

A series of contributions have employed this interpretation to incorporate path dependence and history into Kaldor's (1970) model of cumulative causation. These interpretations start with a formalization of Kaldor's regional growth model, in which faster productivity growth leads to a more rapid growth of exports, hence output, and hence productivity (see Setterfield, 1997a). If the model is stable (this requires, among other things, that the Verdoorn coefficient which relates the rate of growth of output to the rate of growth of productivity is small) it implies that, starting from an initial level of productivity growth, the model will converge to an equilibrium level of productivity growth. This equilibrium, of course, is path independent and the model therefore has no role for history.

Setterfield (1997b) argues that this model can be converted into one where history does play a role by allowing some of the parameters to change 'endogenously'. For example, he argues that as the economy grows by experiencing productivity growth and passes a certain technological threshold, the existence of technological interrelatedness, both within and between firms, can lead to lock-in, which will prevent the economy from adopting new technology. This will lead to a fall in the Verdoorn coefficient, and to a fall in the income elasticity of demand for exports, both of which will shift the curve representing the dynamic equation downwards, implying that the eventual equilibrium will be at a lower level of productivity growth than before. Institutional inertia in growing economies, especially those in labor markets, can also lead to such 'endogenous' parametric changes, reducing the rate of growth. Setterfield claims that upon taking into account these technological and institutional factors, and the parametric changes that they imply, Kaldor's model becomes 'more generally hysterectic', by which he means that their long-run outcomes depend on their path. Setterfield (2001) further argues that lock-in and growth slow-downs are not inevitable, and hence the long-run outcome to the growth path in the model is not deterministic. Roberts (2003) argues that the Kaldorian cumulative causation model may be subjected to a number of parametric changes, some when it reaches a threshold level of productivity, some when it reaches a threshold level of productivity growth, and some when it has been in a certain state for a given length of time. These thresholds are not known for certain, and moreover, what happens when the thresholds are reached cannot be predicted, since they depend on a complex set of political and social factors. These same ideas can be introduced into the growth models discussed earlier, for example, in threshold levels at which some parameters may change. Moreover, there may be threshold levels of real wages when the models experience 'regime shifts' from a neo-Keynesian model to a neo-Marxian one. The crucial issue here is not the precise nature of the thresholds, but the fact that there are no deterministic laws (even in a probabilistic sense) governing the nature and timing of the changes in the parameters of the system.

To appreciate why this is so, consider the following extension of the general framework given by equation (21) where the laws of motion are deterministic. In that system, the equilibrium solution for the vector x depends on the parameters α, so that the equilibrium values can be written as $x(\alpha)$. Now we define a new dynamic system given by

$$d\alpha/dt = A(x(\alpha), \alpha), \tag{24}$$

which specifies the dynamics of α (although some elements in the vector may be taken to be constant). Starting from any initial value of α, if a unique and stable equilibrium exists, this system will arrive at it, and that equilibrium will be path independent. An example of this type of extension was discussed in section 3 by endogenizing the distribution of income by making the dynamics of the profit share depend on the profit share and, more importantly, on labor market conditions, that is, the growth rate of employment. As we saw in that model, making the parameters move over time does not, in itself, therefore give any role to history. Making the system stochastic with white noise error terms does not alter this conclusion.

What may give some role to history is the fact that it may not be possible to write out a system given by equation (24), because the dynamics of α may be too complex to be modeled in any precise manner. It is not possible to know when elements in α will change (for instance, what are the threshold levels), and if they change, by how much they will change. The variables and relationships which can be modeled in systematic terms are included in x, while those that are too complex to precisely model are included in α. The evolution of these parameters over time cannot even be depicted in terms of known probability distributions, and cannot therefore be modeled even in terms of stochastic processes. In this interpretation, however, changes in elements of α will have clear and predictable effects in terms of the system given by (21).

What kinds of (dynamic) relations are less likely to be precisely knowable than others? Although generalizations are difficult because of the broad nature of the question, we can mention a few illustrative examples.

It is possible that events that do not occur on a regular basis, and which depend on a variety of complex factors which include social and political factors, and changes that depend on the collective actions of very large groups or of a small group of people which affect society at large, are arguably less knowable than others. Events that do not occur on a regular basis are less capable of being captured with general laws. Events that are affected by a large number of factors are difficult to portray with a small number of relations between a small number of variables. Collective actions of large groups, or individual actions of powerful groups, are less capable of lending themselves to generalizations: small changes in circumstances may lead to major unpredictable actions and consequences. Another type of relation that may be difficult to generalize about are those involving expectations – which, if we follow Keynes, may be based on flimsy foundations. The distinction between the two kinds of relations can be expressed in terms of Keynes's (1933; 1972, p. 262) distinction between an 'atomic' environment in which elements work in relative isolation in a stable and homogeneous environment and an 'organic' one, 'of discreteness, of discontinuity – the whole is not equal to the sum of the parts, comparisons of quantity fail us, small changes produce large effects, the assumptions of a uniform and homogeneous continuum are not satisfied'.

It should be noted that what elements of a model are considered to be parameters need not only be those that change little or very slowly over time, but may well be elements that change quickly, but in unpredictable ways. Thus, investment can be taken to be given in a simple Keynesian model not because investment is stable, but because it is difficult to theorize about. An implication of this observation is that the variables in the equilibrium model can change more slowly than these parameters change, which makes it all the more necessary to focus on the path of the economy out of equilibrium.

Four implications of the adoption of this interpretation of equilibrium models are worth noting. First, since it is possible to think of all equilibrium models (all of which have some parameters) in this way, this interpretation does not provide a clear criterion for distinguishing between models in which history plays a greater role and those in which it does not (as was the case in the interpretation of parameter *levels* being determined by history). However, it is possible to argue that some equilibrium models include as parameters those whose changes are found to be more interesting and relevant in historical research than the parameters of other equilibrium models. For instance, it is possible that changes in power relations between groups are more important in a particular historical context than changes in the rate of time preference, and therefore to conclude that models in which power relations affect a parameter allow history to play a greater role than models where the time preference rate enters as a parameter.

Second, this conception implies that the model builder recognizes that there are some limits to the extent to which the model can be extended to endogenize more and more parameters as variables. There may, in fact, be no virtue at all to making such extensions, when some of these relationships are too complex for the reasons noted earlier. In this sense, the recognition of the role of history may be expected to have an effect on the construction of equilibrium models.

Third, the recognition of the role of parametric changes implies that equilibrium positions analysed by models should not generally be interpreted as depicting actual economies which are tranquil and not subject to shocks. Two important consequences follow. One, it is not appropriate to incorporate into the model behavior patterns of decision-makers which assumes that the equilibria are tranquil states, or that the dynamic time paths of the model are in fact predictable by the decision-makers, even in a stochastic sense. A great deal of neoclassical analysis, and even some post-Keynesian analysis, assumes this, with arguably misleading consequences. An example of an erroneous claim is that agents do not need to maintain liquidity in equilibrium, since there is full certainty. Two, policy analysts who use equilibrium models should not expect their models to provide precise results, or be surprised that their predictions are far off the mark in a quantitative sense.

Finally, and despite these implications, this interpretation allows the development of equilibrium models and the study of paths in history and its role to proceed – to a large extent – along parallel lines. Economic theorists are left free to specialize in developing equilibrium models in which some historically-conditioned elements are included as parameters, and the effects of such changes on the equilibrium system (they would need to converse with historians about these matters), can be analysed theoretically using the model. In this sense history does not enter economic theory. The next three interpretations of equilibrium models, however, are those in which it does.

6. Instability and multiple equilibria

The next interpretation involves a fundamental modification of the systems given by equation (21) by departing from the assumption that they have unique and stable equilibria. Examples of such systems are shown

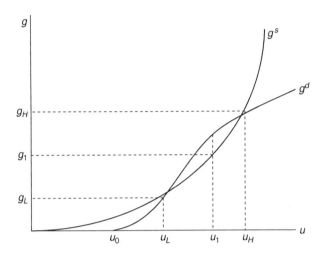

Figure 4.4   Growth model with multiple equilibria

in the simple model depicted in Figure 4.4, and in Figure 4.2(b) for our dynamic model in section 3.

Figure 4.4 depicts a model which modifies the dynamic model of section 3 with non-linear saving and desired investment functions and by assuming that the profit share, π, is constant. The saving function given by $g^s = s\pi u$ with constant s is assumed is assumed to be replaced by one in which s rises with the profit rate, $r = \pi u$, that is, with the marginal propensity to save of capitalists being greater than the average propensity to save. This makes the saving function of Figure 4.4 have an increasing slope. The linear desired investment function given by equation (14) is replaced by the S-shaped one shown in the figure. Assume that a minimum profit is required to bring forth any investment at all (as in Robinson, 1962), then increases in the profit rate do not have a strong effect on desired investment because firms are still cautious, and then further increases in the profit rate bring forth large increases in desired investment, and eventually further increases bring about only small increases in desired investment as firms get cautious with even higher levels of the profit rate. In the short run we have a given rate of accumulation, g, which determines the short-run equilibrium level of u through variations in it which equate g to g^s. In the long run g adjusts to differences between g and g^d as shown by equation (13).

We examine the case in which the g^s and g^d curves intersect, in which case, given our assumptions, they intersect twice. If, initially, g is given at g_1, capacity utilization will be determined at u_1 in the short run. Since g is less than g^d, g will increase and move the economy to the high-growth equilibrium shown by g_H. However, if the economy starts with a g less than g_L, it will experience a cumulative decline. History, or the initial position and subsequent path of the economy will determine where the economy will end up: either with cumulative decline or a high-level long equilibrium growth rate.

Figure 4.2(b) shows the case of saddle-point instability for our dynamic model of section 3. The diagram shows that if the economy starts with a high growth or low profit-share equilibrium above the separatrix shown in the diagram, it will eventually be on a path in which growth increases and the profit share falls (until, presumably the economy reaches some capacity constraint), while if it starts below the separatrix it will experience stagnation and a rise in the profit share. Here again, the initial position and subsequent path of the economy will depend on where the economy goes in the future. More complicated dynamics with the possibility of multiple equilibria are possible if we add non-linearities in the saving and investment function of the type just discussed into this model.

In these examples expectational issues and cumulative processes involving the interaction of goods and labor markets results in instability and path dependence in this sense. There are numerous other examples of such instability in heterodox (and, indeed, orthodox) literature. Kaldor's (1970) analysis of cumulative causation discussed earlier, according to which higher productivity growth leads to even higher productivity growth through scale economies, can become unstable with strong Verdoorn effects. Information cascades and herding behavior can also lead to lock-in, depending on small initial advantages (Arthur, 1994).

The mechanisms that lead to models of this kind are clear from the examples we have discussed here. Increasing returns to scale and learning by doing plays an important role. More generally, it is the existence of what has been called positive feedbacks, which can take a very large variety of forms, ranging from positive externalities, market complementarities, imperfect information, uncertainty, and a variety of non-linearities which abound in the real world. Thus, this way of formalizing path dependence can be argued to be quite appealing and plausible.

However, this approach can also be criticized because of its knife-edge feature: slight changes in initial conditions can have huge effects.

The consequence is that history plays a very small role in determining outcomes, that is, in determining initial conditions and it is not so much history but the internal dynamics of the model which give rise to different outcomes. History can therefore be interpreted simply as bringing about chance small events which determine on which side of the separatrix one starts. However, while this is true in a formal sense, other careful historical analysis can analyse systematically how small events occurred. One can also argue that the approach gives too much weight to the initial condition of the model and the outcome of the system becomes determinate in the sense that it can be defined and reached in terms of the data of the system if we include the initial conditions in that data (Setterfield, 1997a, p. 65). While the models might suggest this, however, a broader interpretation of the model to include forward-looking exceptional issues and stochastic shocks, can make the outcome less deterministic. Krugman (1991) analyses a model in which expectational factors can reduce the determining role of the initial condition to some extent, but does not obliterate it. For instance, if there are positive feedbacks, it is possible that even if we are on one side of the critical point, individuals may expect that a large number of decision-makers to go to the other side, and this may make the economy go to the other side, reversing the movement to a new equilibrium. Such expectational shifts can occur, for instance, due to the ability of the government to influence expectations even without policies which actually change payoffs. If a deterministic model implies that we are on one side of the separatrix or critical point, chance events can lead to shifts which take us to the other side of the critical point. Models of lock-in with some role for chance events are provided in Arthur (1994), for instance. Moreover, such changes may not just be due to chance events. Parametric shifts – such as changes in trade and industrial policy – can play a role in changing an unstable equilibrium case into a stable case, or vice versa, or shifting the system from one side of the separatrix to the other. These parametric shifts in fact can be thought of as being endogenous in terms of a broader model which has not been formally written out (which, when written out can result in sharp changes as in models exhibiting catastrophes), or which may be difficult or impossible to write in formal terms.

7. Zero-root systems

If history can be incorporated into equilibrium model by introducing multiple equilibria, why not go further and allow for a continuum of

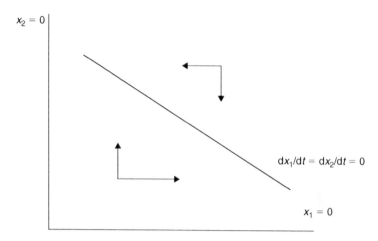

Figure 4.5 Zero-root dynamic model

equilibria? We now turn to models with a continuum of equilibria. Suppose, in a two-variable model, the system of two equations is given in the form

$$dx_1/dt = F^1(x_1, x_2)$$
$$dx_2/dt = F(F^1(x_1, x_2))$$

where $F(0) = 0$. This kind of dynamic system is called a zero-root system because the characteristic roots of the Jacobian matrix of the system are zero. In this case the phase portrait of the system can be represented by a diagram like Figure 4.5, and the system is shown to have an infinite number of equilibria. In this case, the slightest change in the starting point of the system will imply a change in the equilibrium value of the system to which the system will tend, assuming that the equilibria are stable. In this sense, history – or the starting point – determines where the system ends up. If we use stochastic influences in the analysis, stochastic shocks experienced over time will affect the final equilibrium position.

We consider three examples of zero-root models which build on, and are closely related to, the equilibrium growth model of section 3. The first introduces expectations about rates of growth and planned levels of capacity utilization which can change over time, following Dutt (1997) and Lavoie (1995). In it we modify the investment function of equation (6) to the following form

$$g = x + \xi(u - u_d). \tag{25}$$

This introduces three modifications to the model. One, it removes the rate of profit as an explicit determinant of planned investment, to simplify the analysis. Two, it denotes the first term in the investment function by the symbol x to denote the expected rate of growth of the economy which will be endogenous in the long run but is constant in the short run. Finally, the planned addition to capital stock depends on the expected rate of growth plus the difference between actual capacity utilization and the desired or planned level of capacity utilization, u_d. If actual capacity utilization exceeds (is less than) the desired level firms will plan to increase their capital stock at a rate faster (slower) than the expected growth rate, to bring actual capacity utilization down (up) to their planned level. The rest of the equations are the same as in the earlier model.

Short-run equilibrium requires savings and investment to be equal, which implies the short-run equilibrium level of capacity utilization

$$u = \frac{x - \xi u_d}{s\pi - \xi}, \tag{26}$$

where we assume that $s\pi > \xi$ and that the value of x satisfies the inequality $x > \xi u_d$. The resulting short-run equilibrium value of the rate of growth of capital stock, obtained by substituting (26) into (25) is given by

$$g = x + \xi \left(\frac{x - \xi u_d}{s\pi - \xi} - u_d \right) \tag{27}$$

In the long run we assume that x changes adaptively according to the equation[4]

$$dx/dt = \rho(g - x) \tag{28}$$

where $\rho > 0$ is a speed of adjustment constant. Regarding u_d we assume that firms change their planned or desired rate of capacity utilization for strategic considerations. If they expect more competition in the future, they desire more excess capacity to be able to increase to their output quickly to compete with potential competitors, and therefore reduce their desired rate of capacity utilization. We write such an adjustment story in terms of the equation

$$du_d/dt = -\lambda(x - g) \tag{29}$$

where $\lambda > 0$ is a speed of adjustment constant: if firms expected a greater increase in competitors (proxied by the rate of change in capital) than

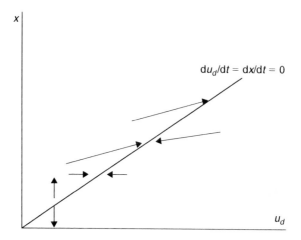

Figure 4.6   A growth model with endogenous desired capacity utilization

the current growth rate, they reduce their desired capacity utilization rate.

Using equation (27) we can write equations (28) and (29) as

$$dx/dt = \rho\xi\left(\frac{x - \xi u_d}{s\pi - \xi} - u_d\right)$$

and

$$du_d/dt = \lambda\xi\left(\frac{x - \xi u_d}{s\pi - \xi} - u_d\right).$$

These equations imply that the $dx/dt = 0$ and $du_d/dt = 0$ isoclines in $<x, u_d>$ space are both given by the same line, the equation for which is $x = s\pi u_d$, as shown in Figure 4.6. The horizontal and vertical arrows show changes in u_d and x. The economy has a continuum of equilibria, and stability requires that $\lambda s\pi > \rho$, that is the destabilizing adjustment of x is weaker than the stabilizing adjustment of u_d. Depending on the initial state of the economy in terms of x and u_d, the economy will end up at different equilibrium levels of these variables, and hence other variables of the model, including g.

A second model takes the investment-capital ratio to be exogenously given in the short run so that capacity utilization adjusts to clear the goods market, and we have, as in the dynamic model of section 3,

$$u = \frac{g}{s\pi}.$$

Assume also, as in the previous model, that firms have a desired rate of capacity utilization, u_d. When firms find that the actual rate of capacity utilization departs from this desired level, they adjust their behavior. Two types of adjustment are usually discussed in the literature. One is that if firms have higher (lower) capacity utilization than they desire, they increase (reduce) their investment levels in an attempt to restore capacity utilization to their desired level. This adjustment can be formalized with the equation

$$\hat{g} = \zeta[u - u^d] \tag{30}$$

where $\zeta > 0$ is a speed of adjustment constant. Having only this adjustment mechanism and keeping all other parameters constant implies that the long-run adjustment, in which the dynamics of g are given by equation (30), implies an unstable adjustment process: substitution of equation (12) into (30) shows that an increase in g increases u, which leads to an increase in the rate of change of g. Another adjustment mechanism is that firms, finding they have excess capacity, reduce their mark-up, z, to increase their sales and hence, capacity utilization. Assuming a similar adjustment which increases the mark-up when they have a degree of capacity utilization than they desire, and noting that $\pi = z/(1 + z)$, we can depict the adjustment with the equation

$$\dot{\pi} = \eta[u - u_d] \tag{31}$$

where $\eta > 0$ is a positive. If we assume that g is a constant, this adjustment implies a stable dynamic adjustment process since, substituting equation (12) into (31) we find that a rise in π reduces u and leads to a fall in the rate of change of π. The long-run equilibrium rate of capacity utilization is given by u_d, and the growth rate of the stock of capital and output are given exogenously by g.

Instead of having these two adjustment mechanisms as alternatives, we can assume that firms actually adjust both g and π when they are not at their desired rate of capacity utilization.[5] In this case the dynamics of the economy can be shown by Figure 4.7. Since the dynamics of the model involve two processes, one unstable and one stable, the overall stability of the model depends on which is stronger: it can be shown that stability requires that $\eta > \zeta$. The stable case is shown in the figure and is seen to be a zero-root model. Depending on where the economy starts from, it will end up at different levels of g and π. Higher equilibrium levels of g are associated with higher equilibrium profit shares.

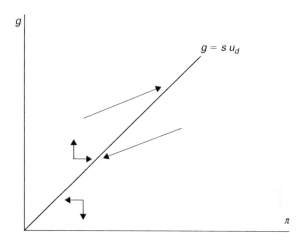

Figure 4.7 A growth model with investment and price adjustment by firms

However if, starting from an equilibrium there is a shock which increases (reduces) the profit share, the equilibrium growth rate will fall (rise) and if there is a shock which increases (reduces) the growth rate, the equilibrium growth rate will rise (fall).

A third example, following Dutt (2006), is a model which incorporates labor markets and technological change into the analysis. We assume, as before that the savings is a constant fraction of profits, so that $S/K = s\pi u$, and that investment takes the simple form

$$g = \gamma + \beta u, \qquad (32)$$

where γ represents the portion of investment which is exogenously given in the short run. The short-run equilibrium, goods-market clearing, value of u is therefore given by

$$u = \frac{\gamma}{s\pi - \beta} \qquad (33)$$

and the rate of capital accumulation by

$$g = \frac{s\gamma}{s\pi - \beta} \qquad (34)$$

In the long run we assume that γ changes according to conditions in the labor market. A simple formulation assumes that

$$\gamma = \Gamma \left(\frac{L}{N} \right)^{-\theta}$$

where N is the size of the labor force (which is given in the short run but grows at the exogenously-fixed rate of growth, n) in the long run, and where Γ and θ are positive parameters. The equation states that in the long-run investment depends on the employment rate. If the employment rate is higher (or the unemployment rate is lower), investment will be lower because of asset market changes considered in neoclassical-synthesis Keynesian macroeconomic models: greater unemployment reduces the wage and the price more, resulting in a larger fall in the demand for money (given a fixed short-run supply of money), resulting in an increase in investment. An alternative mechanism is that greater unemployment will make the government reduce the interest rate more or increase government spending more, which will increase 'autonomous' spending more. This equation implies, differentiating with respect to time, that

$$\overset{\wedge}{\gamma} = -\theta(l - n) \tag{35}$$

where l is the rate of growth of employment. We also assume that in the long run, when there is greater pressure on the labor market and unemployment is low, firms adopt labor-saving techniques at a faster rate in an attempt to economize on labor. Assuming that labor-market pressure is captured by the difference in the rates of growth of employment and labor supply, we assume that

$$\hat{a} = \tau(l - n) \tag{36}$$

where a is the rate of growth of labor productivity, that is, $a = -\overset{\wedge}{a_0}$ where a_0 was defined earlier as the unit labor requirement, and τ is the responsiveness of the rate of technological change to the gap between the rates of growth of labor demand and supply. We assume, for simplicity, that π remains constant throughout, with the real wage rising at the same rate as labor productivity.

With technological change, the rate of growth of employment is given by

$$l = \gamma - a. \tag{37}$$

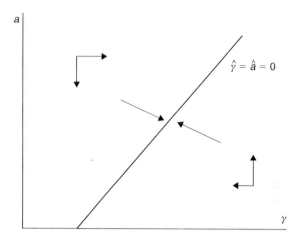

Figure 4.8 Endogenous technological change in a neoclassical-synthesis Keynesian growth model

Using equation (17) which holds by the definition of u, this equation can be written as

$$l = \hat{u} + g - a. \tag{38}$$

Using equations (33) and (34), substituting them in (38) and substituting the result into equation (35) into we get

$$\hat{\gamma} = \frac{\theta}{1 + \theta}\left[n + a - \frac{s\gamma}{s\pi - \beta}\right]. \tag{39}$$

Also substituting equations (33) and (34) in (37) and then into (36), and using (39), we get

$$\hat{a} = \frac{\tau}{1 + \theta}\left[\frac{s\gamma}{s\pi - \beta} - n - a\right]. \tag{40}$$

These last two equations produce a zero-root system involving the state variables γ and a, with the phase diagram shown by Figure 4.8. This model implies that the long-run equilibrium depends on the initial levels of a and γ, and starting from that position, the equilibrium the economy will arrive at an equilibrium determined by the sizes of τ and θ: a higher τ will make the economy go to a long-run equilibrium with a higher a if it starts from a position above the $\hat{a} = \hat{\gamma} = 0$ line. It therefore implies that an exogenous demand shock, which increases γ, can increase a permanently, taking the economy to a higher level of a (rate of productivity growth) and γ. In long-run equilibrium we have $l = n$, which given equation (37) implies that a higher a results in a higher y, and hence, given n, a higher rate of growth of per capita output (assuming that the labor force is equal to the population). Thus, demand shocks have a permanent effect on long-run growth in this model despite the fact that it incorporates the standard property of neoclassical-synthesis Keynesian models that the rate of growth of the economy is equal to its natural rate of growth: what allows demand to have a long-run effect is the responsiveness of the rate of technological change to labor market pressures.

How plausible are these zero-root models? Although these models may appear to be very special, because they require two isoclines to coincide, if we explore the reasons behind this coincidence, they appear to be quite general. The three models we have discussed emphasize three different reasons for getting zero-root models. The first relies on a standard formulation of expectations adjustment, and the assumption that *changes* in the desired level of capacity utilization depend on expectations of growth. In the model, if firms chose their desired level of capacity utilization (as a function between the gap in between expectations and actual outcomes) we would not obtain a zero-root model; it is the fact that they choose changes that obtains this result. It may be supposed that firms are more likely to decide on the *level* of their desired rate of capacity utilization. However, there are good reasons to suppose that firms choose changes rather than levels: it requires less information, and hence is easier, for them to know if what they should plan is too high or too low compared to what they should plan than to know precisely what level they should plan. The change formulation is also consistent with the status quo effect discussed by behavioral economists, according to which decision-makers take the present situation as given and decide on what they should do relative to it. Moreover, it seems plausible to assume that firms choose changes in desired capacity utilization (a first difference) based on a deviation between expected growth of markets compared to the actual rate (another first difference). The second model relies on decision-makers adjusting more than one decision variable in response to some market signal (like the gap between actual and desired capacity utilization). Traditionally, economic models associate changes in one decision variable with one signal – like price adjustment *or* quantity adjustment in response to excess demand. The practical reason for doing so may be to get determinate solutions rather than multiple equilibria, but rationalization of this procedure may be that optimizing firms typically decide on one decision variable, since the market relates this decision to the implied decision about another one (so firms can choose their profit-maximizing price taking into account their demand curve). In reality, firms may not be explicit optimizers, and may not even try to form perceptions about their demand curve, and instead adjust different things in response to external signals they receive. If this is the case, zero-root models are likely to result. The final model makes more than one thing adjust according to conditions in some other thing – like adjustments in investment and the rate of technological change according labor market conditions (measured by the rate of change in unemployment). There is no particular reason to assume that each signal should result in only one kind of adjustment, since the adjustments embody behavior which may be independent of one another. There is therefore even less reason to question this property than when the responses were by the same decision-maker.

In terms of how adequately these models incorporate path dependence and history into equilibrium analysis, although in them a shock to the system which alters the initial conditions without affecting any of the structural parameters of the model has a permanent impact on the final equilibrium, such shocks do not exhibit remanence. That is, if the economy in these models is initially at an equilibrium, and is subjected to a shock, and this is followed by a second shock of the same intensity and in the opposite direction, the economy will return to its initial equilibrium.

8. Hysteresis

If some of the relevant parameters of the equilibrium model are time dependent, so that their values are different when the first shock is applied compared to their values during the reverse shock, the models could imply remanence (see Setterfield, 1997b). This can happen in any equilibrium model for a parameter of the equation. Thus, for instance, if autonomous investment (as a ratio of investment) rises, and then falls at a later date by the same amount, the effect on the equilibrium values of the long-run variables of the model will in general not return to their original level (despite the temporary demand shock) if some parameter like the saving parameter is time dependent, so that the multiplier effects of the identical but opposite-signed demand parameter change will not cancel each other out. Setterfield (1997b) defines this remanence as hysteresis – the economy's equilibrium position do not 'forget' temporary shocks. If the adjustment parameters of the model (like the speed at

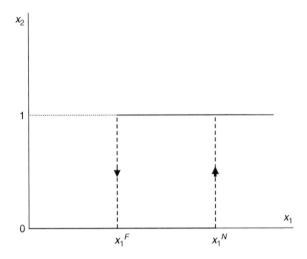

Figure 4.9   A system with hysteresis

which, say, actual accumulation adjusts to desired capacity utilization – which may depend on frictions which are therefore more likely to change capriciously over time – we can still get remanence, but not in standard (stable) equilibrium models (in which the equilibrium is independent of the adjustment parameters) but in multiple equilibrium models (if an equilibrium become unstable) or in zero-root models, because the adjustment coefficients determine the path and hence the final equilibrium of the model.

While there is no reason to rule out such time dependence of parameters, this approach has the problem that it does not provide any reason – let alone a plausible one – why these parameters, and in what systematic manner, they are in fact time dependent. It seems preferable to introduce remanence in growth models using the concept of hysteresis in a more specific sense as the property of systems which retain a memory of their time paths because of differences in the reaction of one variable to another due to changes in different directions (up or down), because they represent different kinds of movement in time (as in its early application in physics by Ewing in the study of electromagnetic fields; see Cross and Allan, 1988).

Simple systems that have different 'switch off' and 'switch on' points for a dependent variable in response to changes in some independent variable in a relationship in the model provide an example of models with remanence. As shown in Figure 4.9, let x_1 be the independent variable, the value of which causes changes in a binary dependent variable x_2, in say a behavioral equation (which states whether a specific action is taken or not). As the value of x_1 increases from 0 to x_1^F (the superscript denoting the switch *off* point) and beyond, x_2 stays at the level 0 till x_1^N (the superscript denoting the switch *on* point) is reached. As x_1 takes the value x_1^N or higher, the system switches on and x_2 takes the value 1. If x_1 then decreases below x_1^N, but stays above x_1^F, x_2 remains at 1. It switches off when x_1 goes below x_1^F. Thus for $x_1 \in [x_1^F, x_1^N]$, x_2 can take the value 0 or 1 depending on what the prior value of x_1 was. Moreover, if the system starts from any point in the interval $[x_1^F, x_1^N]$, and is then shocked to take it to some level outside it, and then brought back to the initial level by a reverse shock, the value of x_2 may change.

If we now introduce a number of such units which can be called hysterons and aggregate over them to get the total value of the dependent variable, given by $X_2 = \Sigma x_2$, and let the values $<x_1^F, x_1^N>$ be different for different units, then history will begin to matter in a more complicated way. The precise time path of x_1 determines exactly how many hysterons are in or out, and hence, the value of X_2 (which will be equal to the number switched in) at any time. The history stored by the system actually consists of the past maxima and minima of the independent variable (which determine how many hysterons are in or out). More general models do not need to feature binary dependent variables but can include continuous variables (denoting the level of the action taken). There are several examples of this type of model in economics, including that of labor markets and unemployment (see Cross, 1995) and of investment (Dixit, 1992).

In the economic growth context a major variable that arguably involves hysteresis is investment. Why investment behavior is likely to involve hysteresis can be understood as follows. Three properties of the investment decision (see Dixit, 1992, for instance) are relevant in this regard: first, it entails some sunk costs involving expenses that cannot be recouped by reversing the decision; second, the economic environment involves uncertainty; and third, the investment opportunity does not vanish, so that the act can be postponed. If there were no sunk costs the decision could be reversed costlessly. If there was no uncertainty, it would be perfectly clear whether – at any given time – investment is profitable or not. If it cannot be postponed, the decision-maker does not have the luxury of waiting. The simultaneous existence of these three characteristics results in hysteresis, which makes decision-makers wait to take an action beyond the level at which the action would be taken in the absence of these characteristics. Hysteresis in this sense can be interpreted as an appropriate way of formalizing the notion of historical time which makes the past become irreversible, at least to some degree: parts of a system which are switched on, for instance, need not be switched off when the system returns to its initial state. Hysteresis of this type has been incorporated into formalizations of investment decisions in a few heterodox growth models (see Dutt, 1997), and seems to be a promising route to introducing path dependence into such models.

Hysteresis, however, can also be interpreted as giving a limited role to history. A property of this kind of model is that although it has a memory of past shocks, that memory is selective in the sense that it remembers the non-dominated sequence of extremum values of shocks to *x*, and not everything that happened in the past. While it is implausible to expect a system to remember *everything* that happens in the past, it is not clear that it should remember *only* such non-dominated extremum values.

It can be argued, however, that the examples that have been analysed in the literature are only a small subset of reasons – sunk costs, uncertainty and postponability – which make hysteresis possible. To the extent that most major economic decisions relevant to the growth process can be postponed and are taken in an uncertain environment, the last two characteristics are likely to be satisfied by most economic activities. But, what about sunk costs? Here the crucial issue is irreversibility, for which sunk costs provides just one cause.

Irreversibility arises in a wide range of situations. Some examples are due to the operation of physical factors: an egg which is broken cannot be put back together again. However, one needs to be careful about this: if eggs are produced every period, then it is possible to replace a broken egg with a new one. There are other related examples as well. A machine can be installed, but once installed, cannot be set aside or converted into something else (at least very easily), except slowly through the process of depreciation or with losses incurred due to disposal in second-hard markets or as scrap. Knowledge can be gained in the form of a new technique or new product, but cannot disappear, unless the knowledge is forgotten after many years of disuse.

The irreversibility of knowledge can be discussed as follows. Increases in knowledge in many models occur due to learning by doing, measured in terms of cumulative output or cumulative investment for example. While some kinds of improvements in efficiency are clearly reversible – if they require large-scale operation – other kinds are irreversible since the knowledge obtained need not be forgotten. As shown in Figure 4.10, suppose that productivity, A_t, increases with K_t, the stock of capital, due to reversible and irreversible improvements in technology. If, when capital

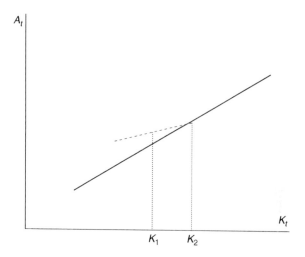

Figure 4.10   A model with knowledge irreversibility

accumulation reaches the level K_2 and begins to fall due to depreciation, the reversible part of productivity improvement disappears while the irreversible part remains, the economy will move down the dashed line. Hence, the level of productivity of the economy will depend not only on the current level of capital stock, but its past peak level.

The examples multiply when we depart from the optimization framework used in the analysis of investment decisions and introduce the habits, norms and the use of heuristics in decision-making. Habits of some types, such as consumption habits, are hard to break. It may be easy to increase consumption when income rises, but after one is used to a higher standard of living, it may be very difficult to adjust back downwards when income falls. This was analysed by Duesenberry (1949) in terms of ratchet effects. In the growth context this implies that changes in policy which are completely reversed may increase aggregate demand. When norms change because some other changes makes them change, and they become widely accepted, they will not be reversed as quickly when the causal factor is reversed. In a growth and distributional context this means that if real wages increase (say, due to a higher rate of growth of employment), as distributional norms change, real wages may not fall to their earlier level if employment growth slows down. Heuristics which lead to biases when people make judgments in uncertain environments also provide explanations of irreversibility (see Kahneman et al., 1982). An example is the availability heuristic according to which the probability of an event is assessed by the ease with which instances of the event come to mind, through retrieval or visual simulation. Which events come to mind, of course, depends on the decision-maker's recent experiences. Biases result not just from the use of simple heuristics, but also from motivational factors, loss aversion and anchoring. Motivational factors lead to a common tendency to attribute success to ability and effort, and failure to bad luck or unfairness. Loss aversion implies that people are much more strongly affected by losses than by gains. Anchoring biases occur when quantities that people estimate are unduly affected by candidate values that people are led to focus their attention on, even when such values may be irrelevant for the quantity being estimated. All of this suggests that current state and immediate experiences will affect how one reacts to changes in circumstances: the reaction of people to changes will depend crucially on the circumstances they find themselves in (which may be different at different states of the economy), and on the direction of change (for instance, due to motivational factors and loss aversion). Such biases may affect investment, wage setting, and asset holding behavior.

These different examples of hysteresis can be introduced to the equilibrium heterodox growth model of section 3 or its modifications in affecting asymmetries in: upward and downward wage adjustments, in saving parameters in periods of rising and falling growth rates and profits; in the coefficient of investment function representing how growth effects technological change in periods of rising and falling growth rates.

This broadening of the discussion of hysteresis has several implications. First, it suggests that hysteresis is omnipresent. It is indeed difficult to imagine major economic relations when such effects can be confidently ruled out. Second, the switch off and switch on points change over time, depending on the evolution of the system. Third, the amount of time spent in a state is likely to affect the degree to which there is irreversibility. Consumption habits, for instance, may be harder to reverse the longer one is used to higher levels of consumption. These considerations imply that the outcome of a process may depend on the path that the economy takes in a more complicated way than suggested by simple models of hysteresis which remember only the non-dominated extremum values of the independent variable.

9. Conclusion

This chapter has examined a number of different methods with which path dependence and history can be, and have been, introduced into heterodox equilibrium models of growth. We have found that these methods suggest that path dependence can fit quite easily and very plausibly into these models, and that path-independent models are no more than simple heuristic devices which can be used only as a basis for introducing more realistic path-dependent features. The methods have different strengths and weaknesses – some introduce history more fundamentally in some sense, some produce models which are simpler to analyse, and some which are more realistic in some sense. Rather than discuss relative merits of the different methods, preference on which may depend more on the personal judgment of the analyst and the type of question being analysed, and which may even profitably be combined, we end by discussing what these methods collectively say about the desirability of, and implications for, introducing path dependence in equilibrium growth models.

First, concerning bringing models closer to our intuitive understanding about the importance of history and time paths in affecting outcomes, our main conclusion is that our intuition may well be correct, but is not very precise. We have examined different ways in which we can interpret why history and paths matter using different methods of departing from equilibrium models. We have also found that even equilibrium models are capable of producing some types of path dependence. Our discussion has shown that many features of the real world can imply path dependence in different precise ways.

Second, concerning the broad issue of 'closedness', we find that the relationship between path dependence and openness is not very clear cut. In terms of the ability to incorporate the role of factors not explicitly considered in the model, standard equilibrium models can suffice, by taking these factors to be parameters of the model. Of course, one can think of examining the impact of parameters, and of parametric changes, as a way of analysing path dependence, and therefore claim that path dependence is necessary for examining the role of these factors in the analysis. However, this is path dependence in a very limited sense because, according to it, all models – because they must have some parameters – are path dependent. It should be noted that to deal with factors outside the model there is no need to have multiple equilibria, as has sometimes been claimed, because these other factors can determine which equilibrium will be 'chosen' by the system. Moreover, having multiple equilibria is sometimes not a useful way of incorporating the role of other factors, because these factors should be explicitly considered – even as given parameters – within the model, rather than not being specified at all. On the issue of free will, path-dependent models do not make any contribution, because even in multiple equilibrium models the initial conditions and the model will determine the outcome in a causal manner, and in hysteretic models the time path of the economy and the structure of the model will determine outcomes. Free will is, of course, involved in some way in individual decision-making, but such decision-making can then imply some behavioral regularities that can be used to model outcomes in terms of models of the economy. Free will and determinism thus operate at different levels and are not incompatible.

Third, concerning the problems with the equilibrium method, some of the criticisms of this method are unwarranted. In some cases it may be fine to analyse the movement of the economy with dynamic equations that result in an equilibrium which can be thought of as a time-less equilibrium in the sense of being a solution of a system of simultaneous equations. The distinction between logical and historical time is therefore not very clear cut. We have found, however, that especially in the presence of uncertainty and increasing returns, the kind of dynamics one gets may not be stable, or may not have unique equilibria, and therefore the use of the equilibrium method without dynamics is problematic for providing a reasonable understanding of the real world. Of course, we can analyse the dynamics with the concept of moving (short-run) equilibrium, and this dynamic analysis may still be equilibrium theorizing in a sense.

It should be emphasized that extending an equilibrium model to introduce path dependence in various ways opens up possibly new and plausible ways of looking at the economy. For instance, models with endogenous excess capacity utilization may be more widely accepted if dynamics involving the adjustment of desired capacity utilization rates which result in a continuum of equilibria, and these models may have novel implications, such as the possibility of a positive relation between the wage share and the rate of capital accumulation. To take another example, aggregate demand shocks can have long-run growth effects, rather than only have short-run consequences that are obliterated in the long run.

Finally, path dependence (except in the weak sense that models have parameters) is not required for policy analysis because policy changes can be interpreted as parametric changes. However, path dependence in several senses can have many important implications for the types of policies that are suitable. In terms of macroeconomic policies for growth, path dependence in the sense of a continuum of equilibria suggest possible dangers of contractionary fiscal and monetary policies because they can slow down growth in the long run. Thus, aggregate demand policies may well be relevant, and one may have to be careful before blindly recommending supply-side policies, such as those that encourage more savings. In terms of the required magnitude of policy changes, some approaches to path dependence (for instance, models with multiple equilibria and instability) suggest that small changes or nudges can have large desirable effects in some circumstances, but in other circumstances may require a big push to move to where positive effects could emerge. In terms of the duration of policy changes, some approaches (such as those with hysteresis) suggest that short-lived policy changes may have long-lasting effects, while others (such as those with a continuum of equilibria) imply that policy reversals can reverse positive effects. In terms of the prediction of effects of policy changes, the models imply that it is difficult to make precise predictions about effects, because where one ends up may depend on the sizes of adjustment parameters, about which firm information may be lacking. What all this implies is that policy-making has to be thought of as an art, and not as an engineering exercise, and requires careful consideration of the types of possible path dependence in the economy being modeled.

Notes

1. This tension seems to exist in Karl Marx's writings, in which economic growth is seen as a dialectical process involving changes in the forces of production and their interaction with the social relations of production, but in which the schemes of simple and expanded reproduction can be given equilibrium interpretations. It is more clearly found in the writings of Joan Robinson and Nicholas Kaldor who criticize the notion of equilibrium but who developed theories of equilibrium growth. See Dutt (2005) for a discussion of Kaldor's and Robinson's views.
2. At the beginning of a presentation I made on history and path dependence at the Faculty of Economics at the University of Notre Dame in September 2003 to both orthodox and heterodox economists, all but one (who abstained) of the 26 present (all economics faculty or graduate students) answered the question – what happens now affects where we end up – in the affirmative. At a conference on Joan Robinson at the University of Vermont, October 2003, immediately preceding my presentation, I asked a large lecture theater full of mostly heterodox economists the same question, and every single person in the room agreed with the statement.
3. The dynamics can also be represented in terms discrete-time systems: see Dutt (2005) for general discussions of both continuous and discrete-time systems.
4. This formulation assumes that firms adjust their expectations by comparing expectations to the actual rate of accumulation. If, instead, they revised expectations on the basis of expectations of actual output growth, we should replace g with the equation $\hat{u} + g$ where the first term can be obtained from

differentiating equation (26) in the text with respect to time. The formulation used here is simpler without changing the results qualitatively.
5. For related models see Van de Klundert and Van Schaik (1990) and Bhaduri (2004).

References

Arthur, Brian (1989), 'Competing technologies, increasing returns, and lock-in by historical events', *Economic Journal*, 99, March, 116–31.

Arthur, Brian (1994), *Increasing Returns and Path Dependence in the Economy*, Ann Arbor: University of Michigan Press.

Bhaduri, Amit (2004), 'On the dynamics of different regimes of demand-led expansion', unpublished, University of Pavia.

Cross, Rod (1995), 'Is the natural rate hypothesis consistent with hysteresis?', in Rod Cross (ed.), *The Natural Rate of Unemployment. Reflections on 25 Years of the Hypothesis*, Cambridge: Cambridge University Press.

Cross, Rod and Allan, A. (1988), 'On the history of hysteresis', in Rod Cross (ed.), *Hysteresis and the Natural Rate Hypothesis*, Oxford: Basil Blackwell.

Dixit, Avinash (1992), 'Investment and hysteresis', *Journal of Economic Perspectives*, 6(1), 107–32.

Duesenberry, James S. (1949), *Income, Saving and the Theory of Consumer Behavior*, Cambridge, Mass.: Harvard University Press.

Dutt, Amitava Krishna (1990), *Growth, Distribution and Uneven Development*, Cambridge: Cambridge University Press.

Dutt, Amitava Krishna (1997), 'Equilibrium, path dependence and hysteresis in post-Keynesian models', in P. Arestis and M. Sawyer (eds), *Essays in Honour of G.C. Harcourt, Vol 2: Markets, Unemployment and Economic Policy*, London: Routledge, 238–53.

Dutt, Amitava Krishna (2005), 'Robinson, history and equilibrium', in Bill Gibson (ed.), *Joan Robinson's Economics: A Centennial Celebration*, Cheltenham, UK and Northampton, Mass.: Edward Elgar, 123–72.

Dutt, Amitava Krishna (2006), 'Aggregate demand, aggregate supply and economic growth', *International Review of Applied Economics*, 20(3), July, 319–36.

Eatwell, John (1997), 'History versus equilibrium', in Philip Arestis, Gabriel Palma and Malcolm Sawyer (eds), *Essays in Honour of G.C. Harcourt, Vol 1: Capital Controversy, Post-Keynesian Economics and the History of Economics*, London: Routledge, p. 386–97.

Kahneman, D., Slovic, P., and Tversky, A. (eds) (1982), *Judgment under uncertainty: Heuristics and biases*, Cambridge: Cambridge University Press.

Kaldor, Nicholas (1934), 'The determinateness of static equilibrium', *Review of Economic Studies*, February, reprinted in F. Tagetti and A.P. Thirlwall (eds), *The Essential Kaldor*, London: Duckworth.

Kaldor, Nicholas (1955–56), 'Alternative Theories of Distribution', *Review of Economic Studies*, 23(2), No. 61, 83–100.

Kaldor, Nicholas (1970), 'The case for regional policies', *Scottish Journal of Political Economy*, 17, 337–48, reprinted in F. Tagetti and A.P. Thirlwall (eds), *The Essential Kaldor*, London: Duckworth.

Kaldor, Nicholas (1972), 'The irrelevance of equilibrium economics', *Economic Journal*, 82, December, 1237–55, reprinted in F. Tagetti and A.P. Thirlwall (eds), *The Essential Kaldor*, London: Duckworth.

Kaldor, Nicholas (1975), 'What is wrong with economic theory', *Quarterly Journal of Economics*, August, reprinted in F. Tagetti and A.P. Thirlwall (eds), *The Essential Kaldor*, London: Duckworth.

Keynes, John Maynard (1933), *Essays in Biography*, London: Macmillan, *Collected Works of John Maynard Keynes, Vol. X*, London: Macmillan, 1972.

Keynes, John Maynard (1936), *The General Theory of Employment, Interest and Money*, London: Macmillan.

Krugman, Paul (1991), 'History versus expectations', *Quarterly Journal of Economics*, 106, 651–67.

Lavoie, Marc (1995), 'The Kaleckian model of growth and distribution and its neo-Ricardian and neo-Marxian critiques', *Cambridge Journal of Economics*, 19(6), 789–818.

Roberts, Mark (2003), 'History versus equilibrium: a debate revisited', Department of Land Economy, University of Cambridge, paper presented at the 4th Analytical Political Economy Conference, Trinity College, Hartford, Connecticut.

Robinson, Joan (1962), *Essays in the Theory of Economic Growth*, London: Macmillan.

Robinson, Joan (1974), 'History versus equilibrium', *Thames Papers in Political Economy*, Thames Polytechnic, London, reprinted in Joan Robinson, *Collected Economic Papers, Vol. V*, Cambridge, Mass: MIT Press, 1980, pp. 48–58.

Setterfield, Mark (1997a), 'Should economists dispense with the notion of equilibrium?' *Journal of Post Keynesian Economics*, Fall, 20(1), 47–76.

Setterfield, Mark (1997b), *Rapid Growth and Relative Decline. Modelling Macroeconomic Dynamic with Hysteresis*, London and Basingstoke: Macmillan.

Setterfield, Mark (2001), 'Cumulative causation, interrelatedness and the theory of economic growth: a reply to Argyrous and Toner', *Cambridge Journal of Economics* 25, 107–12.

Van de Klundert, Theo, C.M.J. and Van Schaik, Anton B.T.M. (1990), 'Unemployment persistence and loss of productive capacity: a Keynesian approach', *Journal of Macroeconomics*, 12(3), 363–80.

5
Money Wage Rigidity, Monopoly Power and Hysteresis

*Alfonso Palacio-Vera**
Universidad Complutense de Madrid, Spain

Abstract

The literature that addresses the effects on the level of aggregate demand of changes in the degree of monopoly typically assumes away the existence of an 'inflation barrier' and an inflation-targeting central bank. The presence of these two institutional factors entails that any aggregate demand change brought about by changes in the functional distribution of income will tend to be offset by changes in real interest rates. We postulate a simple macroeconomic model for a closed economy with a government sector and hypothesize that a change in the average mark-up affects the inflation rate, the 'inflation-barrier' and aggregate demand. The model allows for the analysis of the effects on the employment rate of demand and supply shocks when the economy exhibits asymmetric inflation dynamics (AID) and hysteresis effects. Among other results we find that, if the economy exhibits AID and hysteresis, the effect on the employment rate of a change in the mark up is likely to be either ineffectual or counterproductive even if the associated demand shock is expansionary. We also show that an inadequate functional distribution of income may lead to the occurrence of an aggregate demand deficiency problem.

JEL Classification: B50, E12, E24, E50

Keywords: Neutral interest rate, degree of monopoly, asymmetric inflation dynamics, zero lower bound, hysteresis, reversibility

1. Introduction

An extensive theoretical and empirical literature in the heterodox economics tradition (HET hereafter) has addressed the impact on unemployment of changes in the functional distribution of income stemming from a change in the average degree of monopoly.[1] In this literature, it is commonly postulated that an increase in the wage (profit) share in national income has contradictory effects on the different subaggregates of aggregate demand so its net effect is ambiguous. In general, this literature takes for granted that the level of economic activity is demand-determined in the short and the long run and thus ignores (i) the existence of a short-term 'inflation barrier' determined by the conflict over income distribution between workers and firms, (ii) the impact of changes in the degree of monopoly as captured by changes in the average mark-up on both the 'inflation barrier' and the inflation rate in the short run, and (iii) that a salient feature of the institutional framework that characterizes most present-day economies is that central banks (CBs hereafter) set short-term nominal interest rates in order to achieve an inflation target. When taking all these features into account, it seems to us that it is hardly realistic to study the implications of changes in the degree of monopoly by leaving aside their impact on the supply-side of the economy and, due to their short-run impact on the inflation rate, on real interest rates.

In the last decade or so we have witnessed the emergence of the so-called 'New Consensus' on Macroeconomics (NC hereafter).[2] The NC has been summarized in terms of a simple model with three equations: (i) an aggregate demand equation with the output-gap typically determined by past and expected future output-gap and the ex-ante real interest rate, (ii) a short-run Phillips curve with inflation typically based on current output-gap and past and future inflation and (iii) a monetary policy rule of the Taylor's rule form that endogenizes the setting of interest rates by the CB. The NC strongly suggests that there is no long-run trade-off between inflation and unemployment and that, as a result of it, inflation can be conveniently tamed though interest rate policy using aggregate demand deflation. Unlike the literature referred to above, the NC tends to ignore the impact of the functional income distribution on unemployment. There are (at least) two reasons for this. First and foremost, mainstream economics has traditionally skipped the analysis of a class-ridden socio-economic structure and, hence, the possibility that different social groups have different sources of income and different propensities to spend out of income. Arguably, this is related to the adoption of 'methodological individualism' as a key principle of the Neoclassical Research Programme. Second, proponents of the NC approach tend to view the level of economic activity as hovering in the short run around a supply-determined equilibrium that is assumed to be largely independent of the level and time path of aggregate demand. This supply-determined equilibrium is referred to as the 'natural rate of unemployment' or as the NAIRU, the acronym for 'non-accelerating inflation rate of unemployment'. This study represents an attempt to construct a general framework that encompasses both the HET and the NC as particular cases and to explore its implications for unemployment. Certainly, it incorporates some features of the HET by assuming there are different social groups with different sources of income (i.e., wages and profits) and hysteresis effects, and by adopting Keynesian liquidity preference (LP hereafter) theory. Likewise, it incorporates some key features of the NC as the existence of an 'inflation barrier' and an inflation-targeting CB that sets interest rates.

Economists have recently used the concept of hysteresis especially in the field of unemployment theory since its properties seem to fit well the unemployment dynamics of the last three decades, especially in Western Europe. For instance, Ball (1999) suggests that passive macroeconomic policies are largely to blame for the observed rise in unemployment in several OECD countries since 1985. In countries where policy shifted towards expansion after tight policy had disinflated the economy, unemployment rose only temporarily. By contrast, in those countries where policy remained tight unemployment rose permanently (Ball, 1999, p. 190). Ball blames for this outcome on the presence of hysteresis effects that operated through the impact on 'equilibrium unemployment' of the fraction of the long-term unemployed. Despite an initial wave of studies that lent empirical support to the notion of hysteresis (see the survey in Røed, 1997), the subsequent emergence of controversial evidence in the 1990s, especially for North America, led to an apparent loss of interest in this concept. However, several recent contributions have reopened the debate on the notion of hysteresis. For instance, León-Ledesma (2002) finds strong support for this hypothesis for the EU countries. Likewise, Logeay and Tober (2006) find strong support for the existence of hysteresis in the Euro Area.

There is now a strong body of evidence indicating the presence of 'downward money wage rigidity' (hereafter DMWR) across a wide spectrum of countries (see Lebow et al., 2003, Akerlof, 2007, Holden, 2004 and Holden and Wulfsberg, 2008). Several explanations have been put forward for the existence of such rigidities, such as fairness and social norms (Bewley, 1999, and Akerlof, 2007) or labour market institutions (Holden, 2004). The combination of these factors implies that these nominal rigidities could persist for a long time even in a low inflation environment. Indeed, empirical studies for European countries find that

DMWR persist during low inflation periods (Agell and Lundburg, 2003 and Fehr and Lorenz, 2005). Similarly, the recent Japanese experience shows that, despite the presence of a large negative output-gap for most of the period 1991–2002, inflation turned negative in the second half of the 1990s but, after 1998, core inflation remained stable at moderately negative levels reaching its trough at −0.79 per cent in 2002 (De Veirman, 2007).[3] The presence of DMWR and the recent Japanese experience suggest that, when the output-gap becomes negative and inflation is low or negative, the former is likely to manifest itself in the existence of 'asymmetric inflation dynamics' (AID hereafter) in the sense that inflation decreases more sluggishly when the output-gap is negative and inflation is relatively low than it increases when the output-gap is positive.[4]

The main contributions of this study are the following. First, we find that, in an economy characterized by the presence of an inflation-targeting CB and a short-run 'inflation barrier' that exhibits hysteresis effects, a change in the average mark-up affects the employment rate in the long run through the initial impact on the 'inflation barrier' and the inflation rate. In particular, an increase in the mark-up leads to a long-run decrease in the employment rate and vice versa. Second, we show that, when the economy also exhibits AID, a change in the average mark-up is less effective and may lead to a long-run fall in the employment rate even when it contracts. This is because the long-run impact on the employment rate of the demand shock, even when it is expansionary, is adverse owing to the presence of AID. Therefore, in this second scenario, a contraction in the average mark-up only brings about a long-run increase in the employment rate if the net long-run adverse effect of the demand shock (even when the latter is expansionary) is more than offset by the sum of the favourable effects stemming from the initial fall in the inflation rate and the attenuation of the 'inflation barrier'. More generally, we show that the joint presence of hysteresis effects and AID in the economy (i) helps attenuate macroeconomic volatility and (ii) blocks off the 'reversibility' property typically exhibited by zero/unit root systems. Third, we find that, in the above scenario, whether the economy exhibits a 'wage-led' or a 'profit-led' macroeconomic regime is largely irrelevant for macroeconomic performance as long as the economy does not exhibit an 'aggregate demand deficiency'. Fourth, we show that, despite the previous results, a change in the functional distribution of income may nevertheless impinge favourably on macroeconomic performance if it raises the steady-growth neutral interest rate since this reduces the likelihood that an aggregate demand deficiency occurs. Lastly, we identify a Keynesian and a neoclassical regime according to whether an increase in the actual inflation rate leads to an increase (Keynesian) or to a decrease (neoclassical) in the neutral interest rate and show that the regime the economy exhibits affects the stability conditions of the economy.

The study continues as follows. The following section proposes a definition of an aggregate demand deficiency problem, reviews the NC approach and compares its predictions to those of LP theory. We then present a simple model for a closed economy with a government sector. We work out its steady-growth properties and short-run behaviour. The analysis of the dynamics associated to demand and inflation shocks follows and the final section summarizes and concludes.

2.   Aggregate demand deficiencies and the New Consensus approach

It is well known that short-term nominal interest rates are subject to a zero lower bound constraint. This feature was termed by Kaldor (1939) the 'great constitutional weakness' of monetary policy because it prevents the short-term nominal interest rate from operating equally freely in both directions. In the context of this study, the relevance of the zero lower bound constraint stems from the fact that, if the CB fine-tunes the economy through changes in interest rates, then an inadequate functional distribution of income may bring about an aggregate demand deficiency problem so that the functional distribution of income will affect macroeconomic performance. We define the former as a scenario where, with nominal interest rates at or near zero, the CB is unable to push down real interest rates far enough so as to induce a level of output equal to potential output.[5]

We define the neutral interest rate r^n as the long-term real interest rate which is *neutral* with respect to the inflation rate and tends neither to raise nor to lower it in the absence of transitory supply shocks.[6] In a closed economy with a government sector, there will be an aggregate demand deficiency when planned aggregate saving exceeds the sum of planned private investment plus the government budget deficit at the employment rate consistent with constant inflation even at a zero short-term nominal interest rate. If we denote by ω the *minimum* (ex-ante) real interest rate that a CB can set then the economy will exhibit an aggregate demand deficiency problem if:

$$r^n \prec \omega \tag{1}$$

If we think of r as a short-term real interest rate then the minimum (short-term) nominal interest rate that the CB can set is zero. By contrast, if we think of r as a long-term real interest rate, the minimum (long-term) nominal interest rate that the CB can set is positive because lenders will normally require a (time-varying) term/risk premium $\mu > 0$ to grant credit or purchase long-dated securities.[7] In turn, the size of the term/risk premium will depend positively on the degree of LP. If we assume, for the sake of simplicity, that the expected rate of inflation π^e equals the current inflation rate π we have:

$$\omega = \mu - \pi^e = \mu - \pi \tag{2}$$

Therefore, we say that an economy exhibits an aggregate demand deficiency if:

$$r^n + \pi \prec \mu \tag{3}$$

Expression (3) tells us that the lower are r^n and π, and the higher is μ the more likely it is that an economy that is hit by a shock that pushes either π or r^n (or both) down will exhibit an aggregate demand deficiency. If this is the case, then the current level of output will be lower than potential output and inflation will tend to fall.

A number of mainstream economists have recently evaluated the likelihood of economies exhibiting an aggregate demand deficiency and the policy options that may remove this constraint should it be necessary. A summary of the former is in Blinder (2000) and an evaluation of the different proposals is in Bernanke and Reinhart (2004). There seems to be an emerging consensus on the view that the existence of a zero lower bound constraint on nominal interest rates will lead to a moderate deterioration in macroeconomic volatility as the inflation target approaches zero so it represents a constraint on how monetary policy operates in a low inflation environment (Fuhrer and Madigan, 1997; Reifschneider and Williams, 2000). One aspect these studies address is the possibility that an economy enters a deflationary episode once the zero lower bound constraint binds. The verdict is 'that such episodes are *fairly* rare, even in a low-inflation environment – about once every hundred years if the target rate of inflation is around zero, given the sort of shocks that have characterized the U.S. economy over the past thirty years' (Reifschneider and Williams, 2000, p. 962). Thus, the conclusion is that a deflationary episode may come about only in the wake of unusually large shocks. The studies also recommend setting a low but positive inflation target (preferably 2 per cent). Conversely, there is no consensus as to whether unconventional monetary policy options can take the economy out of a deflationary episode should it be necessary. Yet, as argued in Reifschneider and Williams (2000, p. 943), a summary of the debate is that 'the likely effectiveness of such actions is unclear from a theoretical perspective, and they have never been put to a definitive test'. Only discretionary fiscal policy is viewed as a reliable weapon once the zero lower bound constraint binds (Kuttner and Posen, 2001, pp. 124–40). In this respect, the words of Kazuo Ueda at the 1999 JMCB Conference serve to summarize the conventional wisdom on this subject: 'Don't put yourself in the position of zero interest rates. You'll have to face a lot of difficulties. I can tell you it will be a lot more painful than you can possibly imagine' (Ueda, 2000, p.1109).

The predominant wisdom in the mainstream literature that a deflationary episode may only occur in the wake of unusually large shocks appears to be consistent with the theoretical predictions of the NC approach. In the influential study by Woodford (2003) which, for the purposes of this study, will be taken as the canonical version of the NC approach, he develops a neo-Wicksellian framework based on explicit optimizing foundations where the deviation of the natural interest rate from its steady-growth value is a stochastic process determined by a range of demand and supply shocks (Woodford, 2003, pp. 249–51). In his model, demand shocks include fiscal policy, investment and impatience shocks. The latter modify the rate of time preference of the representative household. Supply shocks consist of productivity shocks to the production function of the firms, shocks to the disutility-of-labour function and changes in the amount of capital. He concludes that real 'interest rates must increase in response to temporary increases in government purchases or in the impatience of households to consume and decrease in response to temporary increases in productivity or in the willingness of households to supply labor' (Woodford, 2003, p. 250). He defines the natural interest rate as 'the equilibrium real rate of return in the case of fully flexible prices' (Woodford, 2003, p. 248). Crucially, he admits the possibility that a range of transitory shocks may make the natural interest rate negative, albeit he suggests that this will be a transitory scenario:

> The present theory allows for variation over time in the natural rate for a variety of reasons, and there is no reason why it should not sometimes be negative. (The model does imply a positive average level of the natural rate, determined by the rate of time preference of the representative household). (Woodford, 2003, p. 251).

We may extrapolate Woodford's results to a growing economy by relying on optimal growth theory. According to it, the optimality condition for saving yields the following 'balanced growth' condition:

$$r^* = \frac{a}{\sigma} + n + \vartheta \tag{i}$$

where r^* is the natural interest rate in steady growth, a is the rate of labour-augmenting technological change, n is the rate of population growth, σ is the inter-temporal elasticity of substitution in consumption and ϑ is the rate of time preference of the representative household.[8] a and n are positive in a growing economy. Hence, the natural interest rate will be positive in steady growth and its lower bound will be ϑ. Finally, in the stationary state we have that $a = n = 0$ and, hence, $r^* = \vartheta$.

Several comments are in order. First, the literature seems to conflate different meanings of the notion of a natural interest rate.[9] This problem was recognized long ago by Myrdal (1939) who noted that monetary equilibrium in Wicksell's theory means that the natural rate of interest must (i) be equal to the marginal productivity of real capital, (ii) equate the supply and the demand for savings at full employment, and (iii) guarantee a stable price level. Only the third meaning is compatible with our previous definition of the neutral interest rate even though it needs to be adapted to a modern setting where it is the inflation rate and not the price level that is stable in the long run.[10] This is because (i) we will assume that the economy operates in the long run at an employment rate that is equal (or lower) than the rate of employment compatible with a constant inflation rate and this, in turn, corresponds to an employment rate that falls short of full employment and (ii) the notion of the marginal productivity of capital is flawed (see Harcourt, 1969). Furthermore, there is nothing *natural* about the natural interest rate since it depends, *inter alia*, on the government budget balance and so we think that the term 'neutral' is preferable. Be that as it may, the role of the natural interest rate in the NC approach is equivalent to the role of the neutral interest rate as defined above, namely, it is the real interest rate that renders the inflation rate constant in the absence of transitory supply shocks or as Woodford (2003, p. 248) notes 'the natural rate of interest is just the real rate of interest required to keep aggregate demand equal at all times to the natural rate of output'.

Second, Woodford's assumption that the average value of the natural interest rate is positive implies that the natural interest rate *returns* in the long-run to a positive gravitation centre provided prices are fully flexible.

The process whereby this occurs is not discussed in Woodford (2003). Presumably, the argument is that, in a hypothetical situation where actual output equals potential output and, in the absence of shocks, economic agents will increase their saving rate whenever the actual real interest rate is above their rate of time preference and vice versa so that, in equilibrium, the former will necessarily equal the latter. The adjustment process can be put forward as follows. Let us assume that the economy initially exhibits an aggregate demand deficiency problem so that the actual real interest rate exceeds the natural interest rate. If so, inflation will start to fall. Since the actual real interest rate (which may be negative) falls short of the average rate of time preference (which is positive), households will increase their consumption so the natural interest rate will increase. This process will continue as long as the actual real interest rate falls short of the rate of time preference. Eventually, the actual real interest rate and the natural interest rate will converge to the average rate of time preference and the economy will reach equilibrium. However, this story faces (at least) one problem; as recognized by most proponents of the NC approach, the economy may end up caught in a deflationary spiral if the initial decrease in the inflation rate endogenously raises the level of the real rate so as to cause aggregate demand to weaken and push inflation down more, thereby raising the real interest rate even further. Therefore, if a deflationary spiral is to be avoided, proponents of the NC approach need to assume that the adjustment process described above will not be short-circuited by the adverse effect upon aggregate demand of a rising actual real interest rate. However, the possibility that, under certain circumstances, a deflationary spiral may set off is readily recognized by proponents of the NC approach so the main theme of our critique to this story needs to rely on a different argument.

We believe that the specific PK critique of the adjustment process described above is that the latter may be short-circuited for reasons *other* than a deflationary spiral. PK theorists insist that individuals make decisions in an environment intrinsically characterized by 'fundamental uncertainty' where probability distributions cannot be the basis for comprehending real world behaviour because they simply do not know all the possible future outcomes and, hence, they cannot attach a probability to them (Davidson, 1991). Consequently, individuals' decisions concerning saving, investment and the allocation of wealth among alternative assets will tend to be dominated by LP considerations. To see this, we may note that in PK theory the real interest rate is the reward obtained for parting with liquidity rather than (as in neoclassical theory) the reward for postponing consumption. In turn, the degree of LP is positively related to the degree of uncertainty (Keynes, 1937, p. 216). PK theorists thus identify the notion of LP with an environment of 'fundamental uncertainty' where the degree of LP is inversely related to the degree of confidence. Crucially, they claim that, if investors' expectations are such that they expect that the holding of real or financial assets other than money will make them incur large capital losses, then there is a rationale for placing wealth in a liquid asset or, alternatively, to use the former to repay outstanding debt. If so, they will postpone consumption plans and increase the liquidity of portfolios. Furthermore, PK theorists insist that reduced LP accompanies conditions that are conducive to increases in economic activity and vice versa. Thus, within a generalized LP theory, a decrease in aggregate demand may be the result of a high degree of LP associated to pessimistic expectations and vice versa or:

> A world of ultimate liquidity preference is a world where firms would refuse to produce for fear of indebtedness, where banks would refuse to lend for fear of loan defaults, and where consumers would refuse to spend for fear of unemployment. (Lavoie, 1996, p. 292)

The existence of 'fundamental uncertainty' will thus tend to dominate saving and investment decisions even if we assume that households exhibit a subjective rate of time preference. In particular, if households are pessimistic about the future, they may well decide to increase their saving rate even if the actual real interest rate falls short of their rate of time preference thus reducing aggregate demand. In addition, an increase in the degree of LP of banks will make them reluctant to grant credit and this will also tend to depress aggregate demand. More generally, the adjustment process posited above *only* applies to a situation where uncertainty is akin to the notion of probabilistic risk. For the purposes of this study, the crucial implication is that the steady-growth neutral interest rate may be negative and will not possess a (positive) centre of gravitation as envisaged in the NC approach.

Lastly, proponents of the NC approach apparently argue that an aggregate demand deficiency problem may only come about when the neutral interest rate is negative. However, expression (3) reflects that an aggregate demand deficiency problem may also occur in a situation where both the neutral interest rate and the inflation rate are positive. This may be the case if the term/risk premium on loan rates becomes large enough so as to satisfy condition (3). The importance of the term/risk premium is recognized in Blinder (2006, pp. 47–8) when he notes that 'long rates are terrible (and biased) predictors of future short rates ... Just why this is so remains a major intellectual puzzle'. Yet, he does not link the size of the term/risk premium to the degree of LP. Likewise, Woodford (2003, p. 244) notes that 'it is a *long-term* real rate of interest rather than a short rate, that determines aggregate demand in this model' and he refers to agents' expectations about future short-term real interest rates as an important determinant of aggregate demand but he does not mention the possibility that the term/risk premium on loan rates may vary as a result of changes in the degree of LP.

3.   The model

We now present the model we will utilize hereafter to analyse a variety of issues related to the impact on the level of economic activity of demand and supply shocks when the CB implements a conventional IT strategy. The exposition is divided into five subsections. The first three subsections contain the different building blocks of the model, the fourth subsection presents the steady-growth analysis and the final one describes the behaviour of the economy in the short run.

3.1   The supply side

Let us consider a one-sector economy with two inputs, labour and capital, and assume that (i) there is a large number of identical firms and (ii) they all utilize the same technology. If we aggregate across all firms in the economy we may define potential output $\overline{Y}$ as:

$$\overline{Y} = \lambda \cdot \overline{N} \leq v \cdot K \tag{4}$$

where $\overline{N}$ is the level of employment that keeps inflation constant in the absence of transitory supply shocks, K is the capital stock, and λ and v are respectively the productivity of labour and capital when the factors are fully utilized. The current rate of capacity utilization is:

$$u = \frac{Y}{v \cdot K} \leq 1 \tag{5}$$

where Y is the actual rate of output. Post Keynesians such as Rowthorn (1977) and Sawyer (1982) postulate the existence of an employment rate compatible with constant inflation in the short run (hereafter CIER) which results from the conflicting income claims of workers and firms.[11] Thus, the CIER represents an 'inflation barrier' even though it may be affected by the level and time path of aggregate demand in the long run if, for instance, hysteresis effects are present. Be that as it may, the presence of an 'inflation barrier' means that the CB will seek to adjust interest rates to affect the level of economic activity so as to balance off the income claims. Therefore, the rate of capacity utilization when $Y = \overline{Y}$ is:

$$\overline{u} = \frac{\overline{Y}}{vK} = \frac{\lambda}{v} \cdot \frac{\overline{N}}{K} = \left(\frac{\lambda}{v}\right) \cdot \left(\frac{\overline{e} \cdot L}{K}\right) \leq 1 \tag{6}$$

where we denote by $\overline{u}$ the 'constant inflation capacity utilization' (CICU hereafter), by $\overline{e}$ the CIER, by L the labour force and where $\overline{N} = \overline{e}(m) \cdot L$.[12]

Let us now assume there is no overhead labour and firms are fully integrated, producing all the materials required for their final output so that prime costs are made up only of labour costs. If we also assume that firms practise mark-up pricing, then the real (product) wage is determined by the firms' profit-maximization objectives:

$$\frac{w}{p} = \frac{\lambda}{m} \tag{7}$$

where w is the money wage, p is the price level and $m > 1$ is one plus the average mark-up set by firms over prime costs,. Furthermore, in the absence of overhead labour, the profit share on national income ρ can be expressed as (Asimakopulos, 1975):

$$\rho = \left(\frac{m-1}{m}\right) = \left(1 - \frac{w/p}{\lambda}\right) \tag{8}$$

where $\partial\rho/\partial m = 1/m^2 > 0$. Hence, ρ depends in a straightforward manner on the mark-up over prime costs used for pricing purposes. Importantly, an increase in m – and hence in ρ – reduces the CIER and vice versa so $\overline{e}_m < 0$ where the subscript denotes a partial derivative. This stems from the fact that, as m rises, employees need to accept a lower real (product) wage relative to average labour productivity if the rate of inflation is to be kept constant.[13] If we assume that workers' bargaining power and/or propensity to shirk depends inversely on the unemployment rate, then a higher m will lead to a higher unemployment rate in the long run. Hence, expression (6) can be re-expressed as:

$$\overline{u}(m) = \left(\frac{\overline{e}(m)}{v}\right) \cdot \left(\frac{\lambda \cdot L}{K}\right) \leq 1 \tag{9}$$

Next, as claimed in Palley (1994) and Akerlof et al. (1996), the lower the inflation rate, the larger the fraction of firms that can only implement real wage cuts through a reduction in the money wage they pay to their workers. According to them, in the presence of DMWR a lower inflation rate thus implies that a larger fraction of firms is forced to pay real wages exceeding the wage they deem optimal. In the model of Akerlof et al. (1996), this increases the long-run sustainable level of unemployment and provides the rationale for the existence of a 'grease' effect of inflation on the labour market whereby a marginal rise in the inflation rate may reduce the equilibrium rate of unemployment when inflation is low. Yet, if firms follow a mark-up pricing strategy and total average costs are roughly constant for a wide range of rates of capacity utilization, the presence of DMWR is more likely to show up in a diminished tendency for the rate of inflation to fall for a given (negative) output-gap as inflation falls below a certain threshold.[14] If we add the proposition that, as observed in the recent Japanese recession, the change in the inflation rate becomes nil (when the output-gap is negative) as the inflation rate gets below a negative level given by $(\phi_\pi \pi^{CR} - \phi_U)/\phi_\pi$, we obtain the expression that captures the AID:

$$\dot{\pi} = \begin{cases} \phi_U(u - \bar{u}(m)) + \varepsilon_\pi & \text{if} \quad u \succ \bar{u}(m) \\ \phi_L(u - \bar{u}(m)) + \varepsilon_\pi & \text{if} \quad u \prec \bar{u}(m) \end{cases} \tag{10}$$

$$\text{where } \phi_L = \begin{cases} \phi_U & \text{if} \quad \pi \geq \pi^{CR} \\ \phi_U + \phi_\pi(\pi - \pi^{CR}) & \text{if} \quad \dfrac{\phi_\pi \pi^{CR} - \phi_U}{\phi_\pi} \prec \pi \prec \pi^{CR} \quad \phi_U, \phi_\pi \succ 0 \\ 0 & \text{if} \quad \pi \leq \dfrac{\phi_\pi \pi^{CR} - \phi_U}{\phi_\pi} \end{cases}$$

where ε_π is a variable that captures transitory cost-push shocks and $\pi^{CR} \succ 0$ represents a (positive) inflation rate below which the downward adjustment of the rate of growth of money wages, and hence of the inflation rate, becomes slower and eventually comes to a halt.[15] The basic proposition is that as the inflation rate decreases and falls below π^{CR}, some firms will need to cut money wages if their product prices are to decrease. In turn, the proportion of firms subject to this constraint will increase as the inflation rate decreases further. In Akerlof et al. (1996), π^{CR} was estimated to be about 3 per cent for the US economy.

Equation (10) also tells us that the inflation rate adjusts differently depending on: (i) whether actual capacity utilization is higher or lower than the CICU and (ii) whether the inflation rate is equal, higher or lower than π^{CR}. As such, ϕ_L may take on three different values. For instance, if the current inflation rate is equal or higher than π^{CR} then inflation dynamics will be symmetric in the sense that the change in the rate of inflation will solely depend on the *absolute* value of the output-gap. If the inflation rate is lower than π^{CR} but higher than the lower threshold $(\phi_\pi \pi^{CR} - \phi_U)/\phi_\pi$ then the adjustment of the inflation rate will be asymmetric since the change in the inflation rate will depend both on the size and sign of the output-gap, that is, a positive output-gap will tend to engender a larger (absolute) change in the inflation rate than a negative one of similar size. The asymmetry will be larger the closer the inflation rate is to the lower threshold. Finally, inflation will stop decreasing when it becomes equal to the former.

3.2 Hysteresis

In economics, the notion of hysteresis has generated a number of different formal characterizations (Amable et al., 1995). Hysteresis is typically associated with dynamic linear models characterized by zero root systems for continuous time models or by unit root systems for models in discrete time (Giavazzi and Wyplosz, 1985). In such systems there is a continuum of equilibria and the final equilibrium reached, selected from within the continuum, depends on the particular features of the system. In a deterministic setting the final equilibrium point depends on the initial conditions of the state variables as well as on the parameters describing the speed of adjustment. In a stochastic setting, the position of the system is determined by the chronicle of exogenous shocks owing to the fact that the latter cumulate forever without progressively vanishing. According to Dutt (1997, p. 240) 'systems of this kind can be called path-dependent systems' since, in these models, history plays a key role in the sense that the starting point and the time path of the economy determine the final outcome.

An important property of these systems is that an initial shock followed by a second one of the same magnitude but opposite sign drives the system back to its initial position. This 'reversibility' property has a crucial implication. If exogenous shocks are generated by a symmetric probability distribution, then negative and positive shocks cancel each other out in the long run. Hence, with zero/unit root systems, any long-run permanent effect on unemployment can solely be caused by (i) exogenous shocks that are generated by an asymmetric probability distribution, (ii) an asymmetric adjustment of prices to shocks of opposite sign or (iii) an asymmetric response to shocks by policy makers (Fontana and Palacio-Vera, 2007). In this study we will focus on the second of these possibilities. This 'reversibility' feature of zero/unit root systems has encouraged some scholars to investigate the properties of systems show-ing hysteresis. Drawing on the work of the Russian mathematician Mark Krasnosel'skii, it has been argued that a system is hysteretic if it exhibits 'remanence', i.e., when the value of the output is permanently affected by an appropriate temporary change in the value of the input (Amable et al., 1995). The crucial point is that, in hysteretic systems, a relevant exogenous force modifying the value of a given parameter λ entails a change in the system dynamics. For instance, the structural modification may move the system out of the initial equilibrium and towards a new equilibrium. By altering the exogenous force such as to bring parameter λ back to the initial value, a structural deformation of equal magnitude but opposite sign is produced. However, and this is a crucial difference with the case of zero/unit root (linear) systems, the system does *not* return to the original equilibrium point. In other words, the temporary change in the value of λ has produced a 'remanent' effect on the final state of the system (Amable et al., 1995, p. 172; see also Dutt, 1997). As we show below, the presence of AID may render a zero/unit root system hysteretic and makes it exhibit 'remanence'. However, instead of rely-ing on an abstract structural modification of the system, our approach builds on Setterfield (1998) by (realistically) assuming the presence of asymmetries in the adjustment of inflation.

Following a suggestion by Hargreaves Heap (1980), we model the dynamics of the CIER as:

$$\dot{\bar{e}} = \zeta(e - \bar{e}) \quad \zeta \geq 0 \tag{11}$$

where the over-dot denotes a time derivative, $\zeta > 0$ measures the speed of adjustment of the CIER whenever it exhibits hysteresis effects and the case $\zeta = 0$ corresponds to the case without hysteresis. Hence, we view the presence of hysteresis effects in the CIER as making it depend on the time path of the actual employment rate so that an increase in the latter tends to raise the CIER up and vice versa.

3.3 The demand side

The equilibrium condition in the goods markets for a closed economy with a government sector when current output is equal to potential output is:

$$s(r^n, z) \cdot \overline{Y} = I + PSBR \tag{12}$$

where s is the saving rate, I is (gross) investment, $PSBR$ is the public sector borrowing requirements, and z is a vector of variables to be filled below.

The real interest rate in (12) is the neutral interest rate which we define as the real interest rate that (in a closed economy) makes planned saving at potential output equal to the sum of planned gross investment and the *PSBR*. It is better thought of as a long-term interest rate (Fuhrer and Madigan, 1997). We denote by $\overline{Y}$ the level of potential output or the level of output that keeps inflation constant in a given period in the absence of transitory supply shocks so that inflation will increase (decrease) when $r < r^n$ $(r > r^n)$. If we divide (12) by the capital stock K, denote the net investment rate by g, the rate of depreciation of capital by ψ and make $b = PSBR/Y$, we can rewrite (12) as:

$$(s - b) \cdot \overline{u}(m) \cdot v = g + \psi \tag{13}$$

The 'natural' rate of growth is:

$$g_n = l + a \tag{14}$$

where l and a are respectively the growth rate of labour force L and labour productivity λ. We now turn our attention to functions s and g. We assume that the saving rate s is a function of the rate of inflation π, the rate of growth of output $\hat{y}$, the mark-up m, the real interest rate r and a measure of shocks ε_s or:

$$s = s(\pi, \hat{y}, r, m, \varepsilon_s) \tag{15}$$

where s_π cannot be signed a priori, $s_{\hat{y}} > 0$, $s_r > 0$, $s_m > 0$, ε_s is a stochastic variable denoting shocks to the saving rate, and the subscripts denote the partial derivatives of s. The positive sign of derivative $s_{\hat{y}}$ stems from Marglin's 'disequilibrium hypothesis' (Marglin, 1984), according to which the saving rate increases when income rises faster than households can adapt their spending habits whereas the opposite occurs when income falls faster than households can rein in their spending. The positive sign of s_r is here attributed to the presence of distribution effects. If we assume (realistically) that the average propensity to consume of net debtors is higher than that of net creditors, then a rise in the real interest rate will redistribute income away from net debtors and towards net creditors thereby raising the *aggregate* saving rate. The positive sign of s_m stems from the fact that the average propensity to save out of profit income is typically higher than the propensity to save out of wage income owing to the fact that (i) firms retain a large fraction of their after-tax net profits in order to fund investment spending, and (ii) ownership of corporate stock tends to be concentrated in the upper income brackets which have higher personal saving rates. Hence, s rises with m and, hence with ρ, and vice versa.

The sign of s_π is ambiguous. Neoclassical economists tend to assume that $s_\pi > 0$ due to the operation of a dynamic version of the 'real balance' effect called the inflation tax whereby increases (decreases) in inflation tend to reduce (increase) the holdings of real balances by economic agents thus making them, in turn, increase (reduce) their saving rate in order to restore the optimum amount of real balances. The empirical relevance of the 'real balance' effect, however, has been criticized by some mainstream economists.[16] By contrast, the case $s_\pi < 0$ is advocated by Keynesians who, taking inspiration in chapter 19 of Keynes's *General Theory* (Keynes, 1936), emphasize the presence of 'inside debt' effects which depress private spending when the price level falls, that is, when inflation becomes negative. However, if the case $s_\pi < 0$ is to be sound, this argument must apply also to the case when the inflation rate decreases but remains positive.

The argument can be explained as follows. Pollin (1985) shows that the stability of the total outstanding debt ratio $S_t = q_t(1 + \hat{Y})/\hat{Y}$ of the US economy's non-financial sectors has displayed essentially no trend throughout the post-Second World War period despite a rising marginal propensity of the aggregate non-financial sector to issue net new debt q_t. He argues that, in an inflationary environment, the nominal value of the debt stock remains fixed while the rate of growth of nominal GNP $\hat{Y}$ rises, so that S_t is biased downwards. With q_t, current-period flow values are in both numerator and denominator, and thus the impact of inflation on the ratio is neutral. Because of this asymmetry, a rising q_t may not engender increases in debt burdens in an inflationary environment. However, for a given q_t, a fall in the rate of inflation will increase net borrowers' real debt burden and vice versa. In the case of net borrower households, the reduction in the inflation rate will make them curtail consumption demand. Presumably, this will be coupled by a rise in net lenders' real financial wealth and, hence, by an increase in their consumption. Yet, the marginal propensity to consume out of wealth of net borrowers is higher than that of net lenders so that *aggregate* consumption will fall when inflation falls and vice versa so that $s_\pi < 0$.

Next, let us assume that firms have a desired rate of capacity utilization $u^* < 1$ so they expand actual capacity when $u > u^*$ and scale investment down when $u < u^*$.[17] A justification for this assumption is that firms operating in imperfect markets keep some capacity idle in order to respond rapidly to unanticipated surges in demand and to deter the potential entry of rivals in the industry (Spence, 1977). Following Skott (1989), we also assume that $u^* = u^*(m)$ where $u^*_m < 0$ is the partial derivative of u^* with respect to m. The rationale for $u^*_m < 0$ is that, for a given value of u, the profit rate on capital is a positive function of ρ and, hence, of m. Since the risk of entry in the industry of new rivals increases as the profit rate rises, one way to deter them is to expand idle capacity. These assumptions can be captured by defining the rate of accumulation, g as:

$$g = v \cdot u \cdot f(u - u^*(m), \varepsilon_g) \qquad (16)$$

where $f_u > 0$ is inversely proportional to the length of the capital goods construction and delivery lags, $f(0) = \bar{f} > 0$ and ε_g captures exogenous shocks hitting g. $\bar{f}$ is the ratio of net investment to output when $u = u^*$ and captures firms' average expected future rate of growth of demand. Therefore, it is affected by the state of long-term profit expectations. As for function b, we assume that:

$$b = b(\hat{y}, r, \pi, \varepsilon_b) \qquad (17)$$

where the partial derivatives satisfy $b_{\hat{y}} < 0$, $b_r > 0$, $b_\pi < 0$ and where ε_b are exogenous shocks affecting b. The negative sign of $b_{\hat{y}}$ is due to the working of fiscal automatic stabilizers so its (absolute) value measures the stabilizing power of (non-discretionary) fiscal policy. The sign of b_π is here attributed to the fact that tax income bases may not be fully indexed so that a rise in the inflation rate will tend to reduce *PSBR* and vice versa. By contrast, the positive sign of b_r captures the impact on *PSBR* of changes in the flow of interest payments due to the holders of government debt resulting from variations in real interest rates. Finally, ε_b captures discretionary changes in the stance of fiscal policy. All this allows us to rewrite (13) as:

$$s(\pi, \hat{y}, r^n, m, \varepsilon_s) - b(\hat{y}, r^n, \pi, \varepsilon_b) = f(\bar{u}(m) - u^*(m), \varepsilon_g) + \frac{\psi}{v\bar{u}(m)} \qquad (18)$$

where (18) represents the equilibrium condition in the goods market when $Y = \bar{Y}$.

3.4   Steady-growth analysis

Steady-growth equilibrium corresponds to a period of sufficient length to enable all the variables in the economy to settle at constant rates in the absence of new shocks. In a hypothetical steady-growth position we have that $\varepsilon_s = \varepsilon_g = \varepsilon_b = 0$, $\hat{y} = g_n = g$, $u = \bar{u} = u^*$ and $\pi = \pi^*$ so the following two conditions must be satisfied:

$$v \cdot u^*(m) \cdot \bar{f} = g_n = \hat{y} \tag{19}$$

and

$$[s(\pi^*, g_n, r^*, m) - b(\pi^*, g_n, r^*)] \cdot v \cdot u^*(m) = g_n + \psi \tag{20}$$

where π^* is the inflation target of the CB. Equation (19) tells us that, in steady growth, the rate of accumulation must equal the 'natural' rate of growth. Equation (20) is the counterpart to equation (18) for the steady-growth equilibrium. In order to get a solution for the steady-growth neutral interest rate r^* we assume that functions s and b adopt a linear form or:

$$s = \bar{s} + s_{\hat{y}}\hat{y} + s_\pi\pi + s_r r + s_m m \tag{21}$$

and

$$b = \bar{b} + b_\pi\pi + b_{\hat{y}}\hat{y} + b_r r \tag{22}$$

where $\bar{s}$ is a shift term determined by individuals' preferences, institutional factors and the degree of LP and $\bar{b}$ denotes the stance of fiscal policy. Substituting equations (21) and (22) into (20) and rearranging we arrive at:

$$r^* = \left[\frac{g_n + \psi}{v \cdot u^*(m)} - c_1 - c_{\hat{y}}g_n - c_\pi\pi^* - s_m m \right] \frac{1}{c_r} \tag{23}$$

where $c_1 = \bar{s} - \bar{b}$ and $c_\pi = s_\pi - b_\pi$ cannot be signed a priori, $c_{\hat{y}} = s_{\hat{y}} - b_{\hat{y}} > 0$ and, for the sake of the argument, we assume that $c_r = s_r - b_r > 0$. Thus, r^* depends *inter alia* on the 'natural' rate of growth, the target rate of inflation, the aggregate saving rate, the stance of fiscal policy and the average mark-up, and it can be interpreted as the real interest rate where 'all markets are in equilibrium and there is therefore no pressure for any resources to be redistributed or growth rates for any variables to change' (Archibald and Hunter, 2001, p. 20). Furthermore, r^* also represents the real interest rate that is compatible with a neutral monetary policy in the long run and, therefore, it is akin to the neutral interest rate embedded in Taylor's rule (1993). The steady-growth properties are:

$$\frac{\partial r^*}{\partial \pi^*} = \frac{-c_\pi}{c_r} \lessgtr 0 \tag{24}$$

$$\frac{\partial r^*}{\partial g_n} = \left(\frac{1}{v \cdot u^*} - c_{\hat{y}} \right) \cdot \frac{1}{c_r} > 0 \tag{25}$$

$$\frac{\partial r^*}{\partial b} = -\frac{\partial r^*}{\partial s} = \frac{1}{c_r} > 0 \tag{26}$$

$$\frac{\partial r^*}{\partial m} = \left(\frac{-(g_n + \psi) \cdot u_m^*}{v \cdot u^*(m)^2} - s_m \right) \cdot \frac{1}{c_r} \underset{>}{\overset{<}{=}} 0 \tag{27}$$

The ambiguous sign of (24) stems from the contradictory effects on aggregate demand of a change in the inflation rate. In principle, the sign of (25) is also ambiguous. However, it will be positive and close to unity for reasonable values of the parameters of the model. The positive sign of (26) reflects the fact that an increase in s pushes r^* down whereas an increase in b raises aggregate demand and, hence, r^*. The ambiguous sign of (27) is here attributed to the fact that a change in m, and hence in ρ, affects the accumulation rate and the saving rate with contradictory effects on aggregate demand. Starting with Bhaduri and Marglin (1990), it is common usage to distinguish between a 'wage-led' regime and a 'profit-led' regime. In the former, an increase in the wage share leads to an increase in aggregate demand whereas, in the latter, an increase in the wage share reduces aggregate demand. Thus, we say that the economy is in a 'wage-led' regime if (27) is negative and in a 'profit-led' regime if the opposite holds. In short, the functional distribution of income along with the inflation target, the aggregate saving rate, the 'natural' growth rate and the fiscal policy stance determines r^* and, hence, the likelihood of the occurrence of an aggregate demand deficiency problem (for a given degree of LP). An increase (decrease) in the mark-up when the economy is 'profit-led' ('wage-led') renders it less likely that the economy exhibits an aggregate demand deficiency and vice versa.

3.5 Short-run dynamics

Steady-growth equilibrium is only valid for explaining a hypothetical long-run scenario where the effects of shocks and lags have already worked themselves out. Admittedly, that scenario is unrealistic because an economy is constantly being shocked away from its steady-growth equilibrium. Yet, the steady-growth analysis provides an equilibrium outcome around which the economy hovers in the short run and may offer some insights. Next, we analyse the behaviour of the economy in the short run where the former is defined as the time it takes for the real interest rate to affect inflation. As before, we assume that the investment function f adopts a linear form or:

$$f(u - u^*(m), \varepsilon_g) = \overline{f} + f_u \cdot (u - u^*(m)) \tag{28}$$

Substituting (28) into (18) and re-arranging we obtain the rate of growth of output $\hat{y}$:

$$\hat{y} = \frac{\overline{f} - c_1 - s_m m - c_\pi \pi - c_r r + f_u \cdot (u - u^*(m))}{c_{\hat{y}}} + \frac{\psi}{c_{\hat{y}} vu} \qquad (29)$$

A solution for r^n can be obtained by setting $u = \overline{u}$ in (29) and rearranging:

$$r^n = \frac{\overline{f} - c_1 - s_m m - c_{\hat{y}} \hat{y}(m) - c_\pi \pi + f_u \cdot (\overline{u}(m) - u^*(m)) + \frac{\psi}{v\overline{u}(m)}}{c_r} \qquad (30)$$

so we have that:

$$\frac{\partial r^n}{\partial \overline{u}(m)} = \frac{c_2}{c_r} \overset{<}{\underset{>}{}} 0 \qquad (31)$$

$$\frac{\partial r^n}{\partial m} = \frac{c_2}{c_r} \cdot \overline{u}_m \overset{<}{\underset{>}{}} 0 \qquad (32)$$

where $c_2 = \left(f_u - \frac{\psi}{v\overline{u}(m)^2} \right) \overset{<}{\underset{>}{}} 0$ and $\overline{u}_m < 0$.

First, expression (31) highlights that a change in the CICU has an ambiguous impact upon r^n. This is because, an increase in the CICU and, hence, in $\overline{Y}$, brings about an increase in the flow of private saving at the higher level of output that may or may not be offset by the result-ing higher rate of investment. If $c_2 < 0$, the increase in the flow of saving will not be offset by the higher rate of investment and vice versa. The standard textbook assumption that at the margin private saving is more responsive than investment to changes in capacity utilization for mak-ing the Keynesian income adjustment process stable requires imposing a negative sign on c_2. Second, we may note that the factors that affect r^n differ from the factors affecting r^*. For instance, a change in the func-tional distribution of income affect r^* through a demand-side channel but, as (32) highlights, it affects r^n through a supply-side channel (i.e., by altering $\overline{u}$). This is because demand shocks affect output growth in the short run and, in turn, the latter affects the saving rate so that the initial impact of the demand shock on r^n – but not the corresponding supply shock that occurs through the induced change in $\overline{u}$ – is *fully* offset by the subsequent variation in the saving rate. Since output growth is equal to the 'natural' growth rate in steady growth, the supply-side effect disappears in the long run thus letting the demand shock reappear.

4. Transient dynamics

The next question we address is the stability of the adjustment process to the new equilibrium after being shocked away in an economy described by the model postulated above. We want to make sure, as Joan Robinson would put it, that the fully-adjusted positions can be reached in historical time. If so, this will imply a successful 'traverse' from one path to another (Hicks, 1965, p. 184). To simplify the discussion, we will side-step the problem that the adjustment process may be short-circuited if the zero lower bound constraint binds at any time and will focus instead on the possibility that the new equilibrium may be unstable even when the zero lower bound constraint does not bind. First, we analyse the stability of the long-run equilibrium when the economy exhibits neither hysteresis effects nor AID and, then, we discuss whether and how the previous results are affected when the economy does exhibit these two features.

4.1 Transient dynamics without hysteresis and AID

In this section we show that an economy described by the model expounded above and that is *not* subject to the zero lower bound constraint at any time during the adjustment process successfully reaches a new steady-growth position provided certain conditions are met. This issue is rather technical so we tackle it in detail in Appendix A where we analyse formally the (local) stability of a non-linear dynamic system extracted from the model presented above when the CB sets real interest rates according to the following Taylor-type policy rule:[18]

$$r = r^*(m) + \alpha(\pi - \pi^*) \tag{33}$$

where α is the response coefficient of monetary policy to changes in the inflation gap, i.e., the difference between the actual and the target inflation rate. We show below that, for a wide range of parameter values, equilibrium $P^* = (\pi^*, u^*(m), u^*(m))$ is (locally) stable if the following three conditions are satisfied:

$$\Delta_1 = \frac{f_u u^*(m) - \frac{\psi}{v u^*(m)}}{c_{\hat{y}}} - g_n - v f_u u^{*^2}(m) < 0 \tag{34}$$

$$c_\pi + \alpha c_r > 0 \tag{35}$$

and

$$\left[\frac{-f_u u^{*^2}(m) + u^*(m) c_{\hat{y}} v + (\psi/v) - c_{\hat{y}} f_u v u^{*^3}}{c_{\hat{y}}} \right] > 0 \tag{36}$$

Conditions (34) and (36) are satisfied for the set of parameter values chosen for the simulation exercise (see Table 5.1 below) so the economy will be (locally) stable if:

$$\alpha > \alpha^* = \frac{-c_\pi}{c_r}$$

This means that, if $c_\pi > 0$, then response coefficient α does not need to satisfy Taylor's principle (Taylor, 1993) (i.e., that $\alpha > 0$) to render the economy locally stable. By contrast, if $c_\pi < 0$, satisfying Taylor's principle does not guarantee the stability of the system. Since $b_\pi < 0$ by assumption, the sign of $c_\pi = s_\pi - b_\pi$ depends on the sign and size of s_π as well as on the size of b_π. Therefore, if the CB is to provide a nominal anchor to the economy, then it will have to be more responsive to changes in the actual inflation rate if the Keynesian 'debt' effect dominates ($c_\pi < 0$) than if the neoclassical 'inflation tax' effect prevails ($c_\pi > 0$). In other words, whether the economy exhibits a Keynesian or a neoclassical regime affects α^* but does not have further repercussions on economic stability as long as $\alpha > \alpha^*$ and the zero lower bound does not bind. Moreover, we have that:

$$\frac{\partial \Delta_1}{\partial u^*(m)} = f_u \left(\frac{1}{c_{\hat{y}}} - 2vu^*(m) + \frac{\psi}{vc_{\hat{y}}u^{*2}(m)} \right) \gtrless 0 \qquad (37)$$

$$\frac{\partial \Delta_1}{\partial c_{\hat{y}}} = \frac{1}{c_{\hat{y}}^2} \cdot u^*(m) \cdot \left(\frac{\psi}{v \cdot u^*(m)^2} - f_u \right) \gtrless 0 \qquad (38)$$

Expression (37) tells us that a change in the desired degree of capacity utilization u^* brought about, for instance, by a change in m may, in principle, make P^* locally unstable – if it makes Δ_1 become positive – even though our own calculations based on the parameter values shown in Table 5.1 suggest that the change would have to be extremely large for this to be the case. We may also note that partial derivative s_m does not show up in the stability conditions above. Thus, changes in m and, hence, in the functional distribution of income, cannot undermine the stability of P^*. In turn, this means that whether the economy exhibits a 'wage-led' or a 'profit-led' regime is irrelevant for macroeconomic stability provided the zero lower bound constraint does not bind. However, the distribution regime the economy exhibits remains an important datum since, as noted above, it affects r^* and, hence, the likelihood that an aggregate demand deficiency occurs. Finally, expression (38) is rather similar to expressions (31) and (32). It tells us that, for example, an increase in the stabilizing power of fiscal automatic stabilizers $b_{\hat{y}}$ and, hence, in $c_{\hat{y}}$, apparently has an ambiguous effect on the sign of Δ_1.

Notwithstanding this, if we look at (34), we see that an increase in $c_{\hat{y}}$ actually renders $\Delta_1 \succ 0$ less likely hence reinforcing stability. Thus, as conventional wisdom has it, the more powerful automatic stabilizers are the more stable the economy becomes.

4.2   Transient dynamics with hysteresis and AID

We now address the consequences for macroeconomic stability of the presence of hysteresis effects and AID. To do so, we need to derive three additional equations for simulation purposes. First, the presence of hysteresis effects means that the CIER is now determined by the time path of the employment rate and that, in turn, changes in the CIER affect the CICU as depicted in expression (9). If we take the logarithms in (9) and differentiate it with respect to time we get:

$$\frac{\dot{\bar{u}}(m)}{\bar{u}(m)} = \frac{\dot{\bar{e}}(m)}{\bar{e}(m)} + g_n - g \tag{39}$$

Next, in order to capture the presence of a zero lower bound constraint on nominal interest rates we need to rewrite the expression that depicts the behaviour of the real interest rate. As before, we assume that the CB knows r^* and that it sets (real) interest rates according to policy rule (33) so that:

$$r_t = \begin{cases} \omega_t = \mu - \pi_t & if \quad r^* + \alpha \cdot (\pi_t - \pi^*) \prec \omega_t \\ r^* + \alpha \cdot (\pi_t - \pi^*) & if \quad r^* + \alpha \cdot (\pi_t - \pi^*) \geq \omega_t \end{cases} \tag{40}$$

Therefore, the (long-term) actual real interest rate is determined by a Taylor-type monetary policy rule when the zero bound constraint does not bind or else is equal to the difference between the term/risk premium on long-term rates and the inflation rate. Finally, differentiation of (5) yields equation (42) in Appendix A which describes the dynamics of capacity utilization. Hence, the model we will use for simulation purposes is made up of the following equations: (10), (11), (14), (16), (23), (28), (29), (39), (40) and (42). Simulation results are shown in Figures 5.1 through 5.22 in Appendix B. Table 5.1 contains the parameter values, the initial conditions and the values of the operators describing the stability conditions. Parameter values are justified in Appendix B. Tables 5.2 and 5.3 summarize the different shocks and scenarios considered in each simulation exercise. The second column in Tables 5.2 and 5.3 explains the type of shock analysed in each exercise whereas the third column identifies those parameter values of each exercise that differ from the values reported in Table 5.1.

4.2.1   The impact on macroeconomic volatility

Figures 5.1 through 5.3 show the behaviour of the inflation rate, capacity utilization and the employment rate in the aftermath of an adverse shock to the inflation rate when the economy exhibits neither hysteresis effects nor AID. For the set of parameter values reported in Table 5.1 the economy exhibits self-sustained oscillations. The former are the result of the interplay in a non-linear context of an (unstable) multiplier-accelerator mechanism and the stabilizing behaviour of real interest rates. Figures 5.4 through 5.6 show the time-path of the same variables when the economy exhibits hysteresis effects. The presence of hysteresis dampens oscillations. This is because, when the employment rate decreases, the CIER decreases along with it and this, in turn, cushions the downward pressure on the inflation rate. Conventional wisdom suggests that this 'cushion' effect should weaken rather than reinforce macroeconomic stability because, as inflation decreases, the CB will lower interest rates and this will spur aggregate spending thereby helping to reverse the initial shock. However, the simulation exercise shows that, at least in the context of our model, the presence of hysteresis ameliorates macroeconomic volatility. The simulation exercise also revealed that the higher parameter ζ is the more dampened oscillations become. Further, Figures 5.7 through 5.9 suggest that the presence of AID also tends to dampen oscillations. In short, the presence of hysteresis and AID appears to *reinforce* the stabilizing power of monetary policy.

4.2.2   The impact of shocks to the inflation rate

As is well known, the existence of (unit-root) hysteresis implies that persistent but nevertheless transitory shocks may have permanent effects on the economy. For instance, Figure 5.6 shows that a disinflation process in the wake of an adverse shock that raised the inflation rate above its target ($\pi_0 = 0.035 \succ \pi^*$) imposes on the economy a permanently *lower* employment rate. However, as pointed out, systems exhibiting (unit-root) hysteresis also possess the 'reversibility' property. Following with the previous example, this means that if the economy is subject to a shock of the same intensity but opposite sign (e.g. $\pi_0 = 0.005 \prec \pi^*$), the employment rate now stabilizes at a *higher* level (see Figure 5.16). Importantly, the long-run decrease in the employment rate brought about by the unfavourable shock is equal to the long-run increase brought about by the favourable supply shock.

Next, we address the consequences for unemployment of inflation shocks when the economy exhibits hysteresis effects *and* AID.[19]

In Figure 5.14, the disinflation process brought about by an adverse inflation shock makes the employment rate settle at 0.884 in the long run, well below its initial level at 0.9. By contrast, in the wake of a shock of equal intensity but opposite sign the employment rate stabilizes at 0.908 (see Figure 5.15) so the 'reversibility' property typically exhibited by zero/unit root systems is violated. The existence of a negative bias to the employment rate is confirmed in the stochastic simulation exercise depicted in Figures 5.17 through 5.19. Figure 5.17 shows the time path of the employment rate when the economy is subject to a sequence of random inflation shocks ε_π. The latter were generated by a normal probability distribution of zero mean and standard deviation equal to 0.0096 (see Figure 5.19). In the absence of AID, the employment rate rapidly drops off and converges to zero. Figure 5.18 shows the replication of the exercise when the economy exhibits hysteresis effects and AID. The employment rate now fluctuates around a *decreasing* trend. Therefore, as far as inflation is concerned, the presence of hysteresis effects and AID reinforces macroeconomic stability, *blocks off* the 'reversibility' property and, crucially, it imparts a long-term *negative* bias on the employment rate in the sense that, if the economy is initially at equilibrium and is subjected to a unfavourable supply shock that raises the inflation rate and this is subsequently followed by a second shock of the same intensity but in the opposite direction then the employment rate does not return to the initial equilibrium but stabilizes at a *lower* level.

4.2.3 *The impact of demand shocks*

We now investigate the long-run effect on the employment rate of demand shocks when the CIER exhibits hysteresis effects. This affects shocks associated to changes in the functional distribution of income as well as to shocks associated to changes in the private saving rate and fiscal policy. The presence of an inflation-targeting CB implies that the short-run impact of a demand shock will be, at least partially, *offset by changes in real interest rates*. This is because the demand shock affects r^* and, if the CB periodically updates its estimate of r^*, the impact on AD is offset by a change in the real interest rate.[20] For instance, if the CB sets interest rates according to a Taylor-type policy rule like (35) then, a rise (fall) in m when the economy is 'profit-led' ('wage-led') (i.e., a favourable demand shock) prompts an upward revision of r^* and, hence, an increase in the actual real interest rate. Figures 5.10 and 5.11 depict the long-run impact on the employment rate of an increase and a decrease in m respectively when the economy is 'profit-led'. In the former case, the increase in m leads to a decrease in u^* that stimulates investment spending and, hence, to an increase in r^* whereas, in the latter case, the opposite holds.[21] The simulation exercise confirmed that, in the absence of AID, shocks do *not* affect the employment rate in the long run. In particular, demand shocks determine the time path of the employment rate but do not affect the level at which it settles in the long run which is equal to the initial (supply-determined) one.

Next, we analyse how the previous results vary when there is both hysteresis effects and AID. Figure 5.12 shows the case of a favourable demand shock whereas Figure 5.13 shows the case of an unfavourable one. In both cases, the employment rate settles below its initial level at 0.9, albeit the long-term decrease is clearly more marked when the shock is unfavourable. Therefore, the presence of AID makes demand shocks have an *adverse* long-term impact on the employment rate even when they are expansionary. This is confirmed in the stochastic simulation exercise depicted in Figures 5.20 through 5.22. As with inflation shocks, we subject the aggregate saving rate to random shocks ε_s drawn from a normal probability distribution of zero mean and standard deviation equal to 0.0084 (see Figure 5.22). Figure 5.20 shows the time path of the employment rate when the economy (only) exhibits hysteresis effects whereas Figure 5.21 shows its time path when the economy exhibits hysteresis effects and AID. In the former case, the employment rate hovers in the short run around a *stationary* trend whereas, in the latter case, the employment rate exhibits a *declining* trend. In short, demand shocks are neutralized by changes in real interest rates induced by the CB so they do affect the employment rate in the short run but do not affect it in the long run unless the economy exhibits AID; in this latter case they affect it adversely even when shocks are expansionary.

To finish off this section let us recall that a change in m gives rise to a short-run change in the actual inflation rate, a permanent demand shock (of ambiguous sign), and an initial supply shock represented by a change in the CIER. The upshot of the previous discussion was that, if the economy exhibits hysteresis effects and AID, the interaction of short-run changes in the inflation rate and demand shocks will lead to a lower employment rate in the long run. To these effects, we need to add the initial favourable (unfavourable) supply shock when m decreases (increases) which will bring about an increase (decrease) in the CIER. If m increases, the (initial) reduction in the CIER will exacerbate the long-run negative bias imparted on the employment rate by the two previous effects. By contrast, if m decreases, the net long-run effect on the employment rate becomes uncertain and depends on the relative strength of the three separate effects.

5. Summary and conclusion

In this study we analysed the long-run impact on the employment rate of a change in the degree of monopoly power as measured by the average mark-up in an economy characterized by the existence of (i) a short-run 'inflation barrier' referred to as the 'constant inflation employment rate' (CIER) that may exhibit hysteresis effects, (ii) a central bank (CB) that sets interest rates in order to hit an inflation target and (iii) the presence of 'asymmetric inflation dynamics' (AID) put down to the existence of downward money wage rigidity. For that purpose, we postulated a macroeconomic model for a closed economy with a government sector that incorporates the above-mentioned features. We identified three different effects of a change in the average mark-up: (i) a permanent change in the level of aggregate demand stemming from a change in the functional distribution of income, (ii) an initial change in the CIER and (iii) a short-run variation in the inflation rate.

We obtained several results. First, we found that, in an economy characterized by the above features except AID, a change in the mark-up only affects the employment rate in the long run insofar as the former initially affects the CIER and the inflation rate. In particular, an increase in the average mark-up leads to a decrease in the employment rate and vice versa. We argued that this occurs because the permanent demand shock brought about by the change in the functional distribution of income leads to a change in the steady-growth neutral interest rate and this, in turn, is passed through into the actual real interest rate by virtue of the monetary policy rule of the CB. Thus, in this scenario a change in the mark up only leads to a long-run increase in the employment rate when it contracts.

Second, we showed that, when the economy also exhibits AID, a change in the average mark-up is less effective and may even be counter-productive. This is because the long-run impact on the employment rate of the demand shock, even when it is expansionary, is adverse. Therefore, in this second scenario, an increase in the average mark-up, even when coupled by an expansionary demand shock, always leads to a long-run decrease in the employment rate. Further, a decrease in the mark-up only brings about a long-run increase in the employment rate if the net adverse effect of the permanent demand shock (even if it is expansionary) is more than offset by the sum of the favourable effects stemming from the initial reduction in the inflation rate and the rise in the CIER. More generally, we showed by means of a sequence of simulation exercises that the joint presence of hysteresis and AID in the type of economy sketched above (i) attenuates macroeconomic volatility and (ii) blocks off the 'reversibility' property exhibited by zero/unit root systems in the wake of inflation shocks. Third, we found that, whether the economy exhibits a 'wage-led' or a 'profit-led' macroeconomic regime is irrelevant for macroeconomic performance as long as the economy does not exhibit an aggregate demand deficiency problem.

Fourth, we argued that, despite the importance of the above results, this does not mean that changes in the functional distribution of income may not affect macroeconomic performance favourably. In this respect, we showed that the functional distribution of income affects the neutral interest rate in the short run and in the long run and, thus, it affects the probability that the economy exhibits an aggregate demand deficiency. We then argued that, although proponents of the NC approach may eventually accept that the functional distribution of income is one potential factor affecting aggregate demand and, hence, the neutral interest rate, they nevertheless reject the notion that it affects the steady-growth neutral interest rate since they assume that the latter is mainly determined by the (positive) rate of time preference of the representative household and the 'natural' growth rate. As a result of this, they fail to perceive the potentially beneficial impact of the functional distribution of income on macroeconomic performance. We then argued that liquidity preference theory precludes the existence of a positive lower threshold to the steady-growth neutral interest rate and this, in turn, implies that factors such as the fiscal policy stance, the functional distribution of income, and the degree of liquidity preference are determinants of macroeconomic performance.

Lastly, we distinguished between a Keynesian regime and a neoclassical regime according to whether an increase in the inflation rate leads to an increase (Keynesian) or to a decrease (neoclassical) in the neutral interest rate and showed that the regime the economy exhibits determines the condition that the monetary policy rule of the CB must satisfy to provide a nominal anchor to the economy. A corollary of our analysis was that Taylor's principle may not hold when changes in the inflation rate affect aggregate demand directly.

Appendix A

This appendix deals with the computation of the equilibrium points and stability conditions of the dynamical system that results from the economic model postulated in section 3. For the sake of the argument, we make a number of simplifying assumptions. First, we assume that the CB knows r^*. Second, we impose the conditions $\phi_U = \phi_L$ and $\overline{f} = (g_n/v \cdot u^*(m))$. The former means that we assume the economy does not exhibit AID whereas the latter means that firms' output growth expectations are firmly anchored to its secular growth rate so we remove any instability that may result from changes in firms' profit expectations. Admittedly, this provides the economy with a built-in stabilizing mechanism but it certainly makes the system much easier to handle. Third, we assume that r^* is positive and high enough so as to make the zero lower bound not bind. Finally, the analysis focuses on the *local* stability of the economy. Taking these limitations into account, we have that:

$$\frac{\dot{u}}{u} = \hat{y} - g \tag{41}$$

and substituting (16), (28), (29) and (33) into (41) yields:

$$\dot{u} = h(u, \pi) \tag{42}$$

Next, if we assume that $\zeta = 0$ (i.e., the CIER does not exhibit hysteresis), we can rewrite (39) as:

$$\dot{\overline{u}} = \overline{u} \cdot (g_n - g) \tag{43}$$

and substituting (28) into (16) and then into (43) yields:

$$\dot{\overline{u}} = \overline{u} \cdot [g_n - v \cdot u \cdot (\overline{f} + f_u \cdot (u - u^*(m))] \tag{44}$$

Therefore, our dynamical system is made up of equations (10) (with $\phi_U = \phi_L$), (42) and (44), so we may obtain the singular points by setting $\dot{\pi} = \dot{u} = \dot{\overline{u}} = 0$ which yields two singular points:

$$u^*_{1,2} = \frac{\overline{f}v - vf_u u^*(m) \pm \sqrt{(-\overline{f}v + vf_u u^*(m))^2 + 4vf_u g_n}}{-2vf_u}$$

and

$$\pi^*_{1,2} = \frac{\overline{f} - c_1 + f_u(u - u^*(m)) - c_r r^* + c_r \alpha \pi^* + \frac{\psi}{vu^*(m)} - c_{\hat{y}} v \overline{f} u^*(m) \atop -c_{\hat{y}} v f_u u^{*^2}(m) + c_{\hat{y}} v f_u u^{*^2}(m)}{c_\pi + c_r \alpha}$$

where the only one with economic meaning is:

$$P^* = (\pi^*, u^*(m), u^*(m))$$

Next, a *necessary* and *sufficient* condition for local stability is:[22]

$$\Delta_1 = \lambda_1 + \lambda_2 + \lambda_3 = 2\delta + \lambda_3 \prec 0 \tag{45}$$

$$\Delta_2 = \lambda_1 \cdot \lambda_2 \cdot \lambda_3 = (\delta^2 + \beta^2) \cdot \lambda_3 \prec 0 \tag{46}$$

$$\Delta_3 = \lambda_1\lambda_2 + \lambda_1\lambda_3 + \lambda_2\lambda_3 = \delta^2 + \beta^2 + 2\delta\lambda_3 \succ 0 \tag{47}$$

and by Orlando's formula (see Gantmacher, 1954, p. 197):

$$\Delta_4 = -(\lambda_1 + \lambda_2)(\lambda_1 + \lambda_3)(\lambda_2 + \lambda_3) = -2\delta(\delta^2 + \beta^2 + 2\delta\lambda_3 + \lambda_3^2) \succ 0 \tag{48}$$

where the λs are the eigenvalues of the (linearized) dynamical system, δ is the real part of the complex conjugate eigenvalues, $\Delta_1 = Tr(J)$, $\Delta_2 = Det(J)$, $\Delta_3 = J_{11} + J_{22} + J_{33}$, $\Delta_4 = -\Delta_1\Delta_3 + \Delta_2$ and J is the Jacobian matrix of the linearized system. In turn, the J_{ii} are the principal minors (of order 2) of J, i.e., the determinants of the matrices that are obtained after deleting the ith row and the ith column. Thus, a *necessary* and *sufficient* condition for the non-linear system made up of equations (10), (42) and (44) to be locally asymptotically stable is:

$$\Delta_1 = \frac{f_u u^*(m) - \frac{\psi}{v u^*(m)}}{c_{\hat{y}}} - g_n - v f_u u^{*2}(m) \prec 0 \tag{49}$$

$$\Delta_2 = \frac{(c_\pi + \alpha c_r) \cdot u^*(m)\phi}{c_{\hat{y}}} \cdot (-g_n - v f_u u^{*2}(m)) \prec 0 \tag{50}$$

$$\Delta_3 = \frac{(c_\pi + \alpha c_r)\phi u^*(m)}{c_{\hat{y}}} \succ 0 \tag{51}$$

and $\quad \Delta_4 = \frac{(c_\pi + c_r\alpha)\phi}{c_{\hat{y}}}\left[\frac{-f_u u^{*2}(m) + u^*(m)c_{\hat{y}}v + (\psi/v) - c_{\hat{y}}f_u v u^{*3}}{c_{\hat{y}}}\right] \succ 0$

$$\tag{52}$$

As a result of this, the stability of the system requires that conditions $c_\pi + \alpha c_r \succ 0$, $\Delta_1 \prec 0$ and $\Delta_4 \succ 0$ be satisfied. Furthermore, there exists a value α^* of the response coefficient of the monetary policy rule of the CB for which the local stability of the system changes dramatically. We may obtain α^* by setting $\Delta_4 = 0$:

$$\alpha^* = \frac{-c_\pi}{c_r} \overset{\succ}{\underset{\prec}{}} 0$$

so the system will be unstable if $\alpha \prec \alpha^*$ and vice versa.

Appendix B

The simulation exercise was aimed at exploring the implications of the existence of hysteresis and AID. Table 5.1 reports the values of the parameters of the model, including r^* and $\overline{f}$, and the initial conditions whereas Tables 5.2 and 5.3 report the values of those parameters and initial conditions whose values may differ in successive simulation exercises from those reported in Table 5.1. The parameters and initial conditions responsible for the single shock are underlined. For the sake of convenience, we assume that $s_m = \overline{u}_m = 0$. The values of the parameters were chosen according to the values typically reported in the literature. For instance, the inflation target for many CBs is 2 per cent. The literature usually reports that the technical output-capital ratio v is about 0.3. Studies for the US economy suggest that the CICU is about 82 per cent (see Garner, 1994 and Corrado and Mattey, 1997) and the value assigned to ϕ_U stems from results in McElhattan (1985) who finds that, for each percentage point that capacity utilization exceeds 82 per cent, inflation accelerates by about 0.15 percentage points. As for π^{CR}, we follow Akerlof et al. (1996) and assume that the presence of DMWR starts to bite when the actual inflation rate is less than 3 per cent. This implies that, if $\phi_\pi = 4$ and $\phi_U = 0.15$, the inflation rate ceases to decrease when it is equal to -0.0075, which is roughly the level at which the Japanese inflation rate settled after 1998. Next, the resulting value for the short-term real interest rate – taking into account that r^* is a long-term interest rate and so we need to subtract the term premium to obtain the former – is roughly the value of the *real* federal funds rate over the 1960–98 period in the US: 2.55 per cent (Reifschneider and Williams, 2000, p. 950). As for the parameters in the saving and investment function, we set them so as to render the economy stable and, as mentioned above, we set $\overline{f}$ equal to its steady-growth value to make the model easier to handle. The standard deviation of the normal distributions used to generate a set of random inflation and demand shocks were taken from Orphanides and Wieland (2000, p. 1373) who estimate a three-equations NC-type model for the Euro Area for the period 1976–98 and report a standard deviation of inflation and demand shocks equal to 0.96 and 0.84 per cent respectively. Finally, the subscripts of the variables in Table 5.1 denote the values that the parameters adopt in different simulation exercises.

Table 5.1 Parameter values, initial conditions and operators

$f_{u,0}=0.015$	$c_r=2.5$	$\zeta_2=0.3$	$u^*=u_0=\bar{u}_0=0.8$	$g_n=0.03$
$f_{u,1}=0.3$	$c_\pi=-0.1$	$s_m=\bar{u}_m=0$	$\alpha^*=0.04\ \alpha=0.5$	$\partial r^*/\partial g_n=1.06$
$\pi^*=0.02$	$\pi_0^{CR}=\phi_{\pi,0}=0$	$\pi_1^{CR}=0.03$	$e_0=\bar{e}_0=0.9$	$\Delta_1=-0.12210$
$c_1=0.14$	$\phi_U=0.15$	$\phi_{\pi,1}=4$	$v=0.3$	$\Delta_2=-0.00302$
$c_2=-0.03$	$\zeta_0=0$	$\bar{f}=0.125$	$\psi=0.035$	$\Delta_3=0.092$
$c_{\hat{y}}=1.5$	$\zeta_1=0.1$	$\mu=0.01$	$r^*=0.035$	$\Delta_4=0.029957$

Table 5.2 Summary of parameter values and initial conditions in the simulation exercises with a single shock

Figure	Single shock	Parameter values (when they differ from those reported in Table 5.1)
5.1	Unfavourable inflation shock	Absence of hysteresis and AID: $\pi_0=0.035$
5.2	Unfavourable inflation shock	Absence of hysteresis and AID: $\pi_0=0.035$
5.3	Unfavourable inflation shock	Absence of hysteresis and AID: $\pi_0=0.035$
5.4	Unfavourable inflation shock	Hysteresis, no AID: $\pi_0=0.035$ and $\zeta_1=0.1$
5.5	Unfavourable inflation shock	Hysteresis, no AID: $\pi_0=0.035$ and $\zeta_1=0.1$
5.6	Unfavourable inflation shock	Hysteresis, no AID: $\pi_0=0.035$ and $\zeta_1=0.1$
5.7	Unfavourable inflation shock	AID, no hysteresis: $\pi_0=0.035$, $\pi_1^{CR}=0.03$ and $\phi_{\pi,1}=4$
5.8	Unfavourable inflation shock	AID, no hysteresis: $\pi_0=0.035$, $\pi_1^{CR}=0.03$ and $\phi_{\pi,1}=4$
5.9	Unfavourable inflation shock	AID, no hysteresis: $\pi_0=0.035$, $\pi_1^{CR}=0.03$ and $\phi_{\pi,1}=4$
5.10	Expansionary demand shock	Hysteresis, no AID: $u^*=0.75$, $f_{u,1}=0.3$, $\pi_0=0.02$ and $\zeta_2=0.3$
5.11	Contractionary demand shock	Hysteresis, no AID: $u^*=0.85$, $f_{u,1}=0.3$, $\pi_0=0.02$ and $\zeta_2=0.3$
5.12	Expansionary demand shock	Hysteresis and AID: $u^*=0.75$, $f_{u,1}=0.3$, $\pi_0=0.02$, $\pi_1^{CR}=0.03$, $\phi_{\pi,1}=4$ and $\zeta_2=0.3$
5.13	Contractionary demand shock	Hysteresis and AID: $u^*=0.85$, $f_{u,1}=0.3$, $\pi_0=0.02$, $\pi_1^{CR}=0.03$, $\phi_{\pi,1}=4$ and $\zeta_2=0.3$
5.14	Unfavourable inflation shock	Hysteresis and AID: $\pi_0=0.035$, $\pi_1^{CR}=0.03$, $\phi_{\pi,1}=4$ and $\zeta_1=0.1$
5.15	Favourable inflation shock	Hysteresis and AID: $\pi_0=0.005$, $\pi_1^{CR}=0.03$, $\phi_{\pi,1}=4$ and $\zeta_1=0.1$
5.16	Favourable inflation shock	Hysteresis, no AID: $\pi_0=0.005$ and $\zeta_1=0.1$

Note: The parameters underlined in the third column are the ones that trigger the shock

Table 5.3 Summary of parameter values and initial conditions in the simulation exercises with a stochastic sequence of shocks

Figure	Shocks	Parameter values (when they differ from those reported in Table 5.1)
5.17	Stochastic inflation shocks	Hysteresis, no AID: $\pi_0 = 0.02$ and $\zeta_2 = 0.3$
5.18	Stochastic inflation shocks	Hysteresis and AID: $\pi_0 = 0.02$, $\pi_1^{CR} = 0.03$, $\phi_{\pi,1} = 4$ and $\zeta_1 = 0.1$
5.19	Stochastic inflation shocks	Drawn from a normal distribution
5.20	Stochastic demand shocks	Hysteresis, no AID: $\pi_0 = 0.02$ and $\zeta_1 = 0.1$
5.21	Stochastic demand shocks	Hysteresis and AID: $\pi_0 = 0.02$, $\pi_1^{CR} = 0.03$, $\phi_{\pi,1} = 4$ and $\zeta_1 = 0.1$
5.22	Stochastic shocks to the saving rate	Drawn from a normal distribution

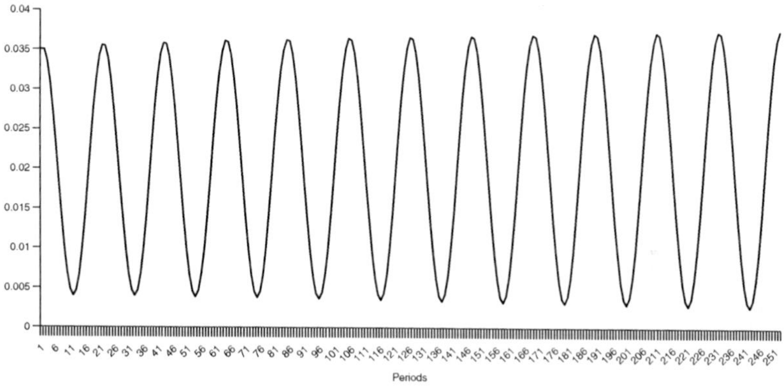

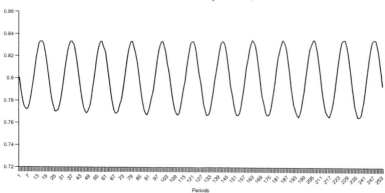

Figure 5.1 Inflation rate (neither AID nor hysteresis)

Figure 5.2 Capacity utilization (neither AID nor hysteresis)

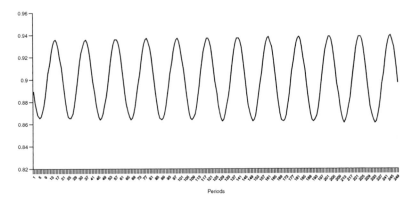

Figure 5.3   Employment rate (neither AID nor hysteresis)

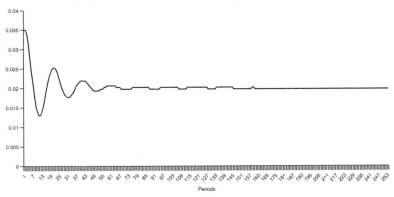

Figure 5.4   Inflation rate (hysteresis, no AID)

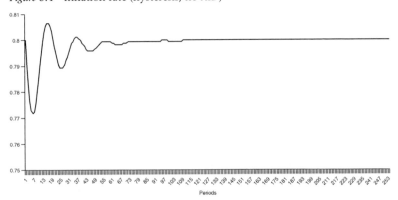

Figure 5.5   Capacity utilization (hysteresis, no AID)

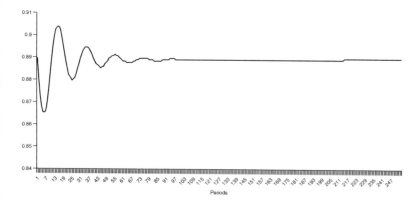

Figure 5.6 Employment rate (hysteresis, no AID)

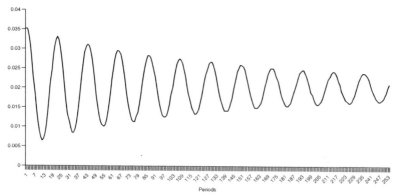

Figure 5.7 Inflation rate (AID, no hysteresis)

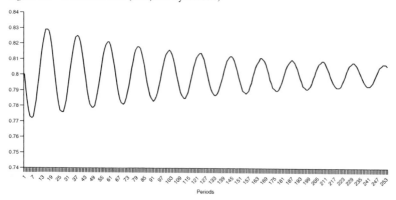

Figure 5.8 Capacity utilization (AID, no hysteresis)

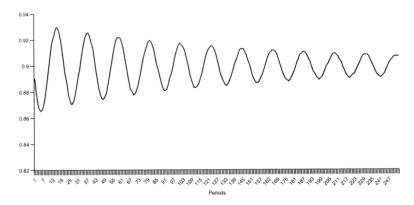

Figure 5.9 Employment rate (AID, no hysteresis)

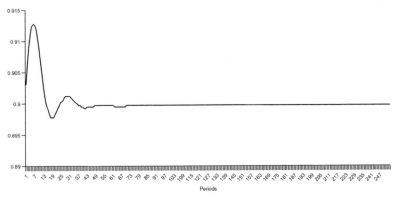

Figure 5.10 Employment rate (hysteresis, no AID)

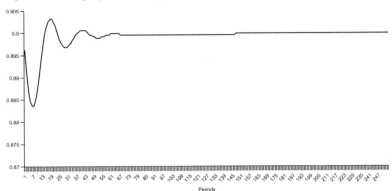

Figure 5.11 Employment rate (hysteresis, no AID)

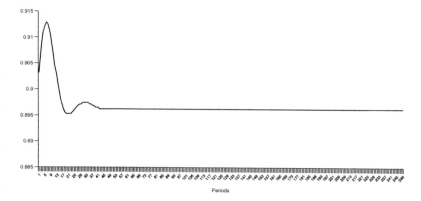

Figure 5.12 Employment rate (hysteresis and AID)

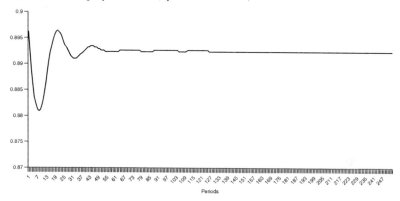

Figure 5.13 Employment rate (hysteresis and AID)

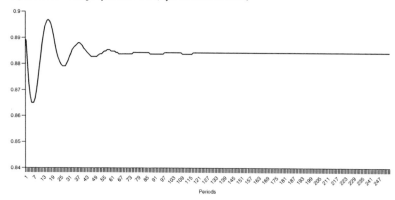

Figure 5.14 Employment rate (hysteresis and AID)

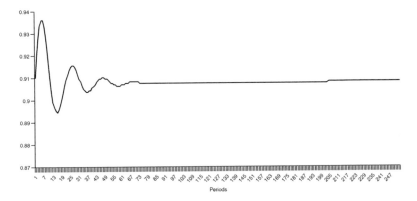

Figure 5.15   Employment rate (hysteresis and AID)

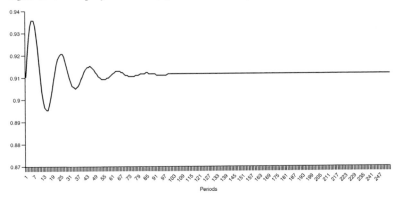

Figure 5.16   Employment rate (hysteresis, no AID)

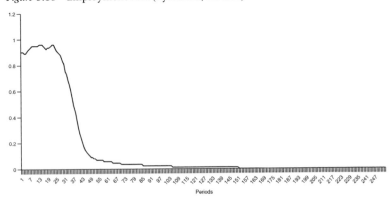

Figure 5.17   Employment rate in the wake of stochastic inflation shocks (hysteresis, no AID)

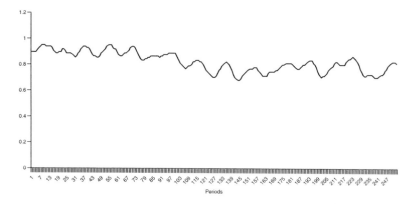

Figure 5.18 Employment rate in the wake of stochastic inflation shocks (hysteresis and AID)

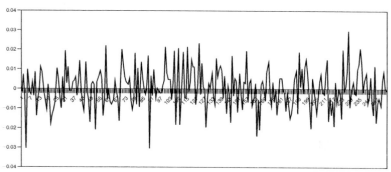

Figure 5.19 Stochastic inflation shocks

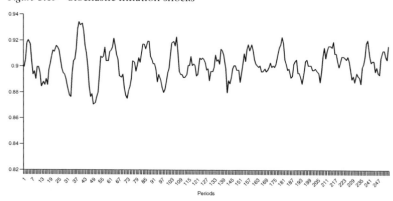

Figure 5.20 Employment rate in the wake of stochastic demand shocks (hysteresis, no AID)

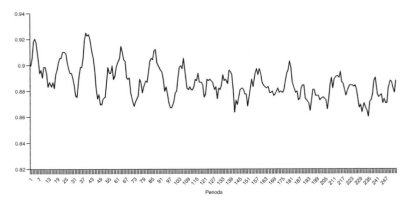

Figure 5.21   Employment rate in the wake of stochastic demand shocks (hysteresis and AID)

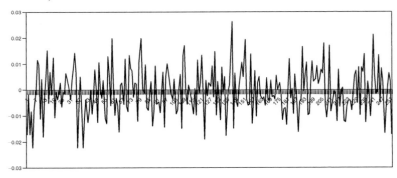

Figure 5.22   Stochastic demand shocks

Notes

*   The author would like to thank Engelbert Stockhammer as well as the participants in the 5th International Conference 'Developments in Economic Theory and Policy', held at the University of the Basque Country in Bilbao (Spain) in July 2008, for their comments and suggestions on a previous draft of this chapter. Of course, the usual disclaimer applies.

1.   Examples of the rapidly growing empirical literature on this topic are the studies by Bowles and Boyer (1995), Gordon (1995), Hein and Ochsen (2003), Stockhammer and Onaran (2004), Naastepad (2006), Naastepad and Storm (2006/7), Hein and Vogel (2007) and Stockhammer et al. (2007).

2.   Detailed expositions of the NC approach can be found in Clarida et al. (1999) and Meyer (2001) and two recent critical reviews are in Arestis and Sawyer (2006, 2008).

3.   In this respect, Krugman (1998) argues that the negative output-gap the Japanese economy exhibited in the late 1990s was largely underestimated

in official statistics. He adds that it could have been as large as 8 per cent of GDP and it may have grown much larger since 1998.

4. For instance, Mourougane and Ibaragi (2004) estimate Phillips curves for Japan and find evidence that at low or negative inflation rates, indicators of demand pressure have no statistically significant effect on price inflation.

5. Of course, current output may also fall short of potential output if the CB purposely sets the real interest rate above the neutral real interest rate in order to trigger a disinflation process. Thus, by an aggregate demand deficiency we mean a situation where the CB *cannot* make current output equal to potential even if the short-term nominal interest rate is equal to zero.

6. This definition of the *neutral* interest rate differs from Keynes's (1936, p. 243) in that he views the former as the long-term interest rate that yields full employment whereas we define it as the long-term interest rate that yields an employment rate that keeps inflation constant.

7. We thus believe, as Keynes (1936, p. 173), that between monetary policy and economic activity 'there may be several slips between the cup and the lip'.

8. For this particular example we assume 'constant relative risk aversion' preferences of the representative household and that the utility of each future generation is weighted equally irrespective of size.

9. The classical presentation of the notion of the natural interest rate is in Wicksell (1936[1898]).

10. This third meaning is emphasized in Cassel (1928).

11. This feature of PK theory is emphasized in Stockhammer (2007). He notes that 'as a theory of inflation the NAIRU model resembles the conflict inflation theory of Post Keynesian origin. This theory...reflects Post Keynesians' long-standing conviction that inflation is the outcome of distributional conflict (and not excessive growth in the money supply) and thus has to be combated through incomes policies' (Stockhammer, 2008, p. 495).

12. The non-accelerating inflation rate of unemployment or NAIRU is hence equal to $1 - \bar{e}$. In this study, we assume that the CIER is equivalent to the notion of 'equilibrium unemployment'. The latter refers to a rate of unemployment that is determined at the intersection of a price-setting function and an upward-sloping wage-setting function in real wage-employment space. Admittedly, a substantive difference between these two concepts is that the NAIRU is typically defined as a situation where the rate of inflation is constant, whereas the only requirement of the concept of 'equilibrium unemployment' is that real wages are constant (when there is no productivity growth) or else grow at the same pace than productivity. Yet, the two approaches can be reconciled by grafting money wage and price dynamics onto the static approach (see Lindbeck, 1993, Appendix B).

13. In terms of the concept of 'equilibrium unemployment' alluded to above, a rise in *m* will lead to a leftward shift in the price-setting curve and, hence, to a higher rate of 'equilibrium unemployment'.

14. Evidence for AID is provided in Peltzman (2000). Unlike in a perfectly competitive economy, in an imperfectly competitive one the price-setting curve may not be negatively-sloped so that, for the relevant range of the curve, there may be a neutral or even a positive relationship between the employment rate and the real (product) wage. The former implies that, in the presence of DMWR, an increase in the real (product) wage paid by the firms once the

actual inflation rate is low or negative may not necessarily result in a higher level of 'equilibrium unemployment'.

15. Hence, the long-term real interest rate exhibits an upper bound equal to $\mu - (\phi_\pi \pi^{CR} - \phi_U)/\phi_\pi$ whenever the short-term nominal interest rate is zero and the inflation rate becomes negative.

16. A pertinent rebuttal to the official position is in Greenwald and Stiglitz (1993) who, referring to the 'real balance' effect, point out that 'quantitatively, it is surely an nth order effect; one calculation put it that, even at the fastest rate at which prices fell in the Great Depression, it would take more than two centuries to restore the economy to full employment. And in the short run even its sign is ambiguous, as inter-temporal substitution effects may (depending on expectations) more than offset the wealth effects' (Greenwald and Stiglitz, 1993, p.36).

17. In general, an asterisk denotes the steady-growth value of the variable. However, in the case of u its steady-growth value coincides with the desired rate of capacity utilization. Likewise, the target inflation rate coincides with the steady-growth value of the inflation rate.

18. An interest rate policy rule like this one can be easily derived from a loss function according to which the CB seeks to minimize the deviation of the actual inflation rate and actual level of output from their respective target levels (see, for instance, Carlin and Soskice, 2005).

19. Henceforth, an 'inflation shock' is a shock to the inflation rate that does not affect the CIER.

20. In this study we assume that the CB estimates the steady-growth neutral interest rate correctly in order to frame our results in the most favourable scenario for the implementation of monetary policy decisions. Of course, we readily admit that any CB faces enormous practical difficulties when estimating it (see, for instance, Weber et al., 2008).

21. Let us note that, for the sake of simplicity, we assume that $s_m = 0$.

22. See the Routh-Hurwitz conditions for the stability of dynamical systems in Gandolfo (1997, pp. 219–23).

References

Agell, J. and Lundburg, P. (2003), 'Survey Evidence on Wage Rigidity: Sweden in the 1990s', *Scandinavian Journal of Economics*, 105(1), pp. 15–29.

Akerlof, G.A. (2007), 'The Missing Motivation in Macroeconomics', *American Economics Review*, 97(1), pp. 5–36.

Akerlof, G.A., Dickens, W.T. and Perry, G.L. (1996), 'The Macroeconomics of Low Inflation', *Brookings Papers in Economic Activity*, 1, pp. 1–59.

Amable, B. Henry, J., Lordon, F. and Topol, R. (1995), 'Hysteresis revisited: A methodological approach', in Cross, R. (ed.) *The Natural Rate of Unemployment: Reflections on 25 Years of the Hypothesis*, Cambridge: Cambridge University Press, pp. 153–79.

Archibald, J. and Hunter, L. (2001), 'What is the Neutral Real Interest Rate, and How Can We Use It?', *Reserve Bank of New Zealand Bulletin*, 64(3), pp. 15–28.

Arestis, P. and Sawyer, M.C. (2006), 'The Nature and Role of Monetary Policy when Money is Endogenous', *Cambridge Journal of Economics*, 30(6), pp. 847–60.

Arestis, P. and Sawyer, M.C. (2008), 'A critical reconsideration of the foundations of monetary policy in the new consensus macroeconomic framework', *Cambridge Journal of Economics*, 32(5), pp. 761–79.

Asimakopulos, A. (1975), 'A Kaleckian Theory of Income Distribution', *Canadian Journal of Economics*, 8(3), August, pp. 313–33.

Ball, L. (1999), 'Aggregate Demand and Long-Run Unemployment', *Brookings Papers on Economic Activity*, 2, pp. 189–236.

Bernanke, B.S. and Reinhart, V.R. (2004), 'Conducting Monetary Policy at Very Low Short-term Interest Rates', *American Economic Review*, Papers and Proceedings, 94(2), May, pp. 85–90.

Bewley, T.F. (1999), *Why Wages Do Not Fall During a Recession?*, Cambridge, MA: Harvard University Press.

Bhaduri, A. and Marglin, S. (1990), 'Unemployment and the Real Wage: The Economic Basis for Contesting Political Ideologies', *Cambridge Journal of Economics*, 14, pp. 375–93.

Blinder, A.S. (2000), 'Monetary Policy at the Zero Lower Bound: Balancing the Risks', *Journal of Money, Credit and Banking*, 32(4), November, pp. 1093–9.

Blinder, A.S. (2006), ,Monetary Policy Today: Sixteen Questions and about Twelve Answers, *CEPS Working Paper* No. 129, July.

Bowles, S. and Boyer, R. (1995), 'Wages, aggregate demand, and employment in an open economy: An empirical investigation', in G. Epstein and H. Gintis (eds) *Macroeconomic Policy after the Conservative Era: Studies in Investment, Saving and Finance,* Cambridge: Cambridge University Press.

Card, D. and Hyslop, D. (1996), 'Does Inflation "Grease the Wheels" of the Labor Market?', *NBER, Working Paper* 5538.

Carlin, W. and Soskice, D. (2005), 'The 3-Equation New Keynesian Model – A Graphical Exposition', *Contributions to Macroeconomics*, 5(1), Article 13.

Cassel, G. (1928), 'The Rate of Interest, the Bank Rate, and the Stabilization of Prices', *Quarterly Journal of Economics*, 42(4), August, pp. 511–29.

Clarida, R., Galí, J. and Gertler, M. (1999), 'The Science of Monetary Policy: A New Keynesian Perspective', *Journal of Economic Literature*, 37, December, pp. 1661–707.

Corrado, C. and Mattey, J. (1997), 'Capacity Utilization', *Journal of Economic Perspectives*, 11(1), Winter, pp. 151–67.

Davidson, P. (1991), 'Is Probability Theory Relevant for Uncertainty? A Post Keynesian Perspective', *Journal of Economic Perspectives*, 5(1), pp. 129–43.

De Veirman, E. (2007), 'Which Nonlinearity in the Phillips Curve? The Absence of Accelerating Deflation in Japan', *Reserve Bank of New Zealand Discussion Paper Series* no. 2007/14.

Dutt, A.K. (1997), 'Equilibrium, Path Dependence and Hysteresis in Post-Keynesian Models', in P. Arestis, G. Palma and M.C. Sawyer (eds), *Capital Controversy, Post Keynesian Economics and the History of Economic Thought: Essays in Honour of Geoff Harcourt*, pp. 238–53, London: Routledge.

Fehr, E. and Lorenz, G. (2005), 'The Robustness and Real Consequences of Nominal Wage Rigidity', *Journal of Monetary Economics*, 52(4), pp. 779–804.

Fontana, G. and Palacio-Vera, A. (2007), 'Are Long-run Price Stability and Short-run Output Stabilization All that Monetary Policy Can Aim For?', *Metroeconomica*, 58(2), pp. 269–98.

Fuhrer, J.C. and Madigan, B.F. (1997), 'Monetary Policy when Interest Rates Are Bounded at Zero', *Review of Economics and Statistics*, 79(4), November, pp. 573–85.

Gandolfo, G. (1997), *Economic Dynamics*, Berlin: Springer-Verlag.

Gantmacher, F.R. (1954), *Theory of Matrices*, Interscience Publishers, New York.

Garner, A. (1994), 'Capacity Utilization and U.S. Inflation', *Federal Reserve Bank of Kansas City*, Fourth Quarter, pp. 5–21.

Giavazzi, F. and Wyplosz, C. (1985), 'The Zero Root Problem: A Note on the Dynamic Determination of the Stationary Equilibrium in Linear Models', *Review of Economic Studies*, 52(2), pp. 353–7.

Gordon, D. (1995), 'Putting the horse (back) before the cart: disentangling the macro relationship between investment and saving', in G. Epstein and H. Gintis (eds) *Macroeconomic Policy after the Conservative Era: Studies in Investment, Saving and Finance*, Cambridge: Cambridge University Press.

Greenwald, B.C. and Stiglitz, J.E. (1993), 'New and Old Keynesians', *Journal of Economic Perspectives*, 7(1), Winter, pp. 23–44.

Grosehn, E.L. and Schweitzer, M.E. (1999), 'Identifying Inflation's Grease and Sand Effect in the Labor Market', in M. Feldstein (ed.) *The Cost and Benefit of Price Stability*, Chicago: Chicago University Press.

Harcourt, G. (1969), 'Some Cambridge Controversies in the Theory of Capital', *Journal of Economic Literature*, 7(2), pp. 369–405.

Hargreaves Heap, S.P. (1980), 'Choosing the Wrong 'Natural' Rate: Accelerating Inflation or Decelerating Employment and Growth', *Economic Journal*, 90(359), pp. 611–20.

Hein, E. and Ochsen, C. (2003), 'Regimes of interest rates, income shares, savings, and investment: A Kaleckian model and empirical estimations for some advanced OECD-economies', *Metroeconomica*, 54(4), pp. 404–33.

Hein, E. and Vogel, L. (2008), 'Distribution and growth reconsidered: empirical results for six OECD countries', *Cambridge Journal of Economics*, 32(3), pp. 479–512.

Hicks, J. (1965), *Capital and Growth*. Oxford: Oxford University Press.

Holden, S. (2004), 'The Cost of Price Stability: Downward Nominal Wage Rigidity in Europe', *Economica*, 71(282), pp. 183–208.

Holden, S. and Wulfsberg, F. (2008), 'Downward Nominal Wage Rigidity in the OECD', *The B.E. Journal of Macroeconomics*, 8(1), Article 15.

Kaldor, N. (1939), 'Speculation and Economic Stability', *Review of Economic Studies*, 7(1), pp. 1–27.

Keynes, J.M. (1936), *The General Theory of Employment, Interest and Money*, Cambridge: Macmillan.

Keynes, J.M. (1937), 'The General Theory of Employment', *Quarterly Journal of Economics*, 51(2), pp. 209–23.

Krugman, P. (1998), 'It's Baaack: Japan's Slump and the Return of the Liquidity Trap', *Brookings Papers on Economic Activity*, 2, pp. 137–205.

Kuttner, K.N. and Posen A.S. (2001), 'The Great Recession: Lessons for Macroeconomic Policy from Japan', *Brookings Papers on Economic Activity*, 2, pp. 93–185.

Lavoie, M. (1996), 'Horizontalism, Structuralism, Liquidity Preference and the Principle of Increasing Risk', *Scottish Journal of Political Economy*, 43(3), August, pp. 275–300.

Lebow, D.E., Saks, R.E. and Wilson, B.A. (2003), 'Downward Nominal Wage Rigidity: Evidence from the Employment Cost Index', *Advances in Macroeconomics*, 3(1), Art.2.

León-Ledesma, M.A. (2002), 'Unemployment Hysteresis in the US States and the EU: A Panel Approach', *Bulletin of Economic Research*, 54(2), pp. 95–103.

Lindbeck, A. (1993), *Unemployment and Macroeconomics*, Cambridge, MA: MIT Press.

Logeay, C. and Tober, S. (2006), 'Hysteresis and the NAIRU in the Euro Area', *Scottish Journal of Political Economy*, 53(4), pp. 409–29.

Marglin, S.A. (1984), *Growth, Distribution and Prices*, Cambridge (MA): Harvard University Press.

McElhattan, R. (1985), 'Inflation, Supply Shocks and the Stable-Inflation Rate of Capacity Utilization', *Federal Reserve Bank of San Francisco Economic Review*, 1, pp. 45–63.

Meyer, L.H. (2001), 'Does Money Matter?', *Federal Reserve Bank of St. Louis Review*, September/October, pp. 1–15.

Mourougane, A. and Ibaragi, H. (2004), 'Is There a Change in the Trade-off Between Output and Inflation at Low or Stable Inflation Rates? Some Evidence in the Case of Japan', *Economics Department Working Paper* No. 379, OECD.

Myrdal, G. (1939), *Monetary Equilibrium*, London: W. Hodge.

Naastepad, R. and Storm, S. (2006/07), 'OECD demand regimes (1960–2000)', *Journal of Post Keynesian Economics*, 29(2), pp. 213–48.

Naastepad, R. (2006), 'Technology, demand and distribution: a cumulative growth model with an application to the Dutch productivity slowdown', *Cambridge Journal of Economics*, 30(3), pp. 403–34.

Orphanides, A. and Wieland, V. (2000), 'Inflation zone targeting, *European Economic Review*, 44, pp. 1351–87.

Palley, T.I. (1994), 'Escalators and Elevators: A Phillips Curve for Keynesians', *Scandinavian Journal of Economics*, 96(1), pp. 111–16.

Peltzman, S. (2000), 'Prices Rise Faster than they Fall', *Journal of Political Economy*, 108(3), pp. 466–502.

Pollin, R. (1985), 'Stability and Instability in the Debt–Income Relationship', *American Economic Review*, Papers and Proceedings, 75(2), May, pp. 344–50.

Reifschneider, D. and Williams, J.C. (2000), 'Three Lessons for Monetary Policy in a Low-Inflation Era', *Journal of Money, Credit and Banking*, 32(4), pp. 936–66.

RØed, K. (1997), 'Hysteresis in unemployment', *Journal of Economic Surveys*, 11(4), pp. 389–418.

Rowthorn, R. (1977), 'Conflict, inflation and money', *Cambridge Journal of Economics*, 1, pp. 215–39.

Sawyer, M.C. (1982), 'Collective Bargaining, Oligopoly and Macro-Economics', *Oxford Economic Papers*, 34(3), pp. 428–48.

Setterfield, M. (1998), 'Adjustment Asymmetries and Hysteresis in Simple Dynamic Models', *Manchester School*, 66(3), pp. 283–301.

Skott, P. (1989), *Conflict and Effective Demand in Economic Growth*, Cambridge: Cambridge University Press.

Spence, A.M. (1977), 'Entry, Capacity, Investment and Oligopolistic Pricing', *Bell Journal of Economics*, 8(2), Autumn, pp. 534–44.

Stockhammer, E. (2008), 'Is the NAIRU Theory a Monetarist, New Keynesian, Post Keynesian or a Marxist Theory?', *Metroeconomica*, 59(3), pp. 479–510.

Stockhammer, E. and Onaran, Ó. (2004), Accumulation, Distribution and Employment: A Structural VAR Approach to a Kaleckian Macro-model, *Structural Change and Economic Dynamics*, 15(4), pp. 421–47.

Stockhammer, E., Onaran, Ó. and Ederer, S. (2007), 'Functional income distribution and aggregate demand in the Euro-area', *Vienna University of Economics & B.A Department of Economics*, Working Paper no. 102.

Taylor, J.B. (1993), 'Discretion Versus Policy Rules in Practice', *Carnegie-Rochester Conference Series on Public Policy*, 39, pp. 195–214.

Ueda, K. (2000), 'Japan's Experience with Zero Interest Rates', *Journal of Money, Credit and Banking*, 32(4), November, pp. 1107–9.

Weber, A.A., Lemke, W. and Worms, A. (2008), 'How useful is the concept of the natural real rate of interest for monetary policy?', *Cambridge Journal of Economics*, 32(1), pp. 49–63.

Wicksell, K. (1936[1898]), *Interest and Prices: A Study of the Causes Regulating the Value of Money*, London: Macmillan.

Woodford, M. (2003), *Interest and Prices: Foundations of a Theory of Monetary Policy*, Princeton, NJ: Princeton University Press.

Yates, T. (2002), 'Monetary Policy and the Zero Bound to Interest Rates: A Review', Working paper No. 190, October, European Central Bank.

6
The Rise and Fall of Spanish Unemployment: A Chain Reaction Theory Perspective[1]

Marika Karanassou
Queen Mary University of London and IZA[2]

Hector Sala
Universitat Autònoma de Barcelona and IZA[3]

Abstract

The evolution of Spanish unemployment has been quite idiosyncratic. The full-employment levels of the early 1970s were followed by unemployment rates that were the highest within the OECD countries in the aftermath of the oil price shocks. While unemployment was extremely persistent during most of the 1980s and 1990s, it experienced its sharpest decline in recent years. We investigate the determinants of this unemployment trajectory using the analytical framework of the chain reaction theory (CRT). We show that unemployment may not gravitate towards its natural rate due to frictional growth, a phenomenon that arises from the interplay of lagged adjustment processes and growing exogenous variables in a dynamic system with spillovers. The empirical analysis distinguishes four periods: (i) 1978–85, (ii) 1986–90, (iii) 1991–94, (iv) 1995–2005, and finds that capital accumulation is a crucial driving force of unemployment. Thus, our theoretical and empirical results question the key role of the natural rate in policy-making.

Keywords: Labour market dynamics, frictional growth, chain reaction theory, capital accumulation, impulse response function

JEL Classification: E22, E24, J21.

1. Introduction

The evolution of Spanish unemployment over the past 35 years has been unique among the OECD countries. The full-employment levels of the early 1970s were, surprisingly, followed by the highest unemployment rates in the aftermath of the oil price shocks, and the most persistent unemployment problem in the 1980s and 1990s. The size and duration of high unemployment rates, in the range of around 10%–20% for approximately 20 years, have been dubbed the 'Spanish disease' (Dolado and Jimeno, 1997). And, somehow, Spain has again surprised by its rapid and prolonged unemployment rate decline over the second half of the 1990s (the fall in unemployment of around 10 percentage points was the sharpest in the OECD area).

Figure 6.1 plots the unemployment rate trajectory by distinguishing four periods: (i) 1978–85, (ii) 1986–90, (iii) 1991–94, and (iv) 1995–2005.[4] Bentolila and Jimeno (2006) refer to the first one as the 'long recession', the next two as the 'EU cycle', and the last one as the 'EMU cycle'.

The consensus view is that a combination of labour unfriendly institutions (e.g. benefits) and adverse macroeconomic shocks (e.g. oil crises) were responsible for the development of the so-called 'Spanish disease'. Although the 'usual suspects' such as wage-push factors, taxes and stock-market swings do matter, we argue that the crucial driving force of unemployment is capital accumulation.

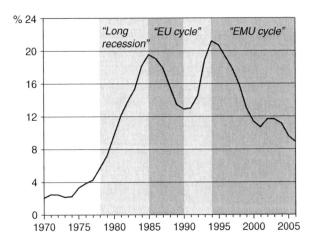

Figure 6.1   Unemployment rate

The conventional wisdom for the rise and fall of Spanish unemployment has evolved along the lines of the natural rate of unemployment, NRU (or NAIRU)[5] story using a variety of methodologies. The econometric models include multi-equations *à la* Layard et al. (1991), single-equations *à la* Phelps (1994), structural vector autoregressions (VARs), and the observable shocks model of Blanchard and Wolfers (2000).

Dolado et al. (1986), using a structural multi-equation model, argue that the policies most suited to reducing unemployment without increasing inflation are lower taxation, a higher degree of labour market flexibility, and more effective incomes policies. Phelps and Zoega (2001) estimate a single-equation model for a panel of OECD countries and find that the long swings in economic activity result from the changes in expected future productivity, which can be proxied by the swings in the stock market. Spain appears as the most sensitive economy to these swings, although the omission of country-specific variables is acknowledged. Dolado and Jimeno (1997), using a structural VAR methodology, attribute the dismal performance of Spanish unemployment to a series of adverse shocks – 'price shocks in the late 1970s, wage shocks in the early 1980s, and demand shocks in the early 90s' (p. 1285) – which were amplified by a rigid system of labour market institutions (e.g. collective bargaining, high firing costs, and barriers to competition in the goods market). Bentolila and Jimeno (2006), using the Blanchard and Wolfers (2000) model of equilibrium unemployment in the OECD, argue that Spain is characterized by a set of 'strongly unemployment generating' labour market institutions (i.e. unemployment benefits, employment protection, and collective bargaining) which aggravate the effects of adverse macroeconomic shocks.

In contrast to the above literature, this chapter examines the Spanish labour market from the perspective of the CRT (chain reaction theory). The CRT uses dynamic structural multi-equation systems and postulates that the unemployment rate is driven by the interplay between interacting lagged adjustment processes and spillover effects. Spillovers arise when shocks to a specific equation feed through the labour market system, where 'shocks' refer to changes in the exogenous variables.

The importance of having distinct equations for labour force and employment in the labour market model, rather than compressing them into a single-equation unemployment rate model, becomes evident from Figure 6.2. According to Figure 6.2, the labour force did not grow much in the 1970s and early 1980s. Although there was an acceleration in the second half of the 1980s, it is since the mid-1990s that this growth has

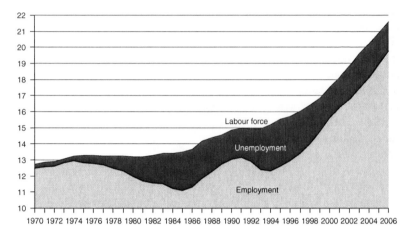

Figure 6.2   Employment, unemployment and labour force
Note: Employment, unemployment and labour force expressed in millions.

been the fastest. On the other hand, employment figures show a much more procyclical behaviour.

The disparity between the time paths of labour force and employment indicates that aggregating them into a single unemployment rate equation will produce a biased summary of their evolution. It can be shown that if the single-equation unemployment rate model and each equation of the multi-equation labour market model have all identical regressors, then the two estimation procedures will yield identical results. However, when structural multi-equation systems are estimated, it is generally the case that the constituent equations do *not* have the same regressors. Therefore, the single-equation model can no longer be viewed as an unbiased summary of the multi-equation model, since it can no longer capture the dynamic interactions among the various lagged adjustment processes portrayed in the multi-equation model. Karanassou et al. (2003) show that the high level of aggregation inherent in single-equation models introduces an interesting bias into the empirical analysis of unemployment movements: the role of the NRU is over-emphasized, while the role of lagged adjustment processes is under-emphasized.

Generally, a CRT labour market model comprises labour demand, labour supply and wage-setting equations. The system is dynamic because of the existence of adjustment costs which are well known in the literature. There are employment adjustment costs due to labour turnover costs, such as the costs of hiring and firing workers; wage setting costs due to nominal wage and price staggering; and labour force adjustment costs, due to monetary and psychic costs of entering and exiting the labour force. Spillovers are created when endogenous variables appear as explanatory variables in other equations (for example, wages in the labour demand and labour force equations, or the unemployment rate in the wage setting equation).

Each shock generates an intertemporal *chain reaction* of effects capturing the interplay between the dynamics and the spillovers of the system. These chain reactions are described in terms of impulse response functions (IRFs). We thus argue that the CRT represents a synthesis of traditional structural macroeconometric models and structural VARs.

The main advantage of the structural VAR methodology, which has dominated the recent empirical literature, is that the overall influence of each shock on the rest of the system is gauged by its IRF. On the other hand, a disadvantage of the structural VAR methodology is its lack of attention to the individual equations of the model (estimated VAR coefficients go unreported, since structural VAR equations do not have an economic interpretation). The advantage of the CRT modelling approach over (structural) VARs is the economic intuition and plausibility that accompanies each of the estimated equations. Consequently, the dynamic structural model of the CRT methodology can measure the contributions of the various exogenous variables to the evolution of the unemployment rate. Nevertheless, the important lesson of the (structural) VAR literature is the use of impulse responses to decide on the plausibility of the labour market model. It is for this reason that we derive the univariate representation of unemployment and use its IRFs to measure the unemployment effects of the various shocks. It is important to note that, since shocks refer to changes in the exogenous variables, our IRF analysis is not subject to biases arising from cross equation correlation.

Another important feature of the CRT is that it allows trended variables, such as capital stock, working-age population, or capital deepening, to influence unemployment. This is in sharp contrast to natural rate models which impose strong a priori restrictions. For example, in the Layard et al. (1991) model any productivity gains arising from capital accumulation are absorbed by the workers' bargaining power, on one hand, and unemployment benefits block the possibility that efficiency gains are translated into employment ones, on the other. This prescription imposes a strong *ex ante* restriction on the capital-unemployment relationship. Unlike the NRU models, the CRT ensures that each equation is balanced (dynamically stable), so that each trended dependent variable is driven by the set of its trended determinants. This distinguishes the CRT from theories that just consider stationary variables as potential determinants of the trendless unemployment rate.

Finally, a key characteristic of the CRT is *frictional growth*, which we define as the interplay of lags (due to adjustment costs in labour market activities) and growing variables (due to the trended nature of the dependent variables). As we show in section 2, in a dynamic framework of analysis the endogenous variable can be decomposed into two parts. The first component is the so-called 'trend', which is a function of the various exogenous variables in the model and their long-run sensitivities. The second is a function of the lagged adjustment processes and the growth rates of the exogenous variables. This second component is identified with the popular concept of the 'cycle' if growth is zero in the long run. If, on the other hand, long-run growth is non-zero the second component gives rise to the phenomenon of frictional growth. We should stress that frictional growth arises under quite plausible conditions, i.e. a dynamic environment with growing variables. Needless to say, frictional growth is zero in static models (due to zero lags) and in single-equation unemployment rate models (due to zero long-run growth, since the exogenous variables are trendless).

Unlike the natural rate and hysteresis approaches,[6] the chain reaction approach focuses explicitly on frictional growth. In the presence of economic growth in the labour market, e.g. capital accumulation leading to a steady rise in labour demand and population growth leading to a steady rise in labour supply, the adjustment processes never have a chance to work themselves out entirely. Employment, labour force and, consequently, unemployment are continually chasing after their moving, frictionless targets, but since the adjustment processes never work themselves out entirely, the frictionless targets are never reached. Therefore, as we show in section 2, long-run unemployment equals its NRU plus frictional growth, and so unemployment cannot be decomposed into 'trend' and cyclical components. In other words, since actual unemployment does not gravitate towards its natural rate, frictional growth challenges the central role attached by the mainstream theories to the NRU for explaining the rise and fall of unemployment. Our analytical results are thus in line with Arestis and Sawyer (Ch. 1 in this volume) and 'run counter to orthodox macroeconomic analysis, which is based on the idea that there is a pre-existing equilibrium path along which the economy can travel and oscillate around it'. The difference is that CRT models may feature rational expectations and ergodic processes, and they only require frictional growth to obtain this 'path dependency' result.

It is also worthwhile pointing out that CRT models are linear, and thus have symmetric responses to shocks. In other words, negative and positive shocks of the same type and size do not affect the time path of unemployment in the long run. Alternatively, CRT models do not display what Cross et al. (1999) call *remanence,* i.e. 'the application and removal of a shock will not be accompanied by a return to the *status quo ante'.* However, since shocks in the CRT models refer to the actual changes in the exogenous variables over time, and it is highly unlikely that, on average, these changes will have the same size but opposite signs, the remanence property is of little practical significance in the chain reaction approach. Nevertheless, as we show in section 2, it is frictional growth which influences the time path of unemployment in the long-run.

Our empirical analysis of labour market dynamics shows that the growth rate of capital stock plays a crucial role in shaping unemployment movements during all the four periods portrayed in Figure 6.1. In particular, our empirical labour market model in section 4 uses trade deficit (foreign demand), capital accumulation, financial wealth, indirect taxes, social security benefits, private consumption, and working-age population in the set of explanatory variables in order to estimate the impact of the various economic developments, which are discussed in section 3, on the Spanish unemployment rate. Direct taxes, oil prices, and social security contributions were also included in our estimation, but did not have any significant effect.

Although benefits, taxes, and financial wealth do influence unemployment, our empirical findings show that capital accumulation is the most substantial contributor to the unemployment trajectory. Since capital accumulation is a significant component of aggregate demand, our empirical findings contradict the macro orthodoxy in which demand plays no role in the long-run unemployment rate.

The rest of the chapter is structured as follows. Section 2 analyses a stylized labour market model to convey the central features of the CRT. Section 3 provides a comprehensive overview of the Spanish experience in the last decades. Section 4 is concerned with the econometric methodology and estimates an augmented version of the stylized labour market system of section 2. Naturally, the model in section 2 is augmented by taking into account the economic developments discussed in section 3. Section 5 uses the estimated equations to evaluate the dynamic contributions of the exogenous variables to the evolution of unemployment. Section 6 uses the empirical model to measure the long-run impact of capital accumulation on the unemployment trajectory. Section 7 concludes.

2.   Chain Reaction Theory (CRT)

To understand the development of the unemployment problem, the chain reaction theory advocates the use of interactive dynamic labour market models, i.e. dynamic multi-equation systems with spillover effects. Spillovers arise when endogenous variables have explanatory power in other equations of the system. By *chain reactions* we refer to the intertemporal responses of the unemployment rate to changes in the exogenous variables ('shocks'). The chain reactions are generated by the interplay between the dynamics and spillovers of the system.

Before we proceed with the analytical details of CRT models, it is useful to briefly compare and contrast the chain reaction, natural rate, and hysteresis theories of unemployment.[7]

2.1   CRT, NRU, and hysteresis

- The short-run (cyclical) and long-run (natural) unemployment rates are
  - interdependent in CRT models
  - compartmentalized in NRU and hysteresis models.
- The effects of temporary shocks on unemployment
  - dissipate through time in CRT and NRU models
  - propagate to its natural rate in hysteresis models.
- While CRT and NRU models can identify the driving forces of the unemployment rate, hysteresis models simply offer statistical representations of its trajectory.
- Whereas CRT estimates a labour market system and then derives the univariate representation of the unemployment rate, NRU single-equation models estimate a reduced-form unemployment rate equation.

It is worthwhile pointing out that linearity is the common ground for all three theories, i.e. the unemployment rate process in NRU, hysteresis and CRT models responds to shocks in a linear fashion. The hysteresis theory in the above discussion refers only to the popular 'unit root hysteresis'. It is beyond the scope of this chapter to discuss hysteretic models that display remanence, i.e. positive and negative shocks of equal size do not cancel out. This type of hysteresis involves economic models with heterogeneous agents that respond non-linearly to shocks (Cross et al., 1999).

2.2 A stylized labour market model

The analytical model below illustrates the workings of the CRT and is in line with our estimated labour market model in section 4. Consider the following labour demand, real wage, and labour supply equations:[8]

$$n_t = \alpha_1 n_{t-1} + \beta_1 k_t - \gamma_1 w_t, \tag{1}$$

$$w_t = \alpha_2 w_{t-1} + \beta_2 x_t - \gamma_2 u_t, \tag{2}$$

$$l_t = \beta_3 z_t + \gamma_3 w_t, \tag{3}$$

and let the unemployment rate be defined as[9]

$$u_t = l_t - n_t, \tag{4}$$

where u_t is the unemployment rate; n_t, w_t, and l_t denote employment, real wage, and labour force, respectively; k_t is real capital stock, x_t represents a wage-push factor, and z_t is working-age population; the βs and γs are positive constants. All variables, except the unemployment rate, are in logs and the error terms are ignored for expositional ease. The autoregressive parameters α_1 and α_2 are positive and less than unity, capturing the employment adjustment and wage/price staggering effects, respectively. Generally, we refer to the lags of the endogenous variables in a CRT model as the lagged adjustment processes.

It is important to note that, unlike the single-equation NRU models, the CRT models may also include trended exogenous variables. The only requirement is that each equation is balanced (i.e. dynamically stable) so that each trended dependent variable is driven by the set of its trended determinants. It can be shown that equilibrating mechanisms in the labour market and other markets jointly act to ensure that the unemployment rate is trendless in the long-run (Karanassou and Snower, 2004). In terms of the above analytical model, these mechanisms can be expressed in the form of restrictions on the relationships between the long-run growth rates of the growing exogenous variables (see section 2.5). Furthermore, unlike multi-equation NRU models, CRT models do not restrict the changes in growing variables, e.g. capital stock, to lead to countervailing shifts in the labour demand, wage setting, and labour supply curves so as to restore the unemployment rate to its original long-run equilibrium. By implication, policies that stimulate capital accumulation can have no effect on the long-run unemployment rate.

The γs generate spillover effects, since changes in an exogenous variable in one equation, say capital stock in labour demand, can also affect the real wage and labour supply equations. Observe that if the wage elasticities are zero ($\gamma_1 = \gamma_3 = 0$), the wage-push factor (x_t) does not influence unemployment. This is because the wage-push factor can only affect employment and labour force via wages. In addition, if unemployment does not put downward pressure on wages ($\gamma_2 = 0$), changes in capital stock (k_t) and working-age population (z_t) do not spill over in the labour market system. This is because labour demand and labour supply are linked via wages. If changes in the capital stock and working-age population do not influence wages ($\gamma_2 = 0$) they cannot spill over to the system, and so their unemployment effects can be adequately captured by the individual labour demand (1) and supply (3) equations.

Therefore, in the presence of spillover effects, the individual labour demand and supply equations cannot provide adequate measures of the sensitivities of unemployment to the exogenous variables. We refer to β as the 'local' short-run elasticities (i.e. the elasticities obtained simply by eye inspection) in order to distinguish them from the 'global' ones, which incorporate all the feedback mechanisms in the labour market model. The global elasticities can be obtained by the univariate representation of unemployment derived below. The univariate representation expresses unemployment as a function of its own lags and the exogenous variables in the system (see equation (11)). Note that (i) the 'local' short-run elasticity of the unemployment rate with respect to capital stock is β_1 (by equations (4) and (1)), whereas the 'global' short-run elasticity is $\theta_z = \frac{\beta_3}{1+\gamma_1\gamma_2+\gamma_2\gamma_3}$ (by equation (11)), and (ii) the 'local' short-run elasticity of the unemployment rate with respect to working-age population is β_3 (by equations (4) and (3)), whereas the 'global' short-run elasticity is $\theta_k = \frac{\beta_1}{1+\gamma_1\gamma_2+\gamma_2\gamma_3}$ (by equation (11)). In other words, the plethora of spillovers in the system may render the 'local' elasticities unreliable, since they could affect both their sign and size. The CRT approach takes this fact into account and uses the univariate representation of the unemployment rate, and its implied IRFs, to diagnose the economic plausibility of the labour market system. In this sense, the CRT is a synthesis of the traditional structural macroeconometric models and the (structural) VARs.

2.3 Univariate representation of unemployment

Rewrite the demand, wage, and supply equations (1)–(3) as

$$(1 - \alpha_1 B)(1 - \alpha_2 B) n_t = \beta_1(1 - \alpha_2 B) k_t - \gamma_1(1 - \alpha_2 B) w_t, \tag{5}$$

$$(1 - \alpha_2 B) w_t = \beta_2 x_t - \gamma_2 u_t, \tag{6}$$

$$(1 - \alpha_1 B)(1 - \alpha_2 B) l_t = \beta_3(1 - \alpha_1 B)(1 - \alpha_2 B) z_t$$
$$+ \gamma_3(1 - \alpha_1 B)(1 - \alpha_2 B) w_t, \tag{7}$$

where B is the backshift operator, and substitute (6) into (5) and (7) to obtain the following equations for employment and labour force:

$$(1 - \alpha_1 B)(1 - \alpha_2 B) n_t = \beta_1(1 - \alpha_2 B) k_t - \gamma_1 \beta_2 x_t + \gamma_1 \gamma_2 u_t, \tag{8}$$

$$(1 - \alpha_1 B)(1 - \alpha_2 B) l_t = \beta_3(1 - \alpha_1 B)(1 - \alpha_2 B) z_t$$
$$+ \gamma_3 \beta_2(1 - \alpha_1 B) x_t - \gamma_3 \gamma_2(1 - \alpha_1 B) u_t, \tag{9}$$

respectively.

As already discussed, a key element of the CRT is that capital stock, a trended variable, influences the time path of the unemployment rate, a stationary variable. We can justify this result as follows. Capital stock initially enters the system as a determinant of employment, a trended variable. Labour demand (1) is a balanced equation since it is dynamically stable ($|\alpha_1| < 1$). Similarly, the trended labour force is driven by working-age population (also a trended variable), and the static labour supply (3) is itself a balanced equation. According to (8)–(9), the labour demand and supply equations remain balanced once the wage (2) has been substituted into them.[10]

The univariate representation (or reduced form dynamics) of the unemployment rate can be obtained by inserting the above equations into (4),[11]

$$[(1 - \alpha_1 B)(1 - \alpha_2 B) + \gamma_3 \gamma_2(1 - \alpha_1 B) + \gamma_1 \gamma_2] u_t = -\beta_1(1 - \alpha_2 B) k_t$$
$$+ \gamma_3 \beta_2(1 - \alpha_1 B) x_t + \gamma_1 \beta_2 x_t + \beta_3(1 - \alpha_1 B)(1 - \alpha_2 B) z_t. \tag{10}$$

The term 'reduced form' relates to the fact that the parameters of the equation are not estimated directly, instead, they are some non-linear function of the parameters of the underlying labour market system (1)–(3).

We can reparameterize the above equation as

$$u_t = \phi_1 u_{t-1} - \phi_2 u_{t-2} - \theta_k k_t + \theta_x(\gamma_1 + \gamma_2) x_t + \theta_z z_t$$
$$+ \alpha_2 \theta_k k_{t-1} - \alpha_1 \gamma_3 \theta_x x_{t-1} - (\alpha_1 + \alpha_2) \theta_z z_{t-1} + \alpha_1 \alpha_2 \theta_z z_{t-2}, \quad (11)$$

where $\phi_1 = \frac{\alpha_1 + \alpha_2 + \alpha_1 \gamma_2 \gamma_3}{1 + \gamma_1 \gamma_2 + \gamma_2 \gamma_3}$, $\phi_2 = \frac{\alpha_1 \alpha_2}{1 + \gamma_1 \gamma_2 + \gamma_2 \gamma_3}$, $\theta_k = \frac{\beta_1}{1 + \gamma_1 \gamma_2 + \gamma_2 \gamma_3}$, $\theta_x = \frac{\beta_2}{1 + \gamma_1 \gamma_2 + \gamma_2 \gamma_3}$,

and $\theta_z = \frac{\beta_3}{1 + \gamma_1 \gamma_2 + \gamma_2 \gamma_3}$.

The univariate representation (11) shows that unemployment is generated by the interplay of lagged adjustment processes and spillovers. In particular, the autoregressive coefficients ϕ_1 and ϕ_2 embody the interactions of the employment adjustment (α_1) and wage-price staggering (α_2) processes. The θs embody the feedback mechanisms built in the system, since they are a function of the semi-elasticities (βs) of the individual equations (1)–(3) and the spillovers (γs). Thus, the θs describe the 'global' short-run sensitivities of unemployment with respect to the exogenous variables. The interplay of dynamics across equations is further emphasized by the lagged structure of the exogenous variables. Using time series jargon, we refer to the lagged exogenous variables as 'moving-average' terms.

2.4   Impulse response functions

The responses of unemployment through time ($R_{t+j}, j \geq 0$) to a one-off unit shock (impulse), occurring at period t, are described by the impulse response function (IRF) of its univariate representation (11). Unemployment persistence (σ) can be defined as the sum of its future responses, i.e. for all periods in the aftermath of the shock:[12] $\sigma \equiv \sum_{j=1}^{\infty} R_{t+j}$.

Note that the responses can be interpreted as the 'global' elasticities (strictly speaking, semi-elasticities or slopes) of the unemployment rate, since shocks in the CRT refer to changes in the exogenous variables. In particular, the contemporaneous response (R_t) captures the 'global' short-run elasticity, whereas the sum of all responses measures the 'global' long-run elasticity. In other words, the short-run elasticity plus persistence equals the long-run elasticity of the specific variable:

$$\text{long} - \text{run elasticity} = \text{short} - \text{run elasticity} + \text{persistence}$$

$$\sum_{j=0}^{\infty} R_{t+j} \qquad\qquad R_t \qquad\qquad \sum_{j=1}^{\infty} R_{t+j} \qquad (12)$$

The most pedagogical illustration of the above concepts is via a simple AR(1) unemployment rate equation:

$$u_t = \alpha u_{t-1} + \beta x_t, \text{ where } |\alpha| < 1. \qquad (13)$$

The impulse response function of the AR(1) stochastic process (13) to one-off unit change in the exogenous variable x_t is as follows:

$$\text{IRF of the AR(1):} \quad \begin{array}{|c|c|c|c|c|c|c|}\hline \text{time} & t & t+1 & t+2 & \ldots & t+10 & \ldots \\ \hline \text{responses} & \beta & \beta\alpha & \beta\alpha^2 & \ldots & \beta\alpha^{10} & \ldots \\ \hline \end{array}. \tag{14}$$

Thus, a one-time unit shock will have an immediate unit impact on the unemployment rate u_t, while the future effects of the shock decline in a geometric fashion. In particular, application of equation (12) gives:

$$\text{long-run elasticity} = \text{short-run elasticity} + \text{persistence}$$
$$\beta/(1-\alpha) \qquad\qquad \beta \qquad\qquad \beta\alpha/(1-\alpha) \tag{15}$$

Furthermore, we can measure the *contributions* of an exogenous variable, say x, to the evolution of unemployment over a specific period of time, say $t=0$ to $t=T$, by sequentially adding up the IRFs of the respective changes during the specific period. Let $\Delta x_j = x_j - x_{j-1}$, where $j=1, 2, \ldots T$, and Δ is the first difference operator. The IRFs of these T shocks are:

$$\begin{array}{lcccc} & t=1 & t=2 & \ldots & t=T \\ \text{IRF}_1: & R_{11} & R_{12} & \ldots & R_{1T} \\ \text{IRF}_2: & - & R_{22} & \ldots & R_{2T} \\ \ldots & - & - & \ldots & \ldots \\ \text{IRF}_T: & - & - & \ldots & R_{TT} \end{array}$$

where IRF_j denotes the response function to the jth shock, and R_{jt} is the response to shock j in time t. Note that the diagonal elements denote the respective contemporaneous responses to the various shocks.

We measure the t-period *contribution* as the sum of all responses at this period. Therefore, the *contributions* of the exogenous variable x to the unemployment trajectory for the given interval are given by the following time series:

$$\begin{array}{ccccc} t=1 & t=2 & t=3 & \ldots & t=T \\ R_{11}, & \displaystyle\sum_{j=1}^{2} R_{j2}, & \displaystyle\sum_{j=1}^{3} R_{j3}, & \ldots & \displaystyle\sum_{j=1}^{T} R_{jT}. \end{array} \tag{16}$$

An important drawback of the traditional structural macroeconometric models is that the IRFs are missing from their analysis. This is because the numerous spillover effects in the system can substantially affect the size and sign of the 'local' elasticities so that the individual equations can be quite misleading regarding the effects of the exogenous variables on unemployment. By focusing on the IRFs of the system, (structural) VARs offer a statistically robust alternative. Unlike the traditional macroeconometric models, the CRT emphasizes the role of IRFs in its investigation and uses the global elasticities as a misspecification tool to diagnose the economic plausibility of the model. Thus, the CRT methodology can be viewed as a synthesis of the traditional structural macroeconometric models and the (structural) VARs.

2.5   Frictional growth

We start by introducing the phenomenon of frictional growth by reparameterizing the pedagogical AR(1) model given by equation (13). For an endogenous variable y_t this yields:

$$y_t = \alpha y_{t-1} + \beta x_t \Leftrightarrow y_t = \underbrace{\frac{\beta}{1-\alpha}x_t}_{\substack{\text{'trend' or steady-state}}} - \underbrace{\frac{\alpha}{1-\alpha}\Delta y_t}_{\substack{\text{'cycke' if lont-run growth=0} \\ \text{'frictional growth' otherwise}}} . \quad (17)$$

Observe that the first term of the above equation is the 'trend' of y_t, while the second term captures the frictional growth of the model. If the exogenous variable does not grow in the long-run, the endogenous variable also stabilizes in the long run (i.e. $\Delta y = 0$ in the long run). In this case frictional growth is zero and the second term of (17) can be interpreted as the 'cyclical' component of the endogenous variable y_t. It is important to note that the long-run elasticity of y with respect to x is $\frac{\beta}{1-\alpha}$ regardless of whether frictional growth is zero or not. We believe that the main interest of economists in elasticities has led them to generally disregard the phenomenon of frictional growth in macroeconometric models. Although frictional growth does not affect single-equation unemployment rate models, it has major implications for dynamic multi-equation labour market systems.

In what follows, we show that frictional growth in the CRT framework of analysis may cause unemployment to substantially deviate in both the short and long run from what is commonly perceived as its natural rate. The disparity between the natural and long-run rates of unemployment was first pointed out by Karanassou and Snower (1997) and opposes to the conventional wisdom that the NRU is the attractor of the unemployment rate.

In the context of the labour market model (1)–(4), we demonstrate this result by making the plausible assumption that capital stock (k_t) and working age population (z_t) are growing variables with growth rates that stabilize in the long run. We also assume, for simplicity and without loss of generality, that the wage-push factor (x_t) does not grow in the long-run. Note that the growth rates of log variables are proxied by their first differences, $\Delta(\cdot)$, and the superscript LR denotes the long-run value of the variable.

The unemployment definition (4) implies that the unemployment rate stabilizes in the long run, $\Delta u^{LR} = 0$, if the growth rate of employment is equal to the growth rate of labour force, say λ,

$$\Delta l^{LR} = \Delta n^{LR} = \lambda. \tag{18}$$

The above restriction can also be expressed in terms of the long-run growth rates of the exogenous variables:

$$\frac{\beta_1}{1 - \alpha_1} \Delta k^{LR} = \Delta z^{LR}. \tag{19}$$

We refer to (19) as the *frictional growth* (FG) *stability condition*, since it ensures that the unemployment rate stabilizes in the long-run.

Let us reparameterize the demand (1) and wage equations (2) as

$$n_t = \frac{\beta_1}{1 - \alpha_1} k_t - \frac{\gamma_1}{1 - \alpha_1} w_t - \frac{\alpha_1}{(1 - \alpha_1)} \Delta n_t, \tag{20}$$

$$w_t = \frac{\beta_2}{1 - \alpha_2} x_t - \frac{\gamma_2}{1 - \alpha_2} u_t - \frac{\alpha_2}{(1 - \alpha_2)} \Delta w_t, \tag{21}$$

respectively. Next, substitute the wage equation (21) into the demand (20) and supply equations (3),

$$n_t = \frac{\beta_1}{1 - \alpha_1} k_t - \frac{\gamma_1 \beta_2}{(1 - \alpha_1)(1 - \alpha_2)} x_t + \frac{\gamma_1 \gamma_2}{(1 - \alpha_1)(1 - \alpha_2)} u_t$$
$$+ \frac{\gamma_1 \alpha_2}{(1 - \alpha_1)(1 - \alpha_2)} \Delta w_t - \frac{\alpha_1}{(1 - \alpha_1)} \Delta n_t, \tag{22}$$

$$l_t = \beta_3 z_t + \frac{\gamma_3 \beta_2}{1 - \alpha_2} x_t - \frac{\gamma_3 \gamma_2}{1 - \alpha_2} u_t - \frac{\gamma_3 \alpha_2}{1 - \alpha_2} \Delta w_t \tag{23}$$

Substitution of the above equations into (4) and some algebraic manipulation yields the following expression for the unemployment rate:

$$u_t = \frac{1}{\zeta}\left[\beta_3 z_t - \frac{\beta_1}{1-\alpha_1}k_t + \frac{(1-\alpha_1)\gamma_3\beta_2 + \gamma_1\beta_2}{(1-\alpha_1)(1-\alpha_2)}x_t\right]$$
$$+\frac{1}{\zeta}\left[\frac{\alpha_1}{(1-\alpha_1)}\Delta n_t - \frac{(1-\alpha_1)\gamma_3\alpha_2 + \gamma_1\alpha_2}{(1-\alpha_1)(1-\alpha_2)}\Delta w_t\right], \tag{24}$$

where $\zeta = \left(1 + \frac{\gamma_1\gamma_2}{(1-\alpha_1)(1-\alpha_2)} - \frac{\gamma_3\gamma_2}{1-\alpha_2}\right)$.

The above leads to the following unemployment rate equation in the long-run:

$$u^{LR} = \frac{1}{\zeta}\left[\underbrace{\left(\beta_3 z^{LR} - \frac{\beta_1}{1-\alpha_1}k^{LR} + \frac{(1-\alpha_1)\gamma_3\beta_2 + \gamma_1\beta_2}{(1-\alpha_1)(1-\alpha_2)}x^{LR}\right)}_{\text{natural rate of unemployment}} + \underbrace{\frac{\alpha_1\beta_1}{(1-\alpha_1)^2}\Delta k^{LR}}_{\text{frictional growth}}\right]$$

$$\tag{25}$$

since $\Delta n^{LR} = \frac{\beta_1}{1-\alpha_1}\Delta k^{LR}$ and $\Delta w^{LR} = 0$. The first term of (25) gives the NRU, whereas the second term of (25) captures frictional growth. Note that when the exogenous variables have non-zero long-run growth rates, unemployment is trendless in the long run under the FG stability condition (19).

According to (24), if the growth rate of employment is zero in the long-run ($\Delta n^{LR} = 0$), the first term of (24) in square brackets is the 'trend' component of unemployment, while the second term in square brackets is its cyclical component (since it is zero in the long-run). However, under frictional growth, this decomposition cannot be obtained. This distinguishes the CRT from models that filter out the cyclical variations of unemployment (e.g. using five-year averages) and then identify its driving forces.

The long-run value (u^{LR}) towards which the unemployment rate converges reduces to the NRU only when frictional growth is zero. In the above CRT model this occurs if (i) the long-run growth rate of capital stock is zero, or (ii) the lagged adjustment effect is zero ($\alpha_1 = 0$). Therefore, frictional growth implies that under quite plausible conditions the natural rate is not an attractor of the moving unemployment rate, and so the relevance of the NRU in policy making is questionable.[13] Reliance on natural rate estimates without taking into account the impact of FG may, for example, lead to a misjudgement of the unemployment effects of labour market reforms.

2.6 Long-run, natural rate, contributions

To sum up, the interplay between lagged adjustment processes and growing exogenous variables generates frictional growth, which has the following implications.

- The NRU is not a reference point for the actual unemployment rate:

$$\text{long-run} = \text{NRU} + \text{frictional growth}$$
$$\text{\tiny(steady-state)}$$

- Unemployment cannot be decomposed into 'trend' and cyclical components. This is in contrast with the standard NRU models:[14]

$$u_t = \alpha u_{t-1} + \beta x_t \text{ or } u_t = \underbrace{\frac{\beta}{1-\alpha} x_t}_{\text{'trend' or NRU}} - \underbrace{\frac{\alpha}{1-\alpha} \Delta u_t}_{\text{cyclical}},$$

since, by construction $\Delta u^{LR} = 0$.

- Since the unemployment rate is trendless, NRU models assert that growing variables can only influence the labour market via their trendless transformations. Unlike NRU models, the CRT models may also include trended exogenous variables. The only requirement is that each equation is balanced (i.e. dynamically stable) so that each trended dependent variable is driven by the set of its trended determinants. Consequently, the univariate representation of unemployment is itself balanced and the frictional growth stability condition (18) ensures that the unemployment rate stabilizes in the long-run.

As we argued above, there may be a substantial disparity between the long-run and natural rates of unemployment due to frictional growth. Our limited knowledge of the long-run values of the growth rates of the exogenous variables implies that we do not have reliable estimates of frictional growth, and consequently of the long-run unemployment rate.

Thus, CRT models do not attempt to determine the factors underlying the natural (or long-run) unemployment rate. Instead, the focus is on the contributions of the exogenous variables to the evolution of the unemployment rate, which were defined by equation (16).

3. Overview of the Spanish experience

Spain enjoyed a long situation of full employment throughout the 1950s and 1960s lasting until 1977. A central feature of the unemployment

Table 6.1 Institutional and policy changes

Labour market changes	Other institutional changes
1980: Workers' Statute	1977: Democracy
1977–86: Incomes policies	1977: Moncloa Pacts
1984: First UB reform	1978: Spanish Constitution
1984: First labour market reform	1986: Entry into the EEC
1992: Second UB reform	1989: Entry into the EMS
1994: Second labour market reform	1992: Maastricht Treaty signed
1997: Third labour market reform	1994: Bank of Spain independence
2001: Fourth labour market reform	1999: Entry into EMU
2002: Third UB reform	1999: Stability and growth pact
2006: Fifth labour market reform	

trajectory is its persistence in the sense that, in the last three decades, it has never recovered the full-employment situation of the past. Table 6.1 summarizes the numerous institutional and labour market related policy changes experienced by the Spanish economy in the aftermath of the Francoist period.

Below we discuss these labour market features, other institutional changes mainly related to the European integration process, and the specific macroeconomic features across business cycles that have accompanied the rise and fall of the Spanish unemployment rate.

3.1 Institutional features

The main issues of interest in the labour market are the wage bargaining system, the implementation of a set of incomes policies in 1977–86, and the legislation on employment and unemployment protection.

During most of the 1970s, the essence of the wage-bargaining system consisted of setting the nominal wage, in period t, as a mark-up over the prices in period $t-1$. This mechanism guaranteed the real wage, on one hand, and allowed the possibility of a wage-price spiral in inflationary periods, on the other. This was the case in the 1970s when Spain witnessed a wage-price spiral that drove the inflation rate over 20 per cent in 1977. Together with an insurmountable growing foreign deficit, this led to a nation-wide set of agreements between unions and employers' organizations (both were legalized in that year), the government, and all political parties, in order to overcome the economic turmoil. These were called the *Moncloa Pacts* and set the policy framework during the early years of the Spanish democracy.

The Moncloa pacts led to a new period of incomes policies according to which unions would reduce their wage claims, so as to avoid massive employment losses and to control inflation; the government would focus on controlling the rise in prices (through a change in the orientation and implementation of the monetary policy, among other things), so as to provide stability and prevent a deterioration of the real wage; and firms, in benefiting from lower wage claims and inflation control (and other economic measures in their support), would avoid massive bankruptcies and be able to face the adjustment. This was combined with a new wage-setting mechanism since 1977 of fixing the nominal wage as a mark-up over expected current prices. These incomes policies were implemented over the 1977 to 1986 period through a succession of tripartite agreements (between unions, firms and the government), and effectively put an end to the wage-price spiral. In the mid-1980s the inflation rate was already below 10 per cent, while the unemployment rate had reached an historical maximum.

The modern system of employment legislation was set up in 1980 when the *Workers' Statute* was passed. Before 1980, the Spanish labour market was paternalistic and highly regulated. The regulations established by the Workers' Statute set the permanent contract as the standard one, and left the temporary contract for specific cases, such as building construction and tourism activities, training periods, temporary replacements of permanent workers or pick-demand needs. The five labour market reforms shown in Table 6.1 (1984, 1994, 1997, 2001 and 2006) are reforms of the Workers' Statute.

The 1984 reform is probably the most significant one. The unemployment rate had been growing intensively for years, Spain was about to enter the European Economic Community (EEC) and, generally, there was a call for enhancing the flexibility of the labour market. This was done by extending the use of temporary contracts to all situations regardless of their justification. As a result, the share of temporary employment was growing until the early 1990s and then stabilized at about a third of total dependent employment. This is one of the salient features of the Spanish labour market, since this share is twice the EU average (see Dolado et al., 2002).

The reforms undertaken in 1994, 1997, 2001 and 2006 are often regarded as 'counter-reforms', since their target was to decrease the excessive use of temporary work. The 1994 reform introduced restrictions in the use of temporary contracts; the 1997 one launched a new highly subsidized permanent contract; the 2001 extended and enhanced the 1997 reform; and the 2006 one gave more incentives to grant permanent contracts to hard-to-place workers, and introduced new measures against the abuse of temporary contracts. Güell and Petrongolo (2007, Table A) provide a useful summary of the legislation on the temporary contracts in Spain since 1980.

The unemployment protection legislation lies in the jurisdiction of the public employment agency, which is the Employment National Institute known as the INEM (Instituto Nacional de Empleo). It was created in 1978 with the aim of managing: (i) the public employment service, with a monopolistic situation until the second labour market reform in 1994 allowed private temporary work agencies; (ii) the unemployment benefits (UB) system; and (iii) the training system for the unemployed. It is financed by the social security contributions of employers and employees, and also by the government (that is, from general taxes).

The UB system is one of the most prominent labour-market institutions in the mainstream literature. The modern UB system in Spain dates from 1980 when contributory and assistance schemes were established. In the contributory scheme the minimum amount of benefits is the national minimum wage (Salario Mínimo Interprofesional, SMI), while the assistance scheme amounts to 75 per cent of the SMI and targets non-eligible unemployed with family responsibilities. This system was reformed in 1984, 1992 and 2002.

The first UB reform, in 1984, changed the composition of the unemployed and left several social groups without any sort of protection. This was essentially due to the sharp reduction in the coverage rate over the 1980–83 period (from about 65% of the unemployed to less than 40%) together with the huge increase in unemployment (see García de Blas, 1985); in particular, casual workers, young workers and the long-term unemployed. This reform was expansionary. It extended the duration of benefits under the contributory scheme by a third, and doubled the allowances under the assistance scheme, which was also extended to protect new groups (for example, casual workers not having completed the minimum contribution period for the contributory scheme).

The 1992 and 2002 reforms were at the opposite end. In 1992, the minimum requirements for entitlement to benefits were made harder, the replacement rate in the first year of benefit was reduced by 10 percentage points, and the maximum duration shortened. The 2002 reform aimed at modernizing the public employment service. In particular, the aim was to achieve more efficiency in the placement of jobseekers and to prevent existing failures within the unemployment insurance system. It also aimed at encouraging the reinsertion of jobseekers, and at extending the unemployment insurance to those particularly disadvantaged.

The main novelty was the need, for all beneficiaries, to sign a 'jobseeker agreement': the worker must prove s/he is actively searching for a job and willing to accept a suitable offer; if not, the unemployment benefit may be interrupted.

3.2 The integration process

Spain joined the EEC in 1986. The reduction in all tariff barriers was the first requirement in order to become a full member of the EEC as a free trade area (see Polo and Sancho, 1993). In the light of the historical levels of high protection, a transitory period was arranged until the end of 1992, i.e. the year scheduled for the creation of a single market for EEC members. In addition to the free movements of goods and services (free trade area), the common market envisaged free movements of labour and capital. In contrast to the several decades that the countries which originally signed the Rome Treaty in 1957 had to adjust, Spain had six years to prepare for the common market. This resulted in one of the most intensive periods of economic changes, in particular with respect to trade, the balance of trade, openness, and the composition of output. The rapid increase in the trade deficit was one of the striking features of this period.

In the second half of the 1980s and early 1990s Spain had, on the trading side, to (i) eliminate both tariff and non-tariff trading barriers for EEC members, (ii) adopt the external common tariff system, and (iii) suppress all sorts of export subsidies. On the fiscal side, the requirement was the implementation of an indirect tax reform to convert the old cascade turnover tax system into the current value-added tax system. On the financial side, Spain had to liberalize the financial sector and free capital movements. This was important, since the historical strict regulation of financial activities in Spain had been blocking the entry of foreign banks for a long time and caused high interest rates.

Indeed, financial liberalization led to an inflow of foreign capital and a fall in the cost of capital. However, like the rest of Europe, the sharp decline in real interest rates was propagated by the fall in the German interest rate in 1995, when the inflation caused by the unification process was under control and the pressure to meet the Maastricht criterion on interest rates increased. The traditional monopolistic power of the incumbent banks in Spain ensured that, even after the financial liberalization of the 1990s, they maintained strong positions in the major industrial firms, and blocked a significant presence of foreign banks in Spain.

In June 1989, Spain joined the European Monetary System (EMS) and adopted the European Exchange Rate Mechanism, according to which the exchange rates of the members' currencies were quasi-fixed and could only fluctuate within some margins – a narrow margin of ±2.25 per cent and a wider one of ±6 per cent. The latter had to be increased to ±15 per cent after the 1992/1993 EMS crisis to accommodate persistent speculation on some currencies, among them the peseta. The strong trade deficit put downward pressure on the peseta, which was overcome by the massive inflow of foreign capital. The strong value of the peseta in the late 1980s and early 1990s was thus dependent on capital movements, which in the early 1990s were mainly driven by currency speculators. This speculation prompted the EMS crisis of 1992/1993 (see Eichengreen, 2000), which forced the peseta to lose more than 20 per cent of its value through successive depreciations (5 per cent and 6 per cent in September and November 1992; 8 per cent in 1993, and 7 per cent in 1995). Spain entered the EMS system with an exchange rate of 65 pesetas per Deutsche Mark, but pegged it at 85.1 in 1998 in view of joining the euro area in January 1999. This, as expected, progressively reduced the trade deficit in the following years, until it reached a balance in 1998.

Discussions on the future European Monetary Union (EMU) across the EEC members had already begun in the late 1980s and early 1990s, posing new challenges for the Spanish economy. In particular, the signing of the Maastricht Treaty in 1992 dominated economic policy until 1999, while the independence of the Bank of Spain took place in 1994 in anticipation of the European Central Bank (ECB). In 1999 Spain joined the EMU, thus entering what currently is the final stage of the European integration process. The fiscal policy is still in national hands, but subject to the stability and growth pact that restricts public deficits and debts.

Last but not least, Spain has been the recipient of a substantial amount of structural and cohesion aid funding through various European programmes, since it first joined the EEC. The impact of such funds is estimated to be, on average, close to 0.4 percentage points of annual GDP growth over the recent decades (Sosvilla-Rivero and Herce, 2008).

Note that our empirical model in section 4 evaluates the influence of the above integration process on the evolution of unemployment by including the trade deficit (foreign demand), indirect taxes, financial wealth, and capital accumulation in the set of explanatory variables.

3.3   The rise and fall of unemployment across business cycles

3.3.1   1977–85

Following the enduring expansion of the 1960s and early 1970s, Spain had to deal with two severe world macroeconomic shocks. The first oil price shock in 1973 had a pronounced effect on inflation and unemployment since the Spanish industry was heavily dependent on oil imports. This was further coupled by a wage-price spiral over the 1973–77 period, in which unions pushed up wages sufficiently to generate real wage growth.

The wage-price spiral was aggravated by accommodating macroeconomic policies. This policy response, in the context of the social and political crises linked with the end of the Francoist period in 1975 and the first democratic elections in 1977, effectively postponed the adjustment to the economic turmoil. As a result, inflation exceeded 20 per cent in 1977, while the unemployment rate remained close to full employment levels until 1977 (in that year it was still 4.2 per cent).

The deep economic crisis was fully felt from 1977 to 1985 with a rapid increase in the unemployment rate, which reached 17.8 per cent in 1985.[15] The second oil price shock in 1979 exacerbated this crisis. A very restrictive monetary policy was implemented during this period to reduce inflation. As a consequence investment and consumption fell dramatically, while interest rates and unemployment rose sharply (the unemployment rate went up by 13.6 percentage points during these years). The profound downturn in the growth rate of capital stock (Figure 6.8 in section 4) is representative of the slump during these years.

In contrast, the fiscal policy was very expansionary, with public expenditures growing much faster than public revenues, and the public deficit reaching around 7 per cent of GDP. The rise in public expenditures is both conjunctural (due to the crisis) and structural (due to the administrative decentralization and the setting up of a modern welfare state).

Regarding the external sector, the peseta was devalued against the US dollar: 20 per cent in 1977 in the context of the Moncloa Pacts, and 7.6 per cent in 1982.

Furthermore, as already explained, the Moncloa Pacts led to the implementation of an incomes policy, whereby the government set an inflation target, the unions agreed to accept moderation in wage increases, and firms agreed to price moderation. Despite the various annual and biannual agreements signed until the mid 1980s, job destruction was significant throughout this period. In 1984, the government introduced a series of labour market reforms, the details of which were discussed in the previous section.

In a nutshell, over the 1977–85 period, whereas inflation and external deficit were brought under control, unemployment and public deficit remained the two main macroeconomic imbalances until 1985.

3.3.2   1986–90

Strong expansion is the characteristic of this period. GDP grew at a 4.5 per cent annual rate, fuelled by strong domestic demand. The unemployment rate went down from 17.7 per cent in 1985 to 12.1 per cent in 1990.

Spain joined the EEC in 1986 after being a closed economy with highly protected product markets. Thus, foreign deficit increased at a rapid pace and the need for international competitiveness put downward pressure on wages and prices (even in the absence of new incomes policies).

Monetary policy was relaxed in 1986 and 1987 (given the subdued inflation rates), while the fiscal policy became restrictive. The expansion was based on the boost in domestic demand and was led by the increase in private consumption and investment. These developments, together with the lagged effects of the labour market reforms of 1984, led to a sharp increase in employment.[16] In the years 1988–90 these policies were reversed, especially after Spain joined the EMS in 1989. To prevent a resurgence of high inflation, monetary policies were tightened in the late 1980s, a move reinforced by the EMS entry. In 1989 the monetary policy became anchored to the foreign sector, aiming at controlling inflation and the value of the peseta, until the ECB would take over in 1999.

3.3.3   1991–94

The 'EU cycle' boom of 1986–90 was followed by the 'EU cycle' recession of 1991–94. Job creation started slowing down and the unemployment rate stopped falling in 1991 as domestic demand collapsed: first private investment, then private consumption. A rise in household indebtedness, the Iraqi war of 1991, the upward pressure on interest rates due to German unification, and the EMS crisis of 1992 and 1993 together pushed the Spanish economy into a short-lived but deep recession. The unemployment rate rose from 12.1 per cent in 1990 to 19.1 per cent in 1994. This recession was accompanied by a decline in the inflation rates, from around 7 per cent in 1990 to less than 4.0 per cent in 1994.

From 1990 the value of the peseta became less credible. On one side, the current account deficit put downward pressure on it. On the other side, high interest rates were attracting short-run foreign capital which increased the demand of pesetas. When Germany raised its interest rates to control the inflation generated by the unification process, this foreign capital flew out to Germany leaving the peseta value unsustainable and subject to strong speculative attacks. The successive devaluations of the peseta following the EMS crisis made Spanish exports more competitive.

3.3.4 1995–2005

This was a prolonged expansionary period with GDP growing around 3.5 per cent on average.[17] In 1994 the Spanish government implemented a second wave of labour market reforms,[18] and the Central Bank became independent, with a mandate to focus exclusively on inflation control. 1997 witnessed a third wave of reforms, which reduced firing costs on permanent contracts thereby partially reversing the trend towards temporary employment.

These two labour market reforms played an important role in containing real wage growth and, along with a new cyclical upturn, provided a strong stimulus to employment in the second half of the 1990s. The peseta devaluation of approximately 20 per cent with respect to the Deutsche Mark in 1992 and 1993 contributed to balance the foreign deficit until 1998, when the exchange rates of the EMU countries were fixed. These developments were reinforced by the monetary policy run-up to Spain's EMU entry in 1999, involving a sharp reduction in interest rates after 1995. Nevertheless, in order to keep inflation under control, the government supplemented its labour market reforms by opening its product markets to foreign competition. Whereas this involved mainly the industrial sector in the second half of the 1980s, in the 1990s it included the service sector, particularly the financial, transport, communication and telecommunication sectors. Several important public companies were privatized, which helped reduce the public sector deficit. As a result, the pronounced increase in employment in the second half of the 1990s was accompanied by a reduction in inflation. However, the labour force expanded (through higher female participation rates) and thus Spain's unemployment rate responded only moderately; in 1998 it was still 14.6 per cent.

The government implemented two fiscal reforms in 1999 and 2003 affecting income tax. The modern income tax system was established with the Moncloa Pacts in 1978 and went through relatively minor changes until 1999. The 1999 reform of the personal income tax reduced the number of tax-brackets from eight to six, which were further reduced to five by the 2003 reform. Moreover, the highest marginal rate fell from 56 per cent before 1999 to 45 per cent after 2003, and the lowest marginal rate fell from 20 per cent to 15 per cent. These changes entailed a reduction in the average tax rate so that, jointly, these reforms increased net real wages by the equivalent of about 1 per cent of GDP according to official figures. In the context of low interest rates, the increase in real wages is one of the main factors behind the strong increase in private consumption until 2007. This, in turn, fed through to the continuous and rapid GDP growth, kept investment high and, thereby, boosted employment.

The immigration boom experienced by the Spanish economy in the early 2000s is another main factor behind the increase in private consumption. In 2000 the Spanish population was 40.5 million people with a tiny share of migrants. In 2006 it had grown to 44.7 million and the proportion of foreigners was above 10 per cent. This rapid population increase boosted private consumption and reinforced building construction, the two characteristic features of the Spanish economy until 2007.

The increase in the labour force resulting from the massive waves of immigrants has also implied a reduction in the speed at which the unemployment rate had been falling in previous years. It went down from 14.6 per cent in 1998 to 10.8 per cent in 2000, and to 8.5 per cent in 2006 (after some stabilization in 2002–03).

4. Empirical analysis

In the spirit of the chain reaction theory model in section 2 and the economic developments discussed above, we identify the driving forces of the unemployment rate by estimating a dynamic structural multi-equation labour market model containing labour demand, labour supply and wage setting equations:

$$\underset{(3\times3)\,(3\times1)}{A_0\ y_t} = \sum_{i=1}^{2} \underset{(3\times3)\,(3\times1)}{A_i\ y_{t-i}} + \sum_{i=0}^{2} \underset{(3\times8)\,(8\times1)}{D_i\ x_{t-i}} + \underset{(3\times1)}{\varepsilon_t}\,, \qquad (26)$$

where y_t is a (3×1) vector of endogenous variables, x_t is an (8×1) vector of exogenous variables, the A_i and D_i are (3×3) and (3×8), respectively, coefficient matrices, and ε_t is a (3×1) vector of strict white noise error terms.

The above dynamic system is stable when all the roots of the determinantal equation: $|A_0 - A_1B - A_2B^2| = 0$ lie outside the unit circle.

4.1 Econometric methodology

We apply the autoregressive distributed lag (ARDL) approach, which was developed by Pesaran and Shin (1999), and Pesaran, Shin and Smith (2001). The ARDL is an alternative to the popular cointegration/error-correction methodology, having the advantage of avoiding the pretesting problem implicit in the standard cointegration techniques (i.e. the Johansen maximum likelihood, and the Phillips–Hansen semi-parametric fully-modified OLS procedures).

It can be shown that the ARDL yields consistent short- and long-run estimates irrespective of whether the regressors are I(1) or I(0). Thus, the ARDL provides us with an econometric tool to conduct our empirical analysis rigorously. To determine the dynamic specification of each equation we rely on the optimal lag-length algorithm of the Schwartz information criterion.

It is important to note that the equations we select are dynamically stable and pass the standard diagnostic tests at conventional significance levels, i.e. they satisfy the conditions of linearity, structural stability, no serial correlation, homoskedasticity, and normality.

To take into account the potential endogeneity and cross equation correlation, we estimate our equations as a system using 3SLS. These estimated equations, together with the unemployment definition (4), are then used to derive the univariate representation of the unemployment rate underlying the rest of our empirical analysis.

In what follows, we present our estimation results and then provide an overall evaluation of the empirical labour market model.

4.2 Data and estimated equations

Our sample covers the 1972–2005 period and the data is obtained by the [1] OECD Economic Outlook, [2] FBBVA, [3] Madrid Stock Exchange, and [4] Bank of Spain. The variables are defined in Table 6.2.[19]

Table 6.2 Definitions of variables

		Source			*Source*
c	constant				
n	employment (log)	[1]	$igbm$	Madrid stock exchange index	[3]
l	labour force (log)	[1]	P	GDP deflator	[1]
u	unemployment rate, $l-n$	[1]	fw	financial wealth, $\log\left(\frac{igmp/P}{\theta}\right)$	[1]
k	real capital stock (log)	[2]	b	social security benefits (% GDP)	[1]
w	real wage per employee (log)	[1]	fd	foreign demand, $\left(\frac{exports-imports}{GDP}\right)$	[1]
tax^i	Indirect taxes (% GDP)	[1]	z	working-age population (log)	[1]
$cons$	private consumption (% GDP)	[1]	zp	$\frac{working\text{-}age\ population}{total\ population}$	[4]
θ	real labour productivity	[1]	d^{00}	dummy, value $= \begin{array}{l} 1,\ 2000\text{--}2005 \\ 0,\ otherwise \end{array}$	

Sources: [1]: OECD, Economic Outlook; [2] FBBVA; [3] Madrid Stock Exchange; [4] Bank of Spain.

In Tables 6.3–6.5 we present the estimates for the labour demand, wage setting and labour force equations, respectively. The first part of each table gives the least squares estimates of the specific equation, while its misspecification tests are shown in the second part of the table. The 3SLS estimates are given in the third part of each table. It is important to note that all three equations are dynamically stable.[20] Finally, according to the reported p-values, all parameters are statistically significant and all three equations are well specified at conventional significance levels.[21]

4.2.1 Labour demand

The labour demand equation is quite standard (see Table 6.3). Employment depends positively on capital stock,[22] and negatively on real wages and indirect taxes. The performance of the stock market enters the labour demand equation with a small coefficient and the expected positive sign.[23] Other product demand-side influences are captured through foreign demand and private consumption, both having the expected positive sign. Finally, observe that the sum of the lagged dependent variable coefficients is 0.66, implying a rather high degree of employment persistence.

Table 6.3 Labour demand equation. Spain, 1972–2005.

OLS			Misspecification tests		3SLS		
	Coeff.	[p-value]		[p-value]		Coeff.	[p-value]
c	1.79	[0.070]			c	2.23	[0.000]
n_{t-1}	0.69	[0.000]	$SC[\chi^2(1)]$	1.07 [0.301]	n_{t-1}	0.66	[0.000]
Δn_{t-1}	0.34	[0.001]	$LIN[\chi^2(1)]$	2.51 [0.113]	Δn_{t-1}	0.36	[0.000]
w_t	−0.31	[0.004]	$NOR[\chi^2(2)]$	0.42 [0.812]	w_t	−0.37	[0.000]
tax_t^i	−0.85	[0.017]	$HET[\chi^2(1)]$	1.75 [0.812]	tax_t^i	−0.96	[0.000]
k_t	0.32	[0.000]	$ARCH[\chi^2(1)]$	0.51 [0.476]	k_t	0.34	*
Δk_t	2.77	[0.001]			Δk_t	2.68	[0.000]
Δk_{t-1}	−1.22	[0.073]	Structural stability tests		Δk_{t-1}	−1.20	[0.014]
fw_{t-1}	0.01	[0.029]	(5% significance)		fw_t	0.01	[0.000]
Δfw_{t-1}	−0.02	[0.033]			Δfw_t	−0.01	[0.001]
fd_{t-1}	0.48	[0.009]	CUSUM	✓	fd_{t-1}	0.40	[0.000]
$cons_t$	0.64	[0.033]	$CUSUM^2$	✓	$cons_t$	0.65	[0.003]
std. error	0.007				std. error	0.007	
R^2	0.998				R^2	0.998	
					(*) Restricted to unity.		

Note: Dependent variable: n_t. Estimation methodology: ARDL.

4.2.2 Wage setting

Real wage depends on its lagged values, the unemployment rate, capital deepening, social security benefits, and indirect taxes (see Table 6.4). Capital deepening is regarded as a good proxy for labour productivity. The advantage of using capital deepening instead of productivity is that we avoid dealing with an additional endogenous variable in our estimation.

In line with the classical assumption, unemployment puts downward pressure on real wages, with a semi-elasticity of 0.23 in the short-run. In addition, if the unemployment rate goes up by 1 percentage point, wages fall by 0.41 per cent in the long run. The effect of capital deepening on wages is captured by a long-run coefficient of 0.52. The significant positive effect of benefits flags their role as the conventional wage-push factor. Finally, although the wage equation depends negatively on taxes, their 'global' effect on unemployment has the expected positive sign.[24] In fact, the 'global' long-run slope of the unemployment rate with respect to the tax rate is 1.36.[25]

4.2.3 Labour supply

In contrast to wage setting, inertia in labour supply decisions is large, with a persistence coefficient of 0.86. Labour supply is driven by the unemployment rate, real wage, and working-age population (see Table 6.5).

Table 6.4 Wage setting equation. Spain, 1972–2005

OLS			Misspecification tests		3SLS		
	Coeff.	[p-value]		[p-value]		Coeff.	[p-value]
c	3.46	[0.008]	SC[$\chi^2(1)$] 0.10 [0.752]		c	3.57	[0.001]
w_{t-1}	0.46	[0.010]	LIN[$\chi^2(1)$] 5.37 [0.020]		w_{t-1}	0.44	[0.003]
Δw_{t-1}	0.48	[0.004]	LIN[$F(1, 24)$] 4.50 [0.044]		Δw_{t-1}	0.46	[0.001]
u_t	−0.23	[0.021]	NOR[$\chi^2(2)$] 0.20 [0.904]		u_t	−0.23	[0.005]
Δu_t	−0.33	[0.077]	HET[$\chi^2(1)$] 0.04 [0.849]		Δu_t	−0.32	[0.047]
$k_t - n_t$	0.28	[0.045]	ARCH[$\chi^2(1)$] 0.55 [0.460]		$k_t - n_t$	0.29	[0.013]
tax_t^i	−1.00	[0.056]			tax_t^i	−1.01	[0.021]
Δtax_t^i	−0.85	[0.087]	Structural stability tests		Δtax_t^i	−1.00	[0.015]
b_t	0.78	[0.067]	(5% significance)		b_t	0.78	[0.030]
std. error		0.011	CUSUM	✓	std. error		0.011
R^2		0.995	CUSUM^2	✓	R^2		0.995

Note: Dependent variable: w_t. Estimation methodology: ARDL.

Table 6.5   Labour force equation. Spain, 1972–2005

OLS			Misspecification tests		3SLS		
	Coeff.	[p-value]		[p-value]		Coeff.	[p-value]
c	−0.69	[0.551]			c	−0.07	[0.175]
l_{t-1}	0.85	[0.000]	$SC[\chi^2(1)]$	0.25 [0.616]	l_{t-1}	0.86	[0.000]
w_t	−0.06	[0.144]	$LIN[\chi^2(1)]$	0.40 [0.529]	w_t	−0.06	[0.045]
Δu_t	−0.21	[0.048]	$NOR[\chi^2(2)]$	2.91 [0.234]	Δu_t	−0.20	[0.011]
z_t	0.19	[0.120]	$HET[\chi^2(1)]$	0.32 [0.570]	z_t	0.14	(*)
zp_t	0.32	[0.154]	$ARCH[\chi^2(1)]$	0.46 [0.495]	zp_t	0.46	[0.003]
Δzp_t	−2.30	[0.195]			Δzp_t	−2.03	[0.083]
d^{00}	0.02	[0.002]	Structural stability tests		d^{00}	0.03	[0.000]
			(5% significance)				
std. error		0.006			std. error		0.007
R^2		0.998	CUSUM	✓	R^2		0.998
			CUSUM^2	✓	(*) Restricted to unity		

Note: Dependent variable: l_t. Estimation methodology: ARDL.

Since it is the change rather than the level of unemployment that enters the labour force equation, we have the so-called *discouraged workers' effect* influencing labour supply. Labour force depends negatively on the real wage, which indicates that the income effect dominates.[26] Both the level of working-age population (z) and its ratio to total population (zp) affect positively the labour force. Note that through zp we can capture demographic influences on the labour supply movements. Finally, the dummy variable (d^{00}) captures the influence of the immigration boom since 2000.

4.3   Model diagnostics

We check the economic plausibility and overall validity of the estimated system by

- looking at the accuracy of the fitted values,
- computing the 'global' (interactive) sensitivities, and
- using the Johansen framework to test for the cointegrating vectors implied by the ARDL.

The fitted values of the unemployment rate can be obtained by using the estimated (3SLS) equations in Tables 6.3–6.5 and the unemployment definition (4). Figure 6.3 plots the actual and fitted values of the unemployment rate and shows that our estimation tracks the data very

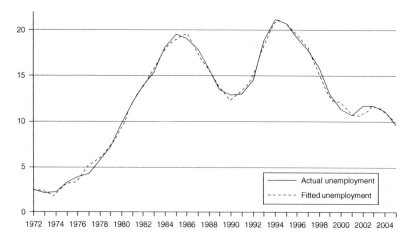

Figure 6.3 Unemployment rate: actual and fitted values

well. We should emphasize that a good fit is much harder to obtain when dynamic multi-equation labour market models are being estimated instead of single unemployment rate equations. This is because of the numerous feedback mechanisms among the endogenous variables that are activated when we solve the model for the unemployment rate.

As explained in Section 2.1, the 'global' slopes or semi-elasticities of an endogenous variable with respect to the exogenous ones incorporate all the spillover effects in the system, and are thus differentiated by the 'local' sensitivities, which are readily displayed by the individual equations. We call them 'global' because (in the short-run) they are the slopes/semi-elasticities of the univariate representation of the unemployment rate. As shown in equation (12), the long-run 'global' sensitivities can be computed by the infinite sum of responses to an impulse. We also argued in section 2.3 that the 'global' sensitivities are an invaluable tool to decide on the economic plausibility of the empirical model. The disadvantage of the traditional structural labour market models is their focus on the 'local' sensitivities whose size and sign can be dramatically affected by the spillovers in the system.

Table 6.6 presents the 'global' long-run sensitivities and the magnitudes of the respective shocks. The latter are measured by the sample average of the change in the specific variable. As expected, taxes, benefits, and working-age population put upward pressure on unemployment, whereas capital stock, foreign demand, the performance of the stock market, and consumption reduce unemployment.

Table 6.6   'Global' long-run unemployment slopes (semi-elasticities)

	tax[i]	b	fw	fd	cons	k	z	zp
LR sensitivity	1.36	1.37	−0.04	−1.31	−2.13	−0.60	0.60	1.93
(Shock size)	(0.02)	(0.02)	(0.71)	(0.03)	(0.02)	(0.36)	(0.10)	(0.03)

Table 6.7   Testing the long-run relationships in the Johansen framework[28]

	ARDL			Johansen			LR test
Labour demand	(N	w	k)	(N	w	k)	
OLS	(1	−1.01	1.02)	(1	−1.09	1.23)	$\chi^2(2) = 0.76$ [0.685]
3SLS	(1	−1.09	1.00)	(1	−1.09	1.23)	$\chi^2(2) = 1.26$ [0.533]
Wage setting	(w	k	n)	(w	k	n)	
OLS	(1	−0.52	0.52)	(1	−0.61	0.74)	$\chi^2(2) = 3.12$ [0.210]
3SLS	(1	−0.52	0.52)	(1	−0.61	0.74)	$\chi^2(2) = 3.12$ [0.210]
Labour force	(L	w	z)	(L	w	z)	
OLS	(1	0.40	−1.29)	(1	0.15	−0.62)	$\chi^2(2) = 0.66$ [0.720]
3SLS	(1	0.38	−1.00)	(1	0.15	−0.62)	$\chi^2(2) = 0.50$ [0.781]

Note: p-values in square brackets; 5% critical values: $\chi^2(2) = 5.99$.

Finally, we test whether the long-run relationships implied by our estimations (second column in Table 6.7) translate to cointegrating vectors within the Johansen framework. Once the maximal eigenvalue and trace statistics confirm that the variables involved in each equation are cointegrated, the Johansen's cointegrating vectors (third column in Table 6.7) are restricted to take the corresponding long-run values of our estimated equations. The last column in Table 6.7 displays the LR tests following a $\chi^2(\cdot)$ distribution.[27] Observe that the restrictions cannot be rejected at any conventional size of the test, indicating that our estimation methodology is consistent with the Johansen procedure.

5.   Dynamic contributions

We examine the influence of (i) social security benefits, (ii) indirect taxes, (iii) financial wealth, (iv) foreign demand, and (v) capital accumulation on the unemployment trajectory over the periods 1978–85, 1986–90, 1991–94, and 1995–2005 by carrying out counterfactual simulations, and applying the technique presented in section 2.3.

We evaluate the contributions of each of the above factors by plotting the actual series of unemployment against its simulated series obtained by fixing each specific factor at its value at the start of a specific period. The disparity between the actual and simulated series of unemployment measures the dynamic contribution of the specific factor to unemployment for the specific period. The evolution of social security benefits, indirect taxes, financial wealth, foreign demand, and capital stock growth, and their contribution to the rise and fall in unemployment, are plotted in Figures 6.4–6.8, respectively.

Figure 6.4 shows that had social security benefits remained constant at its value in:

- 1977, the unemployment rate would have been 6.1 percentage points (pp) below the actual 15.4 pp increase over the 1978–85 recession period;
- 1985, unemployment would have been 0.5 pp above the 6.7 pp decrease over the 1986–91 boom period; per cent;[29]
- 1990, unemployment would have been 2.0 pp below the 8.3 pp increase over the 1991–94 recession period; and
- 1994, unemployment would have been 3.7 pp above the 11.6 pp decrease over the 1995–2005 boom period.

According to Figure 6.5, whereas indirect taxes have negligible contributions during the first three periods, they put upward pressure on unemployment during the boom period 1995–2005. Had taxes not increased, the unemployment rate would have ended the period 1.6 pp below the actual 11.6 pp decrease. We should point out that the substantial increase in the indirect tax rate during the long recession of 1978–85 had virtually no impact on the unemployment rate.

Figure 6.6 displays the downward pressure of the stock market activity on the unemployment rate. Had financial wealth[30] remained fixed at its value in:

- 1977, unemployment would have been 3.5 pp below the 15.4 pp increase over the 1978–85 recession;
- 1985, unemployment would have been 2.3 pp above the 6.7 pp decrease over the 1986–91 boom;
- 1990, unemployment would not have been influenced over the 1991–94 recession;[31] and
- 1994, unemployment would have been 2.5 pp above the 11.6 pp decrease over the 1995–2005 boom years.

The contributions of foreign demand are depicted in Figure 6.7 and are qualitatively similar to the contributions of financial wealth. Both

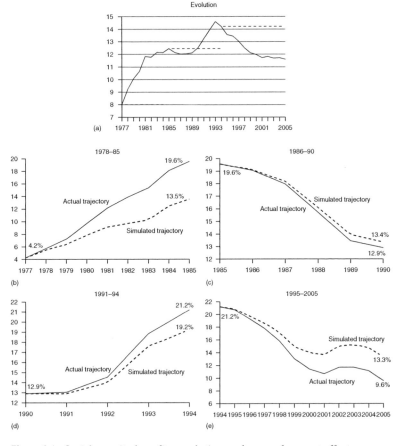

Figure 6.4   Social security benefits: evolution and unemployment effects
Note: Simulated trajectories result from fixing social security benefits at years 1977, 1985, 1990 and 1994.

variables have an inverse relationship with unemployment and do not contribute to the evolution of the unemployment rate over the 1991–94 recession. But in contrast to financial wealth, which has an upward trend during the whole sample, foreign demand is characterized by a downward trend.[32] Furthermore, foreign demand appears to have a stronger impact on the unemployment rate than financial wealth. Had foreign demand stabilized at its value in:

- 1977, unemployment would have been 4.2 pp below the 15.4 pp increase over the 1978–85 recession;

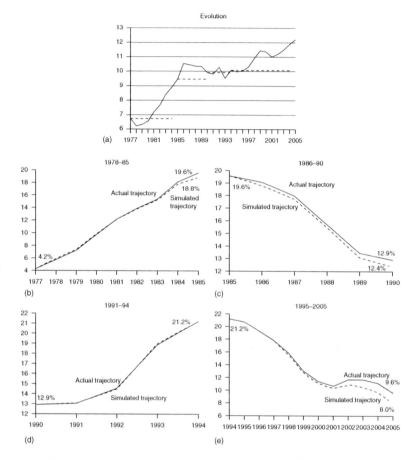

Figure 6.5 Indirect taxes: evolution and unemployment effects
Note: Simulated trajectories result from fixing indirect taxes at years 1977, 1985, 1990 and 1994.

- 1985, unemployment would have been 5.4 pp above the 6.7 pp decrease over the 1986–91 boom period; and
- 1994, unemployment would have been 5.8 pp above the 11.6 pp decrease over the 1995–2005 boom.

Finally, it is clear from the plots in Figure 6.8 that capital stock accumulation has the most profound influence on the evolution of the unemployment rate.[33] In particular:

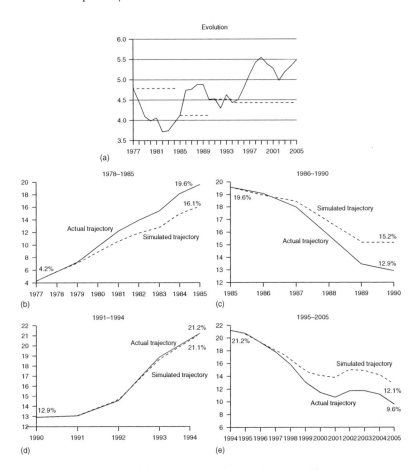

Figure 6.6   Financial wealth: evolution and unemployment effects
Note: Simulated trajectories result from fixing financial wealth at years 1977, 1985, 1990 and 1994.

- Figures 6.8b, c and e show that, for each period, the simulated final value of unemployment is very close to its initial actual value. This indicates that (i) the rise in unemployment during the 1978–85 'long recession' years, (ii) the fall in unemployment during the 1986–91 'EU cycle' boom period, and (iii) the fall in unemployment during the 1995–2005 'EMU cycle' boom years were mostly due to the swings in the growth rate of capital stock.

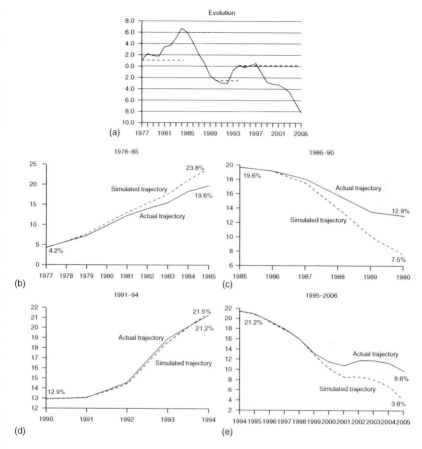

Figure 6.7   Foreign demand: evolution and unemployment effects
Note: Simulated trajectories result from fixing foreign demand at years 1977, 1985, 1990 and 1994.

- Figure 6.8d shows that had the capital stock growth remained constant at its 1990 value, unemployment would have been 6.6 pp below the 8.3 pp increase over the 1991–94 'EU cycle' recession years.

6.   Regime changes in capital accumulation

The simulations in the previous section showed that capital accumulation is the most crucial factor in driving the unemployment movements over each of the four distinct periods in our sample. In what follows we

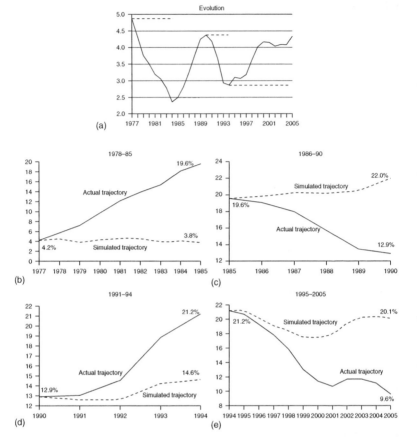

Figure 6.8   Capital stock accumulation: evolution and unemployment effects
Note: Simulated trajectories result from fixing capital stock accumulation at years 1977, 1985, 1990 and 1994.

elaborate on this finding by evaluating the impact of the regime changes in the growth rate of capital stock on the unemployment rate trajectory. We identify the number and longevity of the regimes embedded in the growth rate of the capital stock by estimating its kernel density function.[34]

A stationary time series with different regimes is characterized by a multimodal density of its frequency distribution, the number of modes corresponding to the number of regimes. In particular, a unimodal kernel density indicates that a unique regime exists with mean equal to the value of the mode. On the other hand, a variable with two regimes displays a bimodal kernel density with a 'valley point' dividing the observations in the sample. The data points are grouped in the two regimes depending on whether they lie to the left or to the right of the 'valley point'. The kernel density analysis of the two-regime case can easily be extended to account for three or more regimes.

Naturally, when the variable is characterized by one regime, this is taken to be permanent. For multimodal kernel densities we distinguish between permanent and temporary regimes and identify them as follows. The variable starts in one regime (say, A) in the beginning of the sample, and then moves to another regime (say, B) at some later point in time. If the variable reverses to regime A before the end of the sample, then regime B is temporary and regime A is permanent. On the other hand, if the variable stays in regime B by the end of the sample then both regimes are permanent ones.

The bimodal kernel density in Figure 6.9a indicates that the growth rate of capital stock is characterized by two regimes. According to Figure 6.9b these regimes are permanent, the 'high' regime with mean 6.8 per cent lasts until 1976 when capital stock growth enters the 'low' regime with mean 3.7 per cent. This permanent capital accumulation downturn accompanies, strikingly well, the higher unemployment rates since 1978 (see Figure 6.1).

Finally, 1978 onwards, we evaluate the unemployment impact of the permanent decrease in the growth rate of capital stock as follows. We simulate the steady state of the labour market model (in Tables 6.3–6.5) under two scenarios over the 1978–2005 period: (i) capital stock growing at 6.8 per cent, and (ii) capital stock growing at 3.7 per cent. The reason for simulating the steady state of the model is that we want to measure the effect of the permanent shift in the growth rate of the capital stock net of the lagged adjustments present in the labour market. The difference between the two simulated time paths of the unemployment rate, of around 7 percentage points, is our measure of the long-run contribution of the permanent decline in capital accumulation after 1978 to unemployment. We subtract this contribution from the actual unemployment rate and plot the resulting series in Figure 6.10 (dotted line).

Figure 6.10 shows that had capital stock growth remained at its high regime mean, unemployment would have peaked at 12.5 per cent in 1985 instead of the actual 19.6 per cent. In turn, the actual subsequent fall to around 9.6 per cent in 2005 would have ended up near 2.6 per cent. This result implies that, in the absence of the permanent slowdown in investment after 1978, Spain would have recovered the full-employment levels that had historically characterized its labour market.

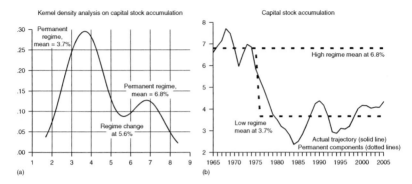

Figure 6.9 Regime changes in capital stock accumulation

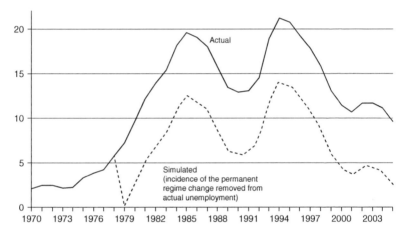

Figure 6.10 Long-run impact on unemployment of the regime change in capital stock accumulation

7. Conclusions

In this chapter we analysed the chain reaction theory (CRT) of unemployment through a stylized labour market model, and showed that the interplay of the dynamics and spillovers in the multi-equation system give rise to the phenomenon of frictional growth. The implications of frictional growth are:

1) unemployment does not gravitate towards its natural rate, since the long-run unemployment rate equals its NRU plus frictional growth;

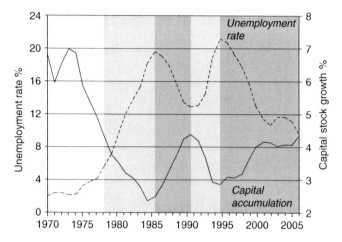

Figure 6.11 Actual capital–unemployment relationship

2) the unemployment rate cannot be decomposed into cyclical (short-run) and 'trend' (long-run) components;
3) trended exogenous variables can be included in CRT models and, thus, are allowed to influence the unemployment rate trajectory.

We applied the CRT to the Spanish economy over the 1970–2005 period by estimating a dynamic system of labour demand, real wage, and labour supply equations with spillover effects. We found that, although variables that are among the conventional wisdom's favourite causes of unemployment (i.e. social security contributions, indirect taxes, and financial wealth) do matter, capital accumulation is the most important driving force of unemployment. Furthermore, foreign demand had a substantial impact on the ups and downs of unemployment, especially during the 'EU cycle' of 1986–1990 and the 'EMU cycle' of 1995–2005.

The finding of capital stock growth as the main determinant of the unemployment rate is in tandem with reality (see Figure 6.11), and supports the literature on the role of capital accumulation in the evolution of unemployment (Rowthorn, 1995, 1999; Gordon, 1997; Arestis and Biefang-Frisancho Mariscal, 2000; Karanassou and Snower, 2004; Blanchard, 2005; Arestis et al., 2007; and Karanassou et al., 2008b).

Our findings indicate that the preoccupation of macroeconomists with the estimation of the NRU, quite often serves as an end to itself and does not provide the means to understand what really matters for the evolution of unemployment. We argue that the unemployment problem can be better addressed by estimating CRT models, and measuring the unemployment contributions of the 'usual suspects' (e.g. wage-push factors) along with those of growing exogenous variables (such as capital stock).

Notes

1. **Acknowledgments:** We are grateful to the editors Philip Arestis and Malcolm Sawyer, and other participants in the 5th International Conference on Developments in Economic Theory and Policy (Bilbao, July 2008), for their insightful comments. Hector Sala is grateful to the Spanish Ministry of Education and Science for financial support through grant SEJ2006-14849/ECON.
2. Department of Economics, Queen Mary, University of London, Mile End Road, London E1 4NS, UK; tel.: +(0)20 7882-8829; email: M.Karanassou@qmul.ac.uk; http://www.karanassou.com
3. Departament d'Economia Aplicada, Universitat Autònoma de Barcelona, 08193 Bellaterra, Spain; tel.: +34 93 5812779; email: hector.sala@uab.es; http://www.ecap.uab.cat/hsala.
4. Some studies use the Spanish labour market figures provided by the quarterly Survey of the Active Population (Encuesta de Población Activa, EPA), which underwent methodological changes in 1987, 1992, 2002, and 2005 (see Garrido and Toharia, 2004). Here we use the homogeneous long-time series provided by the OECD Economic Outlook, which slightly deviate from the EPA series.
5. Tobin (1998) argues that the NAIRU (non accelerating inflation rate of unemployment) and the NRU are not synonymous. However, within our context of analysis, such a distinction is superfluous. See Karanassou, Sala and Snower (2008) for a survey and critique of NAIRU and NRU models.
6. Note that in this chapter, hysteresis refers to the popular 'unit root hysteresis' usage of the term.
7. See Karanassou et al. (2009) for a comprehensive survey and critique of the NRU and hysteresis theories.
8. It can be shown that the above labour market model is compatible with standard microeconomic foundations.
9. Since labour force and employment are in logs, the unemployment rate can be approximated by their difference.
10. Note that (8) and (9) are dynamically stable since the products of polynomials in B which satisfy the stability conditions are also stable.
11. Note that (10) is dynamically stable since (i) products of polynomials in B which satisfy the stability conditions are stable, and (ii) linear combinations of dynamically stable polynomials in B are also stable.
12. Other measures of persistence are the half life of the shock, the sum of the autoregressive parameters, and the largest autoregressive root.
13. For example, Karanassou and Sala (2008a) find that the NRU explains only 33% of the unemployment variation in Denmark, while frictional growth accounts for the remaining 67%.
14. The AR(1) model is used for expositional ease.

15. Recall that we use the OECD Economic Outlook series (rather than the EPA ones).
16. Whereas temporary contracts were infrequent prior to 1984, the ratio of fixed-tem employment to dependent employment rose to 15.6% in 1987 (first year with official data), and further to 32.2% in 1991.
17. In fact, this expansion lasts until 2007. However, data availability at the time this research was conducted restricts the sample period to 2005.
18. This second wave was a response to the first. The main fixed-term contract in the 1984 reform was the 'employment promotion contract', which was used heavily by employers to cover both temporary and permanent tasks, and it gave Spain the highest rate of temporary employment in the EU. Thus, in the second wave of labour market reform, in 1994, the government tried to restrict the use of this contract by substituting it for other temporary contracts, such as the 'contract per task or service' and the 'contract for launching new activities'. These were originally targeted towards some groups of hard-to-place workers, but in fact they were used in the same way as the previous contract. As result, the third wave of reform in 1997 was implemented to favour permanent contracts.
19. Our wider set of explanatory variables also included direct taxes, oil prices, and social security contributions, but they were not significant.
20. If we measure persistence by the sum of the autoregressive coefficients, then wage-setting has the lowest persistence (0.44), followed by labour demand (0.66) and labour supply (0.86).
21. For example, for the wage-setting equation, linearity cannot be rejected at significance levels of (at most) 2% with a chi-square test, or 4.4% with an F-test.
22. The restriction that the elasticity of substitution is unity cannot be rejected. We believe that this restriction has no bearing on our work. If, however, it is interpreted as indicative of an underlying Cobb–Douglas production function, it can only reinforce our results regarding the importance of capital accumulation for the evolution of unemployment (see the next section).
23. This is along the lines of Phelps (1999), who was the first to draw attention to the role played by financial wealth in the (US) labour market.
24. See section 2 for the distinction between 'local' and 'global' sensitivities.
25. If we consider that, on average in our sample, the size of a tax change is 0.02, then the effect of taxes on unemployment is $1.36 \times 0.02 = 0.027$. That is, the overall impact of a tax shock on unemployment is an increase of 0.027 percentage points.
26. This result is also obtained by Bande and Karanassou (2009) using Spanish regional data from 1980 to 1995.
27. It should be noted that the VAR model underlying the Johansen procedure contains all the variables in our labour market model, both the I(0) and I(1) variables. Naturally, the cointegration tests, only consider the I(1) variables in our models: n_t, w_t, l_t, k_t, and z_t. This implies that we test two restrictions in the labour demand, wage setting, and labour supply equations. To conserve space, we do not report the results of the underlying unit root and cointegration tests. These are available upon request.
28. The coefficients are presented up to the second decimal, but the computations take all the information into account. In a couple of cases, this turns

into slight differences with respect to the cointegrating vectors derived from the information provided in Tables 6.2, 6.3 and 6.4.

29. Note that during this period benefits hardly change.

30. Recall that we use the Phelps normalization to describe the stock market performance, i.e. the (log of) ratio of real stock market index to labour market productivity.

31. This is no surprise as financial wealth is rather stable during these years.

32. In fact, Spain has faced a trade deficit since the late 1980s, and this deteriorates over time.

33. Bande and Karanassou (2009) examine the dynamics of Spanish regional unemployment rates over the 1980–95 period and find that capital stock growth was the main driving force of the unemployment rate during the 1985–91 boom and 1991–95 recession years.

34. Raurich et al. (2006), for the EU and the US, and Karanassou et al. (2008b), for the Nordic countries, use the kernel density analysis to evaluate the relationship of unemployment and capital accumulation.

References

Arestis, P. and Biefang-Frisancho Mariscal, I. (2000), 'Capital stock, unemployment and wages in the UK and Germany', *Scottish Journal of Political Economy*, vol. 47 (5), pp. 487–503.

Arestis, P., and Sawyer, M. (2008), 'Path dependency and demand-supply interactions in macroeconomic analysis', Ch. 1, this volume.

Arestis, P., Baddeley, M. and Sawyer, M. (2007), 'The relationship between capital stock, unemployment and wages in nine EMU countries', *Bulletin of Economic Research*, vol. 59 (2), pp. 125–48.

Bande, R. and Karanassou, M. (2009), 'Labour market flexibility and regional unemployment rate dynamics: Spain 1980–1995', *Papers in Regional Science*, vol. 88(1), pp. 181–207.

Bentolila, S. and Blanchard, O.J. (1990), 'Spanish unemployment', *Economic Policy*, vol. 10, pp. 233–81.

Bentolila, S. and Jimeno, J.F. (2006), 'Spanish Unemployment: The End of the Wild Ride?', in M. Werding (ed.), *Structural Unemployment in Western Europe: reasons and remedies*, Cambridge: Mass.: MIT Press.

Blanchard, O. (2005), 'Monetary policy and unemployment', in Semmler, W. (ed.), *Monetary Policy and Unemployment – US, Euro-Area, and Japan*, Routledge, London.

Blanchard, O.J. and Wolfers, J. (2000), 'The Role of Shocks and Institutions in the Rise of European Unemployment: The Aggregate Evidence', *Economic Journal*, 110, March.

Cross R., Darby, J., Ireland, J. and Piscitelli, L. (1999), 'Hysteresis and unemployment: a preliminary investigation', Computing in Economics and Finance, 5th International Conference, Boston.

Dolado, J.J. and Jimeno, J.F. (1997), 'The Causes of Spanish Unemployment: A Structural VAR Approach, *European Economic Review*, vol. 41, pp. 1281–307.

Eichengreen, B. (2000), The EMS Crisis in Retrospect, *NBER Working Paper* No. 8035.

Dolado, J., Malo de Molina, J.L. and Zabalza, A. (1986), 'Spanish industrial unemployment: Some explanatory factors', *Economica*, vol. 53, pp. 313–34.

Dolado, J.J., García-Serrano C. and Jimeno, J.F. (2002), 'Drawing lessons from the boom of temporary jobs in Spain', *Economic Journal*, vol. 112 (480), pp. F270–F295.

García de Blas, A. (1985), 'Unemployment benefits in Spain and other European OECD countries', *International Labour Review*, vol. 124 (2), pp. 147–60.

Güell, M. and Petrongolo, B. (2007), 'How binding are legal limits? Transitions from temporary to permanent work in Spain', *Labour Economics*, vol. 14 (2), pp. 153–83.

Garrido, L. and Toharia, L. (2004), 'What does it take to be (counted as) unemployed? The case of Spain', *Labour Economics*, vol. 11, pp. 507–23.

Gordon, R.J. (1997), 'Is there a trade-off between unemployment and productivity growth?', pp. 433–66, in Snower, D.J. and de la Dehesa, G. (eds), *Unemployment Policy: Government Options for the Labour Market*, Cambridge University Press, Cambridge.

Karanassou, M. and Snower, D.J. (2004), 'Unemployment Invariance', *German Economic Review*, vol. 5 (3), pp. 297–317.

Karanassou, M., Sala, H. and Salvador, P.F. (2008a), 'The (IR)relevance of the NRU for policy making: The case of Denmark', *Scottish Journal of Political Economy*, vol. 55 (3), pp. 369–92.

Karanassou, M., Sala, H. and Salvador, P.F. (2008b), 'Capital Accumulation and Unemployment: New Insights on the Nordic Experience', *Cambridge Journal of Economics*, vol. 32(6), pp. 977–1001.

Karanassou, M., Sala, H. and Snower, D.J. (2003), 'Unemployment in the European Union: A Dynamic Reappraisal', *Economic Modelling*, vol. 20 (2), pp. 237–73.

Karanassou M., Sala, H. and Snower, D.J. (2009), 'Phillips Curves and Unemployment Dynamics: A Critique and a Holistic Perspective', *Journal of Economic Surveys*, forthcoming.

Layard, R., Nickell, S.J. and Jackman, R. (1991), *Unemployment: Macroeconomic Performance and the Labour Market*, Oxford: Oxford University Press.

Phelps, E.S. (1994), *Structural Booms: The Modern Equilibrium Theory of Unemployment, Interest and Assets*, Cambridge, MA: Harvard University Press,

Phelps, E. and Zoega, G. (2001), 'Structural booms: productivity expectations and asset valuations', *Economic Policy*, vol. 32, April, pp. 85–126.

Pesaran, M.H. and Shin, Y. (1999), 'An Autoregressive Distributed-Lag Modelling Approach to Cointegration Analysis', in *Econometrics and Economic Theory in the Twentieth Century: The Ragnar Frisch Centennial Symposium*, edited by Strom, S., Cambridge: Cambridge University Press, pp. 371–413.

Pesaran, M.H., Shin, Y. and Smith, R.J. (2001), 'Bounds testing approaches to the analysis of level relationships', *Journal of Applied Econometrics*, vol. 16, pp. 289–326.

Polo, C. and Sancho, F. (1993), 'An analysis of Spain's integration in the EEC', *Journal of Policy Modeling*, vol. 15 (2), pp. 157–78.

Raurich, X., Sala, H. and Sorolla, V. (2006), 'Unemployment, Growth and Fiscal Policy: New Insights on the Hysteresis Hypotheses', *Macroeconomic Dynamics*, vol. 10 (3), pp. 285–316.

Rowthorn, R. (1995), 'Capital formation and unemployment', *Oxford Review of Economic Policy*, vol. 11 (1), pp. 26–39.

Rowthorn, R. (1999), 'Unemployment, wage bargaining and capital-labour substitution', *Cambridge Journal of Economics*, vol. 23, pp. 413–25.

Sosvilla-Rivero, S. and Herce, J.A. (2008), 'European cohesion policy and the Spanish economy: A policy discussion case', *Journal of Policy Modeling*, vol. 30, pp. 559–70.

Tobin, J. (1998), 'Supply constraints on employment and output: NAIRU versus natural rate', International Conference in Memory of Fausto Vicarelli, Rome, 21–23 Nov.

Index